LANZAROTE
Pages 80–95

0 km   50

0 Miles   50

ISLA DE ALEGRANZA

ISLA DE MONTAÑA CLARA

ISLA GRACIOSA

LANZAROTE

• Arrecife

ISLA DE LOS
LOBOS

• Puerto del Rosario

FUERTEVENTURA

áldar   Las Palmas
              • de Gran Canaria
  • Arucas

GRAN CANARIA

• Maspalomas

FUERTEVENTURA
Pages 66–79

GRAN CANARIA
Pages 40–65

EYEWITNESS TRAVEL GUIDES

CANARY ISLANDS

EYEWITNESS TRAVEL GUIDES

CANARY ISLANDS

Main contributors: PIOTR PASZKIEWICZ
& HANNA FARYNA-PASZKIEWICZ

DORLING KINDERSLEY
LONDON • NEW YORK • MUNICH
MELBOURNE • DELHI
www.dk.com

A DORLING KINDERSLEY BOOK
www.dk.com

Produced by Hachette Livre Polska Sp. z o.o., Warsaw

SENIOR GRAPHIC DESIGNER Paweł Pasternak
CONTRIBUTORS Piotr Paszkiewicz, Hanna Faryna-Paszkiewicz,
Małgorzata Wiśniewska, Barbara Sudnik, Eligiusz Nowakowski
CONSULTANT Carlos Rubio Palomera
GRAPHIC DESIGNERS Paweł Kamiński, Paweł Pasternak,
Piotr Kiedrowski
EDITOR Robert G. Pasieczny
TYPESETTING AND LAYOUT Ewa Roguska, Piotr Kiedrowski

CARTOGRAPHERS
Magdalena Polak, Dariusz Romanowski, Olaf Rodowald

PHOTOGRAPHERS
Paweł Wójcik, Bartłomiej Zaranek

ILLUSTRATORS
Monika Sopińska, Bohdan Wróblewski

Dorling Kindersley
TRANSLATOR Magda Hannay
EDITORS Irene Lyford, Michelle de Larrabeiti, Matthew Tanner
SENIOR DTP DESIGNER Jason Little
PRODUCTION CONTROLLER Melanie Dowland

Printed and bound in China
by Toppan Printing Co. (Shenzhen Ltd)

First published in Great Britain in 2003
by Dorling Kindersley Limited, 80 Strand, London WC2R 0RL
Reprinted with revisions 2006
Copyright © 2003, 2006 Dorling Kindersley, London
A Penguin Company

A CIP CATALOGUE RECORD IS AVAILABLE FROM THE BRITISH LIBRARY.

ISBN 1-4053-1183-5
ISBN 978-1405-31183-0
FLOORS ARE REFERRED TO THROUGHOUT IN ACCORDANCE WITH BRITISH
USAGE; IE THE "FIRST FLOOR" IS THE FLOOR ABOVE GROUND LEVEL.

The information in this
Dorling Kindersley Travel Guide is checked regularly.
Every effort has been made to ensure that this book is as up-to-date
as possible at the time of going to press. Some details, however,
such as telephone numbers, opening hours, prices, gallery hanging
arrangements and travel information are liable to change. The
publishers cannot accept responsibility for any consequences arising
from the use of this book, nor for any material on third party
websites, and cannot guarantee that any website address in this
book will be a suitable source of travel information. We value the
views and suggestions of our readers very highly. Please write to:
Publisher, DK Eyewitness Travel Guides,
Dorling Kindersley, 80 Strand, London WC2R 0RL, Great Britain.

◁ Viewing point by Los Roques at Teide National Park

CONTENTS

Madonna from a church façade at
Santiago del Teide

INTRODUCING
THE CANARY
ISLANDS

Children at the carnival in Las
Palmas de Gran Canaria

Golden sandy beach near Corralejo, on Fuerteventura

TRAVELLERS' NEEDS

Morena frita – a popular local dish

Façade of the parish church in Vega del Río de Palma

SURVIVAL GUIDE

Ceramic candleholder from a factory in La Orotava

Aquatic life of the Canary Islands
(see pp16–17)

How to Use this Guide

THIS GUIDE WILL HELP you to get the most out of your visit to the Canary Islands. It provides recommendations on places to visit, as well as detailed practical information. The section *Introducing the Canary Islands* gives an overview of the geographical position of the islands, their natural environment, their culture and their history. Individual sections describe the main historic sites and star attractions on each of the archipelago's seven inhabited islands. Help with accommodation, restaurants, shopping, entertainment and recreational activities can be found in the *Tourist Information* section, while the *Survival Guide* provides useful practical information and advice for visitors.

THE CANARY ISLANDS AREA BY AREA
Each of the seven inhabited islands has a section devoted to it. Towns and sights of interest on each of the islands are shown on the relevant map.

Colour-coded thumb tabs identify pages devoted to individual islands.

1 Introduction
This section provides a brief overview of each island, describing its history, geographical features and cultural characteristics as well as main tourist attractions.

A locator map indicates the position of the island within the archipelago.

2 Pictorial Map
This shows the main roads and topography of the island. It also locates all the places that are later described in detail.

Boxes contain information about events and people associated with an area.

3 Detailed Information
All the major towns and places of interest are described, listed and numbered to correspond with the island's map. Each entry provides information on the star sights and local attractions.

4 Major Towns
At least two pages are devoted to each major town, with detailed descriptions of historic remains and local curiosities that are worth seeing.

A Visitors' Checklist provides tourist and transport information, including opening hours of tourist attractions, admission charges, and details of local festivals and market days.

A Town Map shows the location of all the main sights within the town centre and provides tourist information on post offices and car parks.

5 The Canary Islands' Star Sights
Two pages are devoted to each major sight. They include an area map and, in the case of larger towns, a street map of the town centre.

An Area Map indicates the main sights, which are numbered for easy reference.

Tourist Information details length of suggested tour plus good stopping places.

6 National Parks
Separate pages in the guide are devoted to the national parks on the islands. Topographic maps in these sections indicate the star sights and any other special features of the park.

Photographs illustrate the most interesting areas and the most scenic spots within the park.

Maps show the area's main roads, walking trails and topography, as well as useful tourist information.

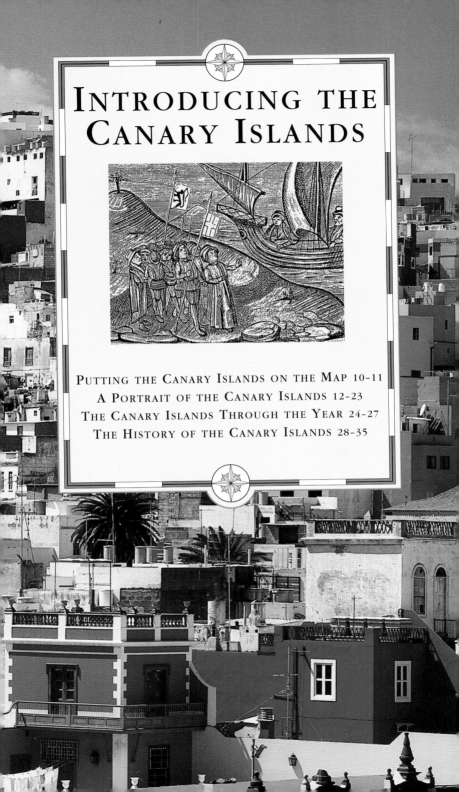

Introducing the Canary Islands

Putting the Canary Islands on the Map

D OTTED IN A GENTLE CURVE, the archipelago of the Canary Islands lies in the Atlantic Ocean to the west of Morocco in Saharan Africa. The seven main islands are inhabited with a total population of more than 1.6 million – the majority living on the larger islands of Gran Canaria and Tenerife. The total area of these volcanic islands is 7,447 sq km (2,875 sq miles) and encompasses a surprisingly rich variety of landscapes, from beaches and desert-like areas to dramatic mountain ranges and green woods. Hot winds from the Sahara ensure that the islands enjoy a warm climate all year round with temperatures averaging 18° C (64° F) in winter and 24° C (75° F) in summer.

Satellite View of Tenerife
This satellite picture shows how Mount Teide, with its volcanic crater, dominates the centre of this rocky island. At 3,718 m (12,195 ft), Teide is the highest peak in the Canaries and Spain.

LA PALMA

Los Llanos de Aridane
Santa Cruz de la Palma

Fuencaliente

La Laguna
Puerto de la Cruz
Santa Cruz de Tenerife
La Orotava

LA GOMERA

Agulo
San Sebastián de la Gomera

TENERIFE

Los Cristianos

Valverde
Puerto de la Estaca

EL HIERRO

0 km   40
0 miles   40

KEY

✈ Airport

▬ Motorway/Highway

▬ Major road

⚓ Ferry port

---- Ferry route

Eastern Coastline of El Hierro
Although there are few beaches here, the island possesses a wild beauty with its rugged coastline and green, misty interior. The smallest of the islands, El Hierro is sparsely populated.

↑ *Cádiz*

Bird's-eye View of Haria
Set in a beautiful valley on Lanzarote, Haria is typical of Canary villages. Its cluster of low, white houses nestles in the shadow of picturesque yet forbidding volcanoes.

ISLA DE ALEGRANZA

ISLA DE MONTAÑA CLARA

ISLA GRACIOSA

Tinajo
San Bartolomé

LANZAROTE

Arrecife

Playa Blanca

Corralejo

ISLA DE LOS LOBOS

FUERTEVENTURA

Puerto del Rosario

Betancuria

Tuineje

Gldar
Las Palmas de Gran Canaria

Agaete
Arucas

Telde

Santa Luca

Morro Jable

Maspalomas

GRAN CANARIA

Location of the Islands
Although just 100 km (62 miles) from Africa, the Canary Islands belong to Spain – a country over 1,100 km (680 miles) away. The islands' population of about 1.6 million, is swollen each year by more than 7.5 million tourists.

WESTERN EUROPE AND NORTH AFRICA

IRELAND
UNITED KINGDOM

FRANCE

ANDORRA

PORTUGAL
SPAIN

AZORES

BALEARICS

MADEIRA

MOROCCO

WESTERN SAHARA
MAURETANIA
ALGERIA

The Formation of the Canary Islands

ALONG WITH OTHER ATLANTIC islands, such as Madeira, the Azores and the Cape Verde Islands, the Canaries are of volcanic origin. They emerged from the sea millions of years ago: Lanzarote and Fuerteventura are believed to be the oldest at between 16 and 20 million years old, with Gran Canaria, Tenerife and La Gomera appearing around 8–13 million years ago. The remaining islands are much younger. Most of the islands lie in the shadow of a central volcanic cone surrounded by smaller cones and areas of solidified lava.

Near El Golfo (see p91) *on Lanzarote is a crater filled with seawater. A black sand beach separates the ocean from the grey-green waters of the lake.*

La Geria's vineyards *on Lanzarote (see p94) flourish in the fertile volcanic soil. Semi-circles of stones protect the vines from the prevailing winds, and the resulting grapes are used to produce the amber-coloured Malvasia wine.*

Atlantic Ocean

Canary Islands

Thin oceanic crust

Upper mantle

Dense lower mantle

THE ORIGIN OF THE ISLANDS

The Canary Islands are the tips of volcanoes pushed up from the floor of the Atlantic Ocean by the movement of the Earth's crust. As the crust buckled along fault lines, hot liquid rock or magma burst up through the cracks.

Los Azulejos *on Gran Canaria show the beauty of the multi-coloured volcanic rocks. Their varied chemical compositions, including copper salts and iron hydrites, create a stunning palette of colours from grey and brown, through ochre and red, to blue and green.*

Malpaís *means "badlands" and refers to this almost completely barren landscape on Fuerteventura (see p78). Only the most desert-hardened flora and fauna survive here.*

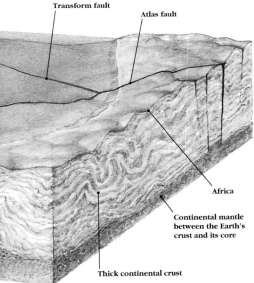

Transform fault
Atlas fault
Africa
Continental mantle between the Earth's crust and its core
Thick continental crust

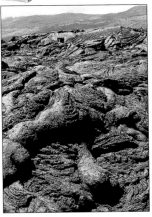

Around La Restinga *on El Hierro, the fields of lava assume fantastic shapes. Fat tongues of lava, that resemble solidified tar, are created by under-water volcanic eruptions. As the flowing lava rapidly cools it forms large areas of magma nodules.*

EVOLUTION OF VOLCANIC ISLANDS

The islands in this archipelago are at various stages in their geological evolution. Tenerife, El Hierro, Lanzarote and La Palma are still volcanically active, with the latter experiencing its most recent eruption in 1971.

Fissures
Feeder dyke
Mantle
Magma chamber
Basalt lava flow
Crust

1 ***The islands of*** *La Gomera, El Hierro and La Palma are really the tops of volcanoes that rise from the ocean's bed. They consist of basalt rock produced by solidified lava. Below, the Earth's crust bends under the weight of the islands.*

Caldera
Shallow magma chamber

2 ***When the magma*** *chamber empties during an eruption, the top of the cone collapses downwards. This creates a crater, known as a caldera – such as the Caldera de Taburiente on La Palma. This stage of an island's evolution is marked by abundant flows of lava.*

Sea level
Exposed solidified magma chamber

3 ***When the eruption*** *has ended, the volcano begins to erode. The mountains of Gran Canaria are in the early stages of erosion, while Fuerteventura's volcanic chambers, with their solidified lava, are typical of a more advanced stage of evolution.*

Flora of the Canary Islands

THE FLORA OF THE Canary Islands is unique. La Gomera, for example, is home to a rare ancient forest that is now a UNESCO world heritage site. More than half of the islands' 1,800 species are indigenous, and the unusual character of these exceptional plants has long attracted the attention of botanists. They are the relics of the old Mediterranean flora, which became extinct throughout the region because of changes in climate. The local flora that remains has survived because of the fairly stable and relatively humid climate of the Canary Islands, along with a variety of colourful, exotic imported plants.

Canary Island pine *is one of the native species, growing at altitudes of over 1,000 m (3,280 ft). Its needles reach over 30 cm (12 in) in length.*

Viper's bugloss (*Echium wildpretii*)

Canary Islands juniper

Canary palm *(Phoenix canariensis), another indigenous species, inhabits scrublands and semi-desert regions. It bears edible fruit, but is regarded mainly as an ornamental plant.*

*The **basalt slopes** of volcanoes are not conducive to plant growth. The few species found here are often indigenous plants, which have evolved to be able to retain water.*

*This type of **spurge olive** has silvery leaves.*

THE DRAGON TREE

One of the most unusual plants in the Canaries, the dragon tree ***(Dracaena draco)*** erupts into numerous, swollen branches that end in tufts of spiky leaves. Its red sap (known as dragon's blood) and its fruit were used as far back as Roman times to make a medicinal powder, and it was used to produce pigments, paints and varnishes. One specimen at Icod de los Vinos, on Tenerife, known as *Drago Milenario*, is said to be 1,000 years old.

Balsamic spurge *grows in semi-desert areas. Its juice is sometimes made into chewing gum, but it is also valued as an ornamental plant.*

Erysimum scoparium, *a woody, native shrub with lilac-pink flowers, grows in the highest regions of the Canary Islands.*

PLANT ZONES

Coastal zones, *mostly rocky, are home to plants that can tolerate salt and temperature variations.*

Semi-desert *plants, found above 400 m (1,300 ft), store water within their fleshy leaves and stalks.*

TYPICAL ISLAND

The mountains of the Canary Islands provide a home for a diverse array of flora, with different plants growing at each level. As the ground rises, the salt-tolerant and semi-desert vegetation gives way to humid rain forests, pine forests and, in the highest regions, to hard-leaf shrubs and rock plants.

Low shrubs *are found above 500 m (1,650 ft), particularly in areas with a low annual rainfall.*

Laurel forests *cover the northern slopes of the islands, where humidity is constantly high.*

Canary Islands spurge (Euphorbia canariensis)

Canary Islands strawflower (Helichrysum gossypium)

Limonium papillatum

Pine woods *occur at up to 2,000 m (6,560 ft). Their undergrowth consists mainly of shade-loving shrubs.*

Canary samphire (Astydamia latifolia) *is found on the coastal basalt rocks of the Canary Islands. This native genus, with its distinctive fleshy, green leaves flowers from December until April.*

Canary Islands holly *is an evergreen shrub, and one of the most common inhabitants of the laurel forests. Its bark has medicinal properties.*

Areas above *2,000 m (6,560 ft) feature cushion-like shrubs. Rock grass covers the highest slopes.*

The Underwater World

D ESPITE THE CANARY ISLANDS' favourable
position on the edge of the tropics, the
waters around the islands are relatively cold.
This explains the lack of coral reefs, which
would normally occur at such latitudes.
Nevertheless, the sea conditions are congenial
to many species of fish, mammal and
seaweed. Divers in coastal and offshore
waters will find a rich variety of marine life,
including several species of whales and
dolphins, shoals of small cardinal fish, huge
crabs, colourful parrot-fish and tiny seahorses.

*Long-finned pilot whales (blackfish)
belong to the dolphin family. The coastal
waters of Tenerife are home to the world's
second-largest colony of these mammals.*

SEA LIFE

The ocean floor around the Canary Islands is
mainly composed of rock with occasional
patches of sand. This environment, illustrated
here, is one reason for the richness of the
local fauna, which includes some
600 species of seaweed.

*Sea horses appear in great
numbers among clumps of
sea-grass, clinging to the
shoots by their tails.
The young hatch
out of spawn that is
laid by the female in the
male's brood pouch.*

*The blue-spotted puffer fish is
so-called due to its habit, when
threatened, of inflating its alimentary
canal with air, to scare off the enemy.*

**Bandtail
puffer**

**Worm
shell**

**Pearly
razorfish**

Starfish

Coral

Sea urchin

*The Parrot-fish is
among the most colourful
inhabitants of the Canary
Islands' waters. Its distinctive, beak-like mouth is
formed by large teeth
fused together.*

Spider crabs hide in the
nooks of the seabed. Their
red shells, which can be as
much as 20 cm (8 in) in
length, are densely covered
with spikes.

*The brown scorpion fish's markings and colour make
it difficult to spot against the rocky sea floor,
despite its large size. The hard spikes
of its dorsal fin deliver venom to its
prey during night hunts. The fish
remains still by day.*

The Moroccan octopus is a common sight in the areas of rocky seabed that lie around the Canary Islands. It catches its prey with its tentacles, which are armed with suckers.

This small mollusc is the *Murex trunculus,* used since antiquity for 2,000 years to make purple dye. It hides inside its thick, striped shell, and eats putrefied matter, including other, dead molluscs.

Limpet

Chiton

DIVING AND SNORKELLING IN THE CANARIES

The Canary Islands provide very attractive diving grounds. Here, beginners can gain experience, while more advanced divers can explore the underwater caves off Gran Canaria, La Palma and El Hierro and the coral reefs near Lanzarote. The water is at its clearest between November and February. The water temperature of 15–20° C (59–68° F) is also conducive to diving and snorkelling. However, strong currents, particularly at greater depths, can present difficulties for divers.

The conger eel has a blackish body, with paler belly, large head and wide mouth. It is active at night, hiding in caves and cracks during the day.

The moray eel, with its elongated, snake-like body and sharp teeth, is one of the fiercest predators of the coastal waters. This marine creature, which can be up to 3 m (10 ft) long, inhabits caves and cracks in the rocks.

Cardinal fish with their scarlet bodies are small, fast-moving fish that may be seen mostly at the entrances to underwater caves. The male carries the spawn in his mouth.

Crafts of the Canary Islands

Ceramic candleholder

T HE INHABITANTS OF THE Canary Islands are enthusiastic about keeping alive their strongly rooted tradition of local handicrafts. These include embroidery, lace-making, basket-weaving, ceramics and woodcarving. Different islands specialize in particular crafts: La Gomera is known for its basketware and pottery that is made without using a wheel, while Tenerife is also a centre for traditional, Guanche-style pots, El Hierro produces beautifully woven rugs and bags and the town of Ingenio *(see p64)* Gran Canaria, produces some of the best embroidery in the islands.

Potter at work in La Orotava workshop, Tenerife

POTTERY

T HANKS TO archaeological discoveries, we now know that pottery was one of the best-developed crafts of the Guanches – the indigenous people of the Canary Islands. Using local clay, they made vessels of various shapes and sizes, which they used for cooking, storing food and carrying water.

Although locally made pottery can be found on all the islands, there are a few centres that pride themselves on their ceramic workshops. La Gomera, Tenerife and La Palma are particularly well known for traditional pottery. Produced from dark clay, without the use of a potter's wheel, this is the most popular style of pottery, and it is regarded as a classic reinterpretation

of Guanche work. Other islands also make pieces that are based on original Guanche designs copied from archaeological finds and produced by traditional methods.

As on the Spanish mainland, there are tiles, plates and vases in the multi-coloured style of the Moorish inspired *azulejos,* for sale in pottery shops.

Colourful displays of pottery adorn many local village shops and most markets will have at least one stall selling ceramics. Workshops where you can view the pots being made also offer an array of wares that makes choosing difficult.

Ornamental water vessel

EMBROIDERY

P RACTISED MAINLY by the women, the skills and styles of Canary Islands' embroidery are passed down from mother to daughter. The craft of embroidery is a source of great pride in the areas that specialize in it. Gran Canaria is famous for embroidery, particularly the villages of Ingenio *(see p64)* and Agaete *(see p57)*, as is La Orotava *(see pp 108–11)* on Tenerife. Original patterns, hand-embroidered onto silk or linen, are among the most exquisite souvenirs that visitors can take home. Richly embroidered bed linen, tablecloths and napkins are among the most popular items. The only drawback is their often very high price, which is a reflection of the skill and time taken by the embroiderer.

Clothing, especially the islands' national costumes, is decorated with embroidery. White shirts, blouses and aprons are all adorned with open-work frills that are threaded with ribbons. Modern, somewhat garish copies of these clothes are on sale in craft markets.

Traditional embroidery in Betancuria Museum, Fuerteventura

LACE-MAKING

LACEWORK IS AMONG the most beautiful and the most striking of the Canary Islands' handicrafts. The subtlety of the designs and colours reflects the continuation of European and Mediterranean traditions.

There are several small, specialized co-operatives on the islands, producing lace tablecloths and curtains. These are very popular among the islanders as well as the tourists. Unlike embroidered items, lacework is not too expensive.

The beautiful openwork tablecloths and placemats are always produced in white and beige. Their designs usually consist of symmetrical patterns with abstract or floral motifs, featuring circles and suns linked together to create uniform compositions.

Experts regard the lace produced in Vilaflor, on Tenerife, as being the most beautiful and best quality.

Lace tablecloth from San Bartolomé on Lanzarote

WEAVING

WEAVING is another traditional handicraft that continues to thrive in the Canary Islands, and there are many established weavers' shops still working in the islands today. As in past centuries, simple hand-looms are still used to produce carpets, which are based on traditional designs. Long and narrow, often with randomly mixed colours,

Weaver's workshop, producing striped carpets

these carpets are very popular with the local population. You will also find carpets with regular stripes or with more sophisticated designs, based on traditional local patterns. Hand-woven cloth is still used to make rugs, tapestries and bags and, until recently, some elements of the local national costumes were also hand-woven. The islands of La Palma and La Gomera are known for their woven products.

Long, multi-coloured striped carpet

OTHER HANDICRAFTS

ALWAYS VERY popular with tourists are items woven from palm leaves or willow. These include baskets and bowls, which are not designed to last forever, but are nevertheless very reasonably priced. Also for sale are the wide-brimmed hats that are an indispensable part of farm workers' clothing.

On religious feast days, the women of the islands wear small hats with an upturned brim. This local fashion has helped to further a demand for these locally produced, plaited straw hats, which are light and airy to wear.

Highly regarded for their artistic merit are local carpentry and woodwork products. The tradition of adorning the surfaces of wooden gates, doors and shutters with carved motifs goes back many centuries. Old gates and shutters, as well as church ornaments, are often masterpieces of woodcarving. The distinctive wooden balconies and oriels, with their carved brackets and balustrades, are based on historic designs. Local trees, including pine, chestnut and beech, provide timber for many household items such as bowls, spoons and ladles.

The *timple* – a small, wooden, five-stringed instrument resembling a ukulele — is a popular souvenir from the Canary Islands. The village of Telde on Lanzarote is renowned for producing these instruments.

***Timple*-maker at work**

Canary Islands Carnivals

OFTEN COMPARED to the extravaganzas in Rio de Janeiro and New Orleans, the Santa Cruz carnival in Tenerife takes place each year in the 10–14 days before Ash Wednesday. It is one of the largest carnivals in Europe, with a spectacular display of costumes and Latin American music. In Gran Canaria, festivities start when the Tenerife carnival ends. The Carnival Fiesta in Lanzarote takes place at the beginning of March, with one in Fuerteventura two weeks later. Although street parties were banned under the Franco regime, the tradition of holding carnivals – renamed "winter festivals" – survived on the islands, re-emerging in their full glory after Spain's return to democracy in 1975.

A candidate for the coveted title of "Carnival Queen"

Colourful procession in the streets of Santa Cruz de Tenerife

STREET PARADES

EACH CARNIVAL has a different theme, usually religious, which dictates the character of the street parades, the costumes worn by revellers and the choice of decorations. Street processions are held every day during the carnival.

Organized marchers are accompanied by floats with tableaux of historical or allegorical scenes. Although just for fun, a lot of care goes into creating the music and costumes for the parades.

THE STAGE

ANOTHER ESSENTIAL element of each carnival is the stage, which is usually built in the town centre. A main venue for night-time revels, this is where the spectacular carnival shows are held each evening, the bands and acrobatic displays attracting huge crowds. Keenly fought competitions are held here, such as one for the best formation dancing team. Comedy shows also attract large audiences. The same stage provides a venue for classical concerts, including programmes of choral works.

THE CARNIVAL QUEEN

THE CARNIVAL begins with the election of its queen. Accompanied by colourful carnival crowds, the hopeful candidates arrive in front of the jury on their lavishly decorated floats.

The contestants are usually local beauties, but any girl may take part in the competition. The beauty and grace of the prospective queens are emphasized by their magnificent costumes. The queen's dress must be unique and command general admiration.

The newly elected queen, accompanied by her equally beautiful ladies-in-waiting, reigns over all the carnival festivities. Her float takes the place of honour in all the parades and the happy "sovereign" looks down from her throne, greeting her cheering carnival subjects as she passes by.

Drag show on the stage in Las Palmas de Gran Canaria

CHILDREN

CARNIVAL means fun and games for everyone, not just the adults – children also enjoy the festivities with many events just for them. They march in separate "small" parades and participate in their own stage shows and competitions. Little girls compete for the title of "Carnival Princess".

Children's costumes, made specially for the occasion, are often tiny masterpieces of dressmaking. They include traditional Spanish folk dresses, Brazilian samba costumes, fairy-tale and circus figures. Pint-sized participants, thrilled with the excitement and their roles, quickly enter into the spirit of carnival.

CARNIVAL COSTUMES AND MAKE-UP

IT OFTEN TAKES months to make the extravagant costumes and masks and to design and construct the floats, so as soon as one carnival ends, the Canarios begin planning the next.

The general aim is always originality, and the ideas for carnival costumes are often unique. The shapes and forms of the outfits are inspired by many cultures, but one indispensable element is an unusual hairstyle – the more extravagant the better.

Another important factor is the make-up, which often sets the theme and is an integral component of the costume. Carnival events often include exhibitions of the most unusual or spectacular body paintings.

DRAG QUEENS

ANOTHER NOTABLE feature of the Canary Islands' carnivals is the drag queens. Mixing with the masquerading crowds they are conspicuously tall as they walk on their high-heeled,

Children's dancing display, in colourful costumes

platform shoes. At night-time, drag queens flaunt their costumes and demonstrate their dancing skills. The one judged most striking and beautiful becomes queen.

A Medusa costume, with equally lurid make-up

MASQUERADERS

IN CONTRAST with the carnival in Rio de Janeiro, where the main procession consists only of organized groups, in the Canary Islands almost everybody wears a mask and costume. Since the masquerade fever also affects tourists, the parade inevitably turns into a huge fancy-dress ball, with druids, pirates, samurai warriors and comedy figures, such as Charlie Chaplin or Disney cartoon characters, packing the streets and squares. The ever-popular game of

pretending to be someone else creates a great sense of euphoria and encourages masqueraders to let their hair down and party.

THE BURIAL OF THE SARDINE

THE SANTA CRUZ carnival ends with a grand funeral procession, called *El Entierro de la Sardina* (the burial of the sardine). This ritual is rooted in the past when carnival was the one occasion when people could deride such powerful institutions as the church. Today, crowds still dress up as clerical figures.

Carried at the head of the procession is an enormous papier-mâché sardine. The "mourners" wail and laugh as they escort the fish to the sea. Here it is set alight and hundreds of fireworks inside it create an explosive display.

Carnival reveller, dressed as a pirate

Sports in the Canary Islands

Extremely favourable year-round weather conditions make the Canary Islands a paradise for all types of sporting activities. The most popular are, naturally, water-based sports such as sailing and windsurfing, but the islands also play host to a variety of spectator sports including golf, international car rallies and soccer matches. Although local sports teams and athletes are not represented at international levels, the islanders are keen on sport and enthusiastically support their soccer teams and the islands' traditional form of wrestling – *lucha canaria*.

Competitor on Caldera de Bandama golf course

Golf

There are 14 excellent golf courses in the Canary Islands – on Gran Canaria, Lanzarote, Tenerife and Fuerteventura – and the all-year-round conditions make this an ideal choice for a golfing holiday. From time to time, the islands host such events as the PGA Spanish Open. The Shell Wonderful World of Golf competition is a fun event held in Tenerife.

Surfing

Local surfing conditions in the Canary Islands are magnificent and, for European enthusiasts, have the advantage of being only a short flight away. Lanzarote and Gran Canaria are regarded as having the best conditions, with good waves and favourable winds. The islands host numerous international competitions, which are attended by world-class surfers. Local surfers, trained in the island schools, often triumph in the minor events.

The best-known "longboard" competitions are Trofeo O'Neil de Surf (*O'Neil surfing trophy*), held on El Socorro beach in Tenerife, and Festival Longboard de Canarias (*Canary Island Longboard Festival*) held at Playa de la Caleta, in Gran Canaria. Copa Federación de Bodyboard (*Bodyboard Federation Cup*) was held here in 2001 as part of the European Championships.

Car Rallies

As in mainland Spain, car rallies are very popular in the Canary Islands and the events held here are attended by many of the world's top competitors.

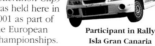

Participant in Rally Isla Gran Canaria

The twisting mountain roads and extensive wilderness areas make these rallies as challenging as the more famous rallies held elsewhere in the world.

Crowds of spectators gather to watch the main events, and the finish of a race is usually heralded with celebrations. The top event is the Michelin Race of Champions held on Gran Canaria every year. The world's best drivers compete to determine the year's professional rankings.

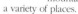

Cycle Racing and Mountain Biking

Spanish cyclists are among the world's best, and cheering spectatators line the routes of the many international events that are held here. Vuelta Ciclista a España, held in Gran Canaria, is considered to be one of the world's top cycling events.

Non-competitive cycling is also popular, and is a great way to enjoy the islands' beauty. There are tour packages or you can rent mountain bikes at a variety of places.

Triathlon

Since 1992, Lanzarote has played host to the Iron-man Triathlon event, which involves a 3.8 km (2.3 miles)

Surfer competing in Gran Canaria

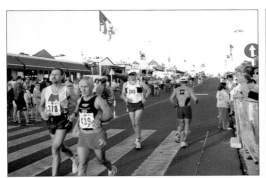

At the finishing line of a triathlon event in Lanzarote

swim, a 42.2 km (26 miles) run and a 180 km (112 miles) cycle ride. This event is held in May at the Playa del Carmen and is very popular with athletes and spectators.

WINDSURFING

THE CANARY ISLANDS rank among the world's best windsurfing venues, and this is borne out by the fact that the world champion of the sport, Björn Dukenberg, lives and trains here. El Médano in Tenerife is acknowledged as one of the world's great windsurfing centres.

The islands play host to several events in the World Cup series, including the Grand Prix de Fuerteventura. Several major regattas are held in Grand Canaria, such as Gran Canaria PWA Gran Slam in Pozo Izquierdo.

SAILING AND DIVING

SAILING enjoys enormous popularity here – one of the great enthusiasts of the sport and a member of the Spanish international team is King Juan Carlos himself. Several sailing events are held in the islands each year. Yachts and dinghies may be also be hired.

The clear warm waters around the islands are attractive for divers, particularly off Tenerife and Lanzarote. Marine parks offer diving packages.

VOLLEYBALL

VOLLEYBALL IS PLAYED on beaches across the resorts of the islands. But this is also a spectator sport of international standard. One of

Windsurfing competition at Pozo Isquiero beach

the top teams is Idecent Guaguas from Las Palmas. Among the leaders of the Spanish league are Hotel Centaur of Gran Canaria. CV Construcciones Marichal of Tenerife is not only one of the best teams in Spain, but also in Europe.

SOCCER

THE SPANISH – and this includes the inhabitants of the Canary Islands – are great soccer fans. Almost every small town on the islands has its own football stadium. At present two Canary teams – Unión Deportivo Las Palmas and Club Deportivo Tenerife – play in Spain's premier league. Although not the best in the league, they have their faithful supporters, as do the minor teams from lower ranking leagues.

Apart from the regular league games, there are also a number of major soccer events. The traditional soccer tournament in Maspalomas takes place during the winter months. Its participants include some well-known first-league teams from Germany, Denmark and England. The Mundialito (the little world cup), held in Gran Canaria, attracts thousands of young soccer players from around the world.

LUCHA CANARIA

The local version of wrestling – *lucha canaria* – is an extremely popular sport in the Canary Islands. Each team consists of two members, but the competitors fight individually. Each pair plays a match consisting of three rounds and the winning team is the one that wins most rounds. The rules forbid the competitors to kick, hit or pinch. During the fight they are allowed to touch the floor only with the soles of their feet. Competitors fight in a ring measuring 9–10 m (30–33 ft) in diameter, covered with sand.

Two competitors in a *Lucha canaria* wrestling match

THE CANARY ISLANDS
THROUGH THE YEAR

THE INHABITANTS of the Canary Islands are deeply devoted to tradition – a fact that is reflected in the numerous religious feast days, or fiestas, that they celebrate. Some of these traditions go back to the time of the Guanches (see pp30–31). Fiestas are normally associated with the cult of saints, and in particular with various patron saints. In agricultural areas, fiestas mark the end of the harvest. During

Tenerife 1996 carnival souvenir

the fiesta, people abandon their work to pray, dance and join colourful parades. Fiestas in the Canary Islands tend to last for several days, some for as long as two or three weeks. In the Islands' larger cities such fiestas are often accompanied by music, theatre and cinema festivals, and some have an international flavour. Of the other events on the islands, sporting events, and particularly *lucha canaria* and soccer, attract enormous crowds.

Flowering apple trees at the foot of Roque Nublo, Gran Canaria

SPRING

ALTHOUGH THE year-round mild climate of the Canary Islands gives the impression of perpetual spring, true spring weather is most noticeable between March and May. Then the landscape is at its greenest. This is also the season of intense rainfall, particularly on Tenerife.

MARCH

Fiesta del Almendro en Flor (*early Mar*) all islands. The fiesta of almond blossom, is celebrated on a grand scale in the towns of Tejeda and Valsequillo, Gran Canaria.

There are displays of classic folk dancing, and almonds, wines and sweets are distributed by each village.
Rally El Corte Inglés (*Mar/Apr*), Gran Canaria. Car rally attracting international competitors.
Semana Santa (*Mar/Apr*), all islands. Holy Week, with a Good Friday procession.

APRIL

Fiesta de Juventud (*5 Apr*), Lajita, Fuerteventura. Feast day of the Virgin Mary.
Fiesta de los Pastores (*25 Apr*). La Dehesa, El Hierro. The annual feast of the island's shepherds.
Fiesta de Ansite (*29 Apr*),

Bunch of ripe bananas

Gran Canaria. Music and dancing mark the final uprising of the Guanches against the Spanish and Spain's victory over the island.

MAY

Festival de Ballet y Danza (*May*), Las Palmas de Gran Canaria. Concerts and dance performances.
Fiesta del Queso del Flor (*30 Apr– 7 May*), Santa María de Guía, Gran Canaria. Much eating of cheese in this small town famed for its production.
Feria del Caballo (*1 May*) in Valsequillo is an annual horse market.
Romería de San Isidro (*15 May*) in Uga, Lanzarote. Elaborate procession.

Traditional fiesta procession on El Hierro

AVERAGE DAILY HOURS OF SUNSHINE

Hours

Jan Feb Mar Apr May Jun Jul Aug Sep Oct Nov Dec

Hours of Sunshne
The islands differ considerably in their daily hours of sunshine: Lanzarote and Fuerteventura enjoy only about 12 sunny days in August; northern parts of Tenerife and Gran Ganaria can sometimes be cloudy, while the southern regions of the islands bask in sunshine.

SUMMER

IN SUMMER, temperatures in the islands can reach 35° C (95° F). During July and August, there is very little rainfall, except in the region of Las Palmas de Gran Canaria. In August, the crowds of foreign tourists are swollen by holiday-makers from the Spanish mainland. This is when most fiestas take place.

Gathering cochineal insects on a prickly pear plantation

JUNE

Corpus Christi *(Jun)*, all islands. Celebrations include processions, and are at their most colourful in Las Palmas, Gran Canaria, and La Laguna, and La Orotava, Tenerife.
Festival Internacional de Música Popular *(Jun)*, Las Palmas. Folk music and dancing performed by both local and visiting groups.
Día de San Juan *(24 Jun)*, Las Palmas de Gran Canaria.

Crowded beaches of Puerto del Carmen, Lanzarote

Commemorates the town's foundation with a big party.
Bajada de Nuestra Señora de las Nieves *(every 5 years, end Jun)*, Santa Cruz de la Palma. Amazing costumes, and a lavish procession at this important festival.
Día de San Pedro y San Pablo *(29 Jun)*, is the feast of St Peter and St Paul.

JULY

Bajada de la Virgen de los Reyes *(every 4 years, early Jul)*. El Hierro. A fabulous procession and party.
Festival Internacional Canarias Jazz & Mas Heineken *(three weeks in Jul)*, all islands. Jazz concerts by international musicians.
Fiesta de San Marcial del Rubicon *(one week in Jul)*, Femés and Yaiza. Celebrates Lanzarote's patron saint.
Día de San Buenaventura *(14 Jul)*, Bentacuria, Fuerteventura. The town's patron saint processes through the streets.
Fiesta del Carmen *(16 Jul)*, Gáldar, Gran Canaria. Party and procession in honour of

the patron saint of fishermen.
Día de Santiago Apóstol *(25 Jul)*, Santa Cruz, Tenerife. Celebrates the island's patron saint and the town's defeat of the English and Nelson.

AUGUST

Bajada de la Rama *(4 Aug)*, Agaete, Gran Canaria. This colourful fiesta has its roots in the Guanches' rain dance.
Día de San Bartolomé *(24 Aug)*, in San Bartolomé, Lanzarote. Processions, music and dancing honour the saint.
Fiesta de San Ginés *(25 Aug)*, Arrecife, Lanzarote. Feast of St Gines, the patron saint of the town of Arrecife.

Bajada de Nuestra Señora de las Nieves, La Palma

AVERAGE MONTHLY RAINFALL

mm
60
50
40
30
20
10
0

Jan Feb Mar Apr May Jun Jul Aug Sep Oct Nov Dec

Rainfall
The average monthly rainfall in the Canary Islands rarely exceeds 50 mm (2 in). La Palma and La Gomera have the highest rainfall, Lanzarote and Fuerteventura the lowest. The rain is more frequent in Tenerife and Gran Canaria, particularly on the northern shores of the islands.

Fiesta of San Miguel Arcangel in Tuineje

AUTUMN

AUTUMN DOES not differ much from summer, except that high daytime temperatures give way to somewhat cooler nights. Large temperature differences may be felt at higher altitudes on Tenerife or Gran Canaria, where you can find yourself suddenly enveloped in fog, with a rapid drop in temperature.

SEPTEMBER

Encuentro Internacional Tres Continentes (*Sep*), Agüimes, Gran Canaria. Exciting international theatre festival, with European, Latin American and African groups.
Columbus Week (*1–6 Sep*), San Sebastián, La Gomera. Shows and processions celebrate Christopher Columbus.
Fiesta de la Virgen del Pino (*6–8 Sep*) Teror, Gran Canaria. The island's most important celebration includes an evening procession with offerings of

produce to the patron saint of Gran Canaria.
Fiesta del Charco (*7–11 Sep*), San Nicolás, La Palma. Participants jump into a pool of salt water to catch fish.
Romería de Nuestra Señora de Los Dolores (*21 Sep*), Lanzarote. A pilgrimage to the sanctuary of Los Dolores (St Mary of the Volcanoes), in Mancha Blanca.

Fishing, an all-year-round occupation in the Canary Islands

Fiesta de la Virgen de la Peña (*3rd Sat in Sep*). Celebration of the patron saint of Fuerteventura.
Fiesta del Santísimo Cristo (*late Sep*) La Laguna, Tenerife. A spectacular fiesta featuring firework displays, a vintage car rally and *lucha canaria* tournaments.

OCTOBER

Bajada de la Virgen de Guadelupe (*5 Oct*), La Gomera. Fishermen carry a statue of the Virgin Mary from Puntallana to San Sebastián by sea.
Fiesta de la Naval (*6 Oct*), Las Palmas, Gran Canaria. Festival to celebrate victory over Sir Francis Drake.
Romería de Nuestra Señora de la Luz (*mid-Oct*), Las Palmas, Gran Canaria. Procession of boats at sea celebrate the Virgin.
Festival Internacional de Cine de Las Palmas (*Oct–Nov*), Gran Canaria. Film festival attracting many international movie stars.

NOVEMBER

International Ecological Film Festival Puerto de la Cruz, Tenerife. Shows films that are devoted mainly to the Canary Islands.
Feast of the Teide Volcano (*16 Nov*) Guía de Isora, Tenerife. Celebrates Spain's highest mountain.
Atlantic Rally for Cruisers (*last Sun in Nov*), Gran Canaria. A transatlantic rally for yachts from Las Palmas to the Caribbean.

AVERAGE MONTHLY TEMPERATURE

°C
30
25
20
15
10
5
0
Jan Feb Mar Apr May Jun Jul Aug Sep Oct Nov Dec

Temperature
The mild climate produces average temperatures of between 18° C (64° F) in the winter and 24° C (75° F) in the summer. The climate on Fuerteventura and Lanzarote is harsher than that in Tenerife and Gran Canaria. In El Hierro, the western-most island, it is often cool and damp.

WINTER

MANY PEOPLE decide to spend the winter months on the Canary Islands, not least because of the mild climate at this time of the year. For this reason, the height of the tourist season on the Canary Islands is from December to February. Although the peak of the Teide volcano is sometimes covered with snow, the coastal areas remain warm.

DECEMBER

Día de Santa Lucia *(13 Dec)*, Gran Canaria. Churches and villages are illuminated for this celebration.
Santos Inocentes *(28 Dec)*, all islands. This is the Spanish equivalent of April Fools' Day, when tricks are played.
Carrera de San Silvestre *(31 Dec)*, Maspalomas, Gran Canaria. This is the annual New Year's Eve run.
Noche Vieja *(31 Dec)* is the New Year's Eve celebration.

Gale-stricken ship listing off the coast of Lanzarote

JANUARY

Festival de Música de Canarias *(Jan/Mar)*, most islands. Classical music concerts with international orchestra and soloists.
Soccer Tournament *(Jan/Feb)*, Maspalomas, Gran Canaria. For European clubs.
Día de los Reyes *(6 Jan)*, all islands. The three kings throw sweets to the children at this Epiphany celebration with colourful processions.

FEBRUARY

Festival de Opera *(Feb/Mar)* most islands. An international opera festival held principally in Las Palmas' Teatro Pérez Daldós and Tenerife's Teatro Guimerá.
Carnival *(Feb/Mar)*, all islands. Several weeks of partying and masquerades commence with the election of the carnival queen.
Romería de la Virgen de Candelaria *(2 Feb and 15 Aug)*, Candelaria, Tenerife. Candlemas. The Feast of the Virgin Mary, the patron saint of the islands, is celebrated in style to commemorate the day on which the Virgin appeared to the Guanches.

PUBLIC HOLIDAYS

Año Nuevo *New Year's Day (1 Jan)*
Día de los Reyes *Epiphany (6 Jan)*
Jueves Santo *Maundy Thursday (Mar/Apr)*
Viernes Santo *Good Friday (Mar/Apr)*
Día de Pascua *Easter (Mar/Apr)*
Fiesta de Trabajo *Labour Day (1 May)*
Día de las Islas Canarias *Canary Islands Day (30 May)*
Corpus Christi *(early Jun)*
Asunción *Assumption of the Virgin Mary (15 Aug)*
Día de la Hispanidad *National Day (12 Oct)*
Todos los Santos *All Saints' Day (1 Nov)*
Día de la Constitución *Day of the Constitution (6 Dec)*
Inmaculada Concepción *(8 Dec)*
Navidad *Christmas (25 Dec)*

Drag queen in procession during carnival

THE HISTORY OF THE CANARY ISLANDS

*T*HE EARLY HISTORY *of the Canary Islands is shrouded in myth and legend. Some believed the islands to be the lost land of Atlantis, which, according to Plato, was destroyed by an earthquake. To others they were known as the Fortunate Islands, poised at the edge of the world, whose inhabitants knew no sorrow.*

It is believed that the first inhabitants of the Canary Islands came from North Africa, and probably arrived here around 3,000 BC. Although scholars disagree about the origins of the islands' early dwellers, one prominent theory is that they were Neolithic people from the Cro-Magnon era. Typically thet were tall and well-built with narrow skulls.

Around the second century BC, the islands became populated by the next wave of arrivals – the Guanches. Their origins have also not been clearly established. It is believed that prior to the conquest of the islands by Spain in the 15th century, the Guanche population of the islands consisted of some 30,000 in Gran Canaria and Tenerife, over 4,000 in La Palma, over 1,000 in El Hierro and a few hundred in Fuerteventura and Lanzarote.

The ancients knew about the islands: their sailors used to visit them and information about the archipelago can be found in the writings of Roman historians. In AD 150, a fairly accurate map by the

Idol from Tara – a statuette from the time of the Guanches

Egyptian geographer, Ptolemy, represented the islands as the edge of the world. Following the fall of the Roman Empire, Europe forgot the Canaries for over 1,000 years.

CONQUEST OF THE CANARY ISLANDS

The Canary Islands were rediscovered by Mediterranean sailors. In 1312, Captain Lanzarotto (or Lancelotto) Malocello, a native of Genoa, reached the furthest northeast island, where he encountered the native population, the Guanches. The island was subsequently named after him – Lanzarote.

Throughout the 14th century, Italians, Portuguese and Catalans sent their ships to the islands to bring back slaves and furs.

The rapid process of the islands' conquest began in 1402, when the Norman knight, Jean de Béthencourt, arrived in Lanzarote. Two years later, he returned with the backing of the Castilian crown. Encountering little resistance, the conquistadors took over the sparsely populated islands of El Hierro, La Gomera and Fuerteventura.

TIMELINE

2nd–1st century BC Arrival of Guanches	**AD 24** Campaign of the Moorish King Juba II		**1402–1405** Jean de Béthencourt conquers Lanzarote, Fuerteventura and El Hierro
3350 BC	AD 1	350	700	1050	1400
3,000 BC Arrival of African migrants	**AD 150** Ptolemy plots the position of the Canary Islands on his world map		**1312** Lanzarotto Malocello lands on the most north-easterly island of the archipelago

Anaterue – Guanche chieftain

◁ **Christopher Columbus, discoverer of the Americas**

The Guanches

Guanche clay pot

THE ANCIENT INHABITANTS of the Canary Islands were known as the Guanches from the words "guan", (meaning "man") and "che", (meaning "white mountain"), referring to the snow-capped Teide volcano on Tenerife. According to Spanish historical records, the Guanches were tall, strongly built, blue-eyed and blond-haired. Their origins and date of arrival on the islands are still unknown, as is the language they spoke. Their society was based on a tribal structure, with a king or chieftain at its head. They worshipped Abor – a powerful god who could bring rain and stop the flow of lava. Their tools and weapons were produced from roughly cut wood, stone and bone.

Rock Carvings
These rock carvings, many of which have been pre-served, once adorned caves inhabited by the Guanches.

Rock Paintings
Cave paintings bear testimony to the artistic skill of the Guanches. Cueva Pintada, near Gáldar on Gran Canaria, is decorated with striking red, white and black geometric patterns.

Quern
The Guanches used querns (mills) made from lava to grind barley, to make their staple, a porridge known as gofio.

Guanche family in their cave

COSTUMBRES DE L

DAILY LIFE OF THE GUANCHES
One of three small mosaics in the town park in Santa Cruz de Tenerife illustrates the life of the Guanche tribe during peacetime. In a landscape and climate similar to that of the present day, the Guanches cultivated land and raised animals.

Cave Dwelling
The Guanches lived in natural caves, such as Cueva de Belmaco, or in grottos carved into the rocks. Caves also served as granaries and as places of worship, and were also used to bury the dead.

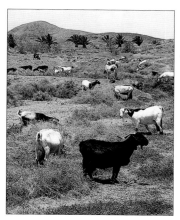

Domestic Animals
Goats and sheep are the only animals that can find food in the hard mountainous terrain of the Canary Islands. The Guanches depended on these animals to supply them with skins, milk and meat.

Shepherds fought daily battles for better grazing grounds for their flocks of sheep and goats. In the face of external dangers, they would unite and become warriors.

Guanche Chief
Guanches were led into battles by their tribal kings, known as "guanarteme" in Gran Canaria and as "menceyes" in Tenerife and La Palma.

Long, strong poles or spears were used as weapons in battles and were also useful when traversing the difficult mountainous terrain.

REMAINS OF THE GUANCHE CULTURE

Apart from the caves, the early indiginous population lived in somewhat primitive, low huts built of stone, such as those that have been partially reconstructed in the ethnographic park Mundo Aborigen, in Gran Canaria. The bodies of the tribal elders were mummified, and you can see them today in Canary museums, along with stone and bone ornaments, clay pots and woven bags.

The mummified skull of a Guanche, its orifices plugged with beeswax, is one of many such items kept in the Museo de la Naturaleza y el Hombre in Tenerife.

Circular Guanche tombs in Mundo Aborigen

Founding of Santa Cruz de Tenerife

THE 15TH CENTURY

The Portuguese followed in the footsteps of the Spanish conquistadors in the mid-15th century. The rivalry between the two seafaring powers lasted until 1479, when the Alcáçovas Treaty gave the Canary Islands to Spain, who, in return, let Portugal annex the Azores, the Cape Verde Islands and Madeira.

Mosaic depicting the ship of Christopher Columbus

The following years brought a new wave of bloody conquests: 1483 saw the fall of Gran Canaria, followed five years later by La Gomera and, in 1496, La Palma. In 1495, following three years of intense battles, Tenerife, which had put up the fiercest resistance, fell into the hands of the Spanish. The Guanches, deprived of their land and forced into slavery, were soon dying out. Those who survived were forcibly converted to Christianity and became assimilated.

In 1541, Girolamo Benzoni, an Italian visiting the islands, noted that the Guanches were "nearly extinct" and that their language had not survived the century following their subjugation by Spain.

THE SUGAR ERA

The 16th century brought about a rapid growth in the numbers of European settlers on the islands, particularly in Gran Canaria and Tenerife. Sugar cane, imported from Madeira, was used to produce sugar, which quickly became the main export from each island. Large sugar-cane plantations sprang up, employing European workers and African slaves, despite the ban on the slave trade introduced by Spain in 1537. This industry resulted in the transformation of the local ecosystem. Stripped of their trees, forests gave way to sugar-cane fields and bare slopes became prone to erosion.

The growth of the sugar industry was halted by the colonization of America and the Caribbean where sugar could be produced more cheaply.

Castillo San Miguel, guarding Garachico against pirates

TIMELINE

1478–1483 The Spanish, led by Juan Rejón and Pedro de Vera, occupy Gran Canaria	**1494–1496** Occupation of Tenerife by Alonso Fernández de Lugo completes the conquest of the archipelago	**1537** The Spanish introduce a ban on the slave trade, which is not observed in the Canary Islands

1450	1500	1550	1600

1479 The Alcáçovas Treaty gives the Canary Islands to Spain

Christopher Columbus stopped in the Canary Islands to provision his ships

1590 *Descripción de las Islas Canarias*, by Leonardo Torriani

THE WINE TRADE

The Canary Islands' economy was saved by the growing export demand for wine, which was produced mainly in Tenerife and Gran Canaria. So popular was the local *vino seco* that it was praised by the character

Map from around 1600 showing the Canary Islands situated off the west coast of Africa

Falstaff in Shakespeare's play, Henry IV part II. The Canary Islands' Company was founded in 1665 in London, and came to monopolize the Canary wine trade in Great Britain.

At the turn of the 18th century, however, income from wine production fell drastically. One of the reasons was a plague of locusts from 1685 to 1687 that destroyed the vineyards. In addition, the emergence of competition from new brands of wine from Madeira and Málaga, and the War of the Spanish Succession, which Spain fought with England and Portugal, reduced the demand.

The closing years of the 18th century witnessed a further reduction in wine production and export. This led to the near total collapse of the economy on the islands. It was at this time that carmine – a natural dye obtained from cochineal insects – became a major export. To this day the islands are major exporters of cochineal, used to produce dye for the food industry.

THE ISLANDS UNDER ATTACK

Spanish rule of the Canary Islands was threatened almost from the start. Throughout the 16th and 17th centuries, pirates and slave traders, from Europe and the northwest coast of Africa, harassed the islands. Several castles were built during this period to defend port entries from French, Dutch and British fleets; they also provided shelter for the local population when under attack. The last attempt at conquering the Canary Islands was made in 1797 by Admiral Horatio Nelson, who launched an attack on Santa Cruz de Tenerife. He not only failed to take the town, but lost his arm in the battle. The Governor of Santa Cruz, in a truly magnanimous gesture, presented the vanquished enemy with some of the local wine.

Ornate Baroque altar from the church, Iglesia de Nuestra Señora de la Regla, in Pájara, Fuerteventura

1665 Establishment of the Canary Islands' company, in London

British fleet attacking San Sebastián de la Gomera

1797 British fleet, commanded by Admiral Horatio Nelson, attacks Santa Cruz de Tenerife

1650	1700	1750	1800

1666 Peasants destroy English *bodegas* in Garachico

1706 Garachico destroyed by the eruption of Volcán Negra

1744 Benedict XIV permits Augustine monks to establish a university in La Laguna

El Tigre gun from Santa Cruz de Tenerife

19TH-CENTURY ISLAND RIVALRIES

In 1821, the Canary Islands became a province of Spain, with its capital in Santa Cruz de Tenerife. This situation served to intensify the rivalry between the two largest islands in the archipelago – Tenerife and Gran Canaria. In 1852, Queen Isabella II granted duty-free status to the Canary Islands.

Casa de la Coroneles, seat of the Colonels who ruled Fuerteventura

In view of the growing domination of Tenerife in 1911, local rule was re-established on individual islands, thus weakening the control that Santa Cruz de Tenerife exercised over the whole archipelago. In 1927, the rivalry between Santa Cruz de Tenerife and Las Palmas de Gran Canaria led to the division of the archipelago into two provinces: the western province including the islands of Tenerife, La Gomera, La Palma and El Hierro, and the eastern province including Gran Canaria, Fuerteventura and Lanzarote. This division remains in force to this day.

Manuel Velásquez Cabrera – fighter for Canary autonomy

THE BANANA TRADE

The collapse of cochineal production in the 1870s led to a period of mass emigration of Canarios to Latin America. The archipelago's economy was saved by bananas, which at that time became the main export product. Their cultivation on an industrial scale was introduced by the French Consul, S. Berthelot, in 1855. Production reached a peak in 1913, when more than 3 million bunches of bananas were exported from Tenerife, Gran Canaria and La Palma.

The outbreak of World War I and the Allied blockade of the European continent ruined international trade, and banana exports dropped by more than 80 per cent. The ensuing harsh economic conditions resulted in a second wave of emigration.

Elected representatives of the first provincial government of Tenerife, in 1912

THE FRANCO ERA

The proclamation of the Second Spanish Republic in Madrid, in 1931, led to increased tension. In 1936, fearing a coup d'état, the Republican government

TIMELINE

1852 Queen Isabella II proclaims the Canary Islands a free-trade zone

1882 Works commence on the construction of Las Palmas harbour (Puerto de la Luz)

1912 Formation of the first island-by-island provincial government

| 1825 | 1850 | 1875 | 1900 |

1821 The Canary Islands proclaimed a province of Spain, with its capital in Santa Cruz de Tenerife

1888 First steamer ferry service begins between the islands

Emigrants Monument

"exiled" General Francisco Franco, a hero of the Moroccan wars, to Tenerife. In July 1936, Franco seized control of the islands, marking the beginning of the Spanish Civil War, which lasted until 1939. Franco's Spain was ostracized by the international community. This hampered economic development in the Canary Islands, and resulted in yet more inhabitants emigrating during the 1950s. Opening the borders to sun-seeking European tourists in the 1960s failed to improve the situation. Growing resistance to Franco fed on the fertile ground of revived Canary nationalism. The MPAIC movement, founded in 1963, became the vehicle of the islands' drive for independence. In the late 1970s, companies and military establishments on the Spanish mainland became targets for terrorist attacks by the nationalists.

General Francisco Franco, the ruler of Spain until 1975

THE CANARY ISLANDS TODAY

Changes following Franco's death in 1975 brought about the devolution of power in Spain and, in August 1982, the Canary Islands were granted autonomy. Local authorities are now in control of education, health services, and transport, leaving matters of defence, foreign policy and finances in the hands of the central government. In 1986, Spain became a member of the European Union (EU).

Today, mass tourism accounts for some 80 per cent of the islands' revenue. However, on the smaller islands the economy still relies on agriculture and fishing. High unemployment and low wages continue to create problems. These, along with the need to protect the environment, present the greatest challenge to today's provincial authorities.

Golden beaches of Maspalomas, crowded with tourists

7 Division of
e archipelago
into two
provinces

Mass tourism begins to develop in the 1960s

1982 The Canary Islands become an autonomous region of Spain

1986 Entry of Spain and the Canary Islands into the EU

| 1925 | 1950 | 1975 | 2000 |

1930 Building of an airport in Gran Canaria

1936 General Franco seizes control of the Canary Islands, leading to the outbreak of the Spanish Civil War

Colourful carnival is the most popular fiesta on the islands

THE CANARY ISLANDS AREA BY AREA

The Canary Islands at a Glance

THE CANARY ISLANDS are diverse enough to cater for all tastes, from the individual traveller to groups on package holidays. Those who shy away from the noisy modern resorts of Tenerife and Gran Canaria can find repose in the islands' interior. Fuerteventura can be recommended to admirers of beautiful windswept beaches, while Lanzarote offers a lunar landscape, spotted with craters and featuring curious architectural edifices built by the most famous Canary artist – César Manrique. The wild, lush island of La Gomera and the perpetually green La Palma provide a paradise for hikers. El Hierro attracts lovers of nature, regional cuisine and handicrafts.

Pico del Teide (see pp118–19), *the highest mountain in Spain and an active volcano, is one of few places on the Canary Islands where snow can be sometimes seen.*

In Santa Cruz de la Palma (see pp144–5) *stands a replica of the* Santa Maria, *the ship in which Christopher Columbus "discovered" the Americas.*

LA PALMA
(see pp140–51)

LA GOMERA
(see pp122–31)

TENERIFE
(see pp96–121)

EL HIERRO
(see pp132–39)

Hermigua (see p126), *nestles in a beautiful ravine, with steep slopes covered by the picturesque terraces of a banana plantation.*

El Sabinar (see p137), *a remote point on El Hierro, is named after the ancient juniper trees that grow here, twisted into strange shapes by ceaseless winds.*

| 0 km | | 30 |
| 0 miles | | 50 |

◁ **Yachts in Puerto Rico marina, Gran Canaria**

Haria (see p88), *a small town lying in a valley, is reminiscent of a Saharan oasis with its low, whitewashed houses shaded by palm trees, acacias and rubber plants.*

Goats *are the most frequently encountered animals in Fuerteventura. Unsurprisingly, they are a symbol of the island.*

LANZAROTE
(see pp80–95)

Orchids, *in a host of fabulous colours, along with numerous species of exotic birds and butterflies from all over the world, attract tourists to Palmitos Parque (see p61).*

FUERTEVENTURA
(see pp66–79)

GRAN CANARIA
(see pp40–65)

Puerto Rico (see p60) *is a modern resort on the south coast of Gran Canaria, offering facilities for all kinds of water sports and fishing and diving trips.*

Ibis, *a wading bird with a long, sabre-like beak, is one of the main attractions of Guinate Tropical Parque (see p88), one of many theme parks to be found throughout the larger islands.*

GRAN CANARIA

L YING AT THE HEART *of the archipelago and occupying an area of 1,533 sq km (599 sq miles), Gran Canaria is the third largest of the Canary Islands. It is one of the most densely populated islands, with 710,000 inhabitants – more than half of the entire population of the archipelago. It is also the one of the most popular islands, attracting some 1.5 million visitors each year.*

The centre of Gran Canaria is occupied by the rocky volcano summit of Pico de las Nieves *(see pp62–3)*. The mountain sides, sloping towards the ocean, are criss-crossed by deep canyons.

The island is divided by a mountain range into two climatic zones. The northern part is more humid and fertile, with long stretches of banana plantations running along the coast, while the southern part is dry and hot.

The island's landscape displays similar diversity, with the northern and western coasts steep and rocky, and the eastern and southern slopes falling gently towards the sea. This diversity has given Gran Canaria the nickname of a "miniature continent".

Farmer with his donkey

Gran Canaria enjoys a mild climate throughout the year, with an average air temperature of 21° C (70° F). Water temperature, however, is somewhat lower than average for these latitudes, due to a cool current flowing from the Gulf of Mexico.

The island was conquered between 1478 and 1483 by the Spanish, led by Pedro de Vera, and fully colonized during the 1520s. Today it offers a multitude of tourist attractions. Las Palmas has museums and historic buildings alongside its own beach, the Playa de las Canteras, with its nightclubs, cafés and shops. In contrast, in the rugged environs of Pico de las Nieves hikers can follow the trails of the Guanches' culture.

Stage in a square in Puerto de Mogán

◁ **Tourists on the dunes around Maspalomas**

Exploring Gran Canaria

Gran Canaria is the most frequently visited island of the archipelago. Each year it receives around 1.5 million visitors, who are attracted by its fine scenery, consistently mild climate and numerous tourist attractions. The island's capital, Las Palmas, is situated in the northeast; it is a city with a fascinating history *(see pp29–35)*, and its colonial past is reflected in its delightful old town and many museums. Sun-seekers favour the warmer, southern parts of the island, where sunny weather is guaranteed all year round. Maspalomas is one of the largest, purpose-built tourist developments in Spain. At its heart is the Playa del Inglés with its vast hotels, restaurants, bars, discotheques and, above all, golden sandy beaches.

LOCATOR MAP

GETTING THERE

Gran Canaria has scheduled flight connections with all the islands in the archipelago, and with mainland Spain, as well as charter flights from many European cities. There are regular ferries and hydrofoil services to Tenerife, Lanzarote and Fuerteventura. Gran Canaria has a good network of bus routes, but to reach some of the villages, particularly those at the centre of the island, you will need to hire a car. Most roads, major and minor, are well surfaced.

SEE ALSO

- **Where to Stay** pp156–157
- **Where to Eat** pp168–170

Walking trail in the mountainous region of Presa de los Hornos, near Pico de las Nieves

KEY

- ▬ Motorway/Highway
- ▬ Major road
- ▬ Minor road
- ▬ Scenic route
- ✈ Airport
- ⛴ Ferry port
- ✲ Viewpoint

Village of Sardina, on the coast near Gáldar

① *LAS PALMAS DE GRAN CANARIA*

ARUCAS ⑦
GC 2
GC 23

⑧ FIRGAS

GC 21

TEROR ⑥

TAFIRA ALTA ② C 811

SANTA BRÍGIDA ④

③ CALDERA DE BANDAMA

GC 15

⑤ VEGA DE SAN MATEO GC 41 TELDE ㉓

GC 130 GC 100 GC 1

SAN BARTOLOMÉ DE TIRAJANA ⑰ BARRANCO DE GUAYADEQUE ㉒ INGENIO ㉑ ✈

⑲ SANTA LUCÍA

㉒ ㉑ ㉒ ㉒ ㉑

㉒⓴ AGÜIMES

GC 65

VECINDARIO ●

GC 1

● SAN AGUSTÍN

● PLAYA DEL INGLÉS

ALOMAS

0 km   5
0 miles   5

SIGHTS AT A GLANCE

Agaete ⑫
Agüimes ⑳
Arucas ⑦
Barranco de Guayadeque ㉒
Caldera de Bandama ③
Firgas ⑧
Gáldar ⑪
Ingenio ㉑
Las Palmas de Gran Canaria pp44–51 ①
Maspalomas ⑯
Moya ⑨
Puerto de Mogán ⑭
Puerto Rico ⑮
San Bartolomé de Tirajana ⑰
San Nicolás de Tolentino ⑬
Santa Brígida ④
Santa Lucía ⑲
Santa María de Guía de Gran Canaria ⑩
Tafira Alta ②
Telde ㉓
Teror ⑥
Vega de San Mateo ⑤

Tours

Around Pico de las Nieves pp62–63 ⑱

Orchids in Palmitos Parque, near Maspalomas

Street-by-Street: Las Palmas de Gran Canaria ❶

Las Palmas town crest

THE LARGEST TOWN of the archipelago, Las Palmas was founded on 24 June 1478 by the Spanish conquistadors. It soon became an important port for ships sailing around the African continent and heading for America. The town's wealth attracted the attention of pirates – in 1599, Dutch adventurers plundered Las Palmas. In the late 19th century, Sir Alfred Lewis Jones founded the Gran Canaria Coal Company here and the town began to flourish. The port became the main stopping point on the transatlantic route and a new town sprang up around it. In 1927, Las Palmas became the capital of the eastern province of the Canary Islands, encompassing Gran Canaria, Fuerteventura and Lanzarote.

★ **Catedral de Santa Ana**
Construction began on the church in 1497.

Plaza de Santa Ana
The entrances to this square are guarded by bronze statues of dogs – symbolizing the legendary dog which, since 1506, has appeared in the town's crest.

0 m   200
0 yards   200

Caldera de Bandama

Plaza del Espíritu Santo
This charming square, to the south of the cathedral, has a striking, monumental fountain at its centre. There are also a number of historic houses and the Chapel of the Holy Spirit.

★ **Museo Canario**
The museum houses the Canary Islands' largest collection of exhibits relating to the history and culture of the Guanches.

San Antonio Abad
*This small church was built
in the late 17th century. It is
said that Columbus prayed
here before setting off on his
great expedition.*

Triana

PLAZA DEL MERCADO

MENDIZÁBAL

MATADERO

BOTAS

R. MORERA

LOS BALCONES

AGUSTÍN MILLARES

S. AGUSTÍN

AVENIDA DE CANARIAS

OR CHIL

E. DORESTE

A TELLO

REYES CATÓLICOS

DOLORES DE LA ROCHA

DOMINGO DORESTE

PEDRO CERÓN

PADRE JOSÉ DE SOSA

VISITORS' CHECKLIST

370,000. 16 km
(10 miles) south. 928 579
138, 928 579 094. Estación
de Guaguas. 928 368 335.
Parque de Santa Catalina.
928 264 623. FAX 928 229
820. Sun.
Carnival (Jan–Feb); Festival
Internacional de Cine de Las
Palmas (Mar); Día de San Juan
(24 Jun).

**Centro Atlántico
de Arte Moderno (CAAM)**
*The Atlantic Centre of Modern Art
was opened in 1989.*

**Museo
Diocesano
de Arte Sacro**
*This museum has
a fine collection
of Spanish
woodcarvings
dating from the
16th to the
19th century.*

★ Casa de Colón
*This is one of the most
beautiful buildings in
Las Palmas, with
typical Canary
wooden balconies.
Since 1952, it has
housed a museum
(see pp46–7).*

STAR SIGHTS

★ Casa de Colón

★ Catedral de Sta Ana

★ Museo Canario

Casa de Colón

I**N THE OLDEST DISTRICT** of Las Palmas stands the palace of the first governors of the island. According to tradition, Christopher Columbus stayed here in 1492 during a break in his voyage while one of his ships was repaired, hence the name Casa de Colón, or Columbus House. This charming building, with its beautiful wooden balconies, was rebuilt in 1777. Since 1952 it has housed a museum that includes models and artifacts relating to voyages made by the famous navigator.

Ship's Interior
A reconstructed, full-size fragment of the interior of La Niña, *one of the ships that sailed with Columbus's expedition, demonstrates the living conditions that sailors endured while crossing the oceans.*

Ground floor

Main entrance

Santa Maria
Models of the three ships from Columbus's fleet (Santa Maria, La Niña, La Pinta), *and navigation instruments, illustrate the equipment available to mariners in the early 16th century.*

Astrolabe
One of the early navigational instruments, the astrolabe was developed in the 2nd century BC. It was used to measure the height of heavenly bodies above the horizon. The collection here includes a bronze astrolabe from the first half of the 16th century.

KEY

☐	Ecuadorian art
☐	Mexican culture
☐	Yanomami culture
☐	Marine charts and navigational instruments
☐	Columbus and his voyages
■	Canary Islands and discovery of America
☐	Las Palmas de Gran Canaria
☐	Gran Canaria
☐	16th–20th century painting

GALLERY GUIDE

The exhibits are arranged on three levels, in 12 rooms surrounding two inner courtyards and in underground chambers. The underground chambers contain treasures of pre-Columbian art. The ground floor is given to Columbus's expeditions, the development of cartography and the history of the Canary Islands as the gateway to the New World. The first-floor rooms present an overview of Las Palmas history, from the 15th until the 19th century. There are also separate rooms displaying items on loan from Madrid's Prado Museum.

★ St Lucia

This painting by Guamart de Amberes is one of the museum's collection of works by 16th-century Dutch and Italian painters, some of which belong to the Prado Museum. They include paintings by Guido Reni, the Carracc brothers and Guercino.

First Floor

★ External Portal

Casa de Colón features a magnificent portal crowned by a Tudor arch. This exquisite ornament combines plant and animal motifs, with two lions supporting the town's crests.

Courtyard

At the centre of the inner courtyard stands an old well. Centuries-old galleries and arcades, in typical Canary style, keep the rooms cool and shady.

Basement vaults

★ Pre-Columbian Art

An extensive collection of pre-Columbian artifacts of gold and other metals includes original items and replicas associated with the Spanish conquests in Central and South America.

STAR EXHIBITS

- ★ External Portal
- ★ Pre-Columbian Art
- ★ St Lucia

Façade of the cathedral of Santa Ana

Exploring La Vegueta

La Vegueta, the oldest district of Las Palmas, consists of a labyrinth of narrow streets, lined with historic houses with wooden balconies and beautiful patios. Equally charming are the old town squares, such as **Plaza de Santo Domingo**, with St Dominic Church dating from the early 18th century. Also noteworthy is the Baroque church of **San Francisco de Borja** (1644) formerly belonging to the Augustine monks and now serving as a law court.

Right at the edge of the district are large market halls selling a variety of goods, including fruit, vegetables, fish, meat and local cheeses, as well as local handicrafts.

🏛 Museo Canario

C/Dr Verneau, 2. 📞 928 336 800. ⭕ 10am–8pm Mon–Fri; 10am–2pm Sat–Sun. 🈳
🔲 www.elmuseocanario.com

The Canary Islands' Museum was opened in 1879. A refurbishment carried out in the mid-1980s has transformed it into a modern establishment.

The collection includes such archaeological finds as statuettes of gods, pottery, jewellery and tools of the Guanches, as well as skulls, skeletons and mummies. The displays, which are diverse, also include models of historic houses. Among the star attractions are copies of the paintings discovered in

Cueva Pintada de Gáldar, as well as *pintaderas* – terracotta "stamps" used for printing geometric patterns on clothes.

🔒 Catedral de Santa Ana

Plaza Santa Ana.

The building of the cathedral began in 1497 and took 400 years to complete. The lengthy gestation affected both its architectural form and interior furnishings.

The Neo-Classical façade hides Gothic vaults resting on slender columns, altar retables, Baroque pulpits and sculptures by José Luján Pérez. The crypt contains the tomb of José de Viera y Clavijo, Canary traveller, historian of the Enlightenment period and the author of *Noticias de la Historia General de Canarias*. Another chapel is the resting place of diplomat Fernando de León y Castillo *(see p65)*.

A lift in the south tower whisks visitors to the viewing terrace, which offers fine views of the town and harbour.

🏛 Museo Diocesano de Arte Sacro

C/Espíritu Santo, 20. ⭕
📞 928 314 989. ⭕
10am–4:30pm Mon–Fri;
10am–1:30pm Sat. 🈳

Opened in 1984, this museum of sacred art adjoins the cathedral. It has a collection of Spanish sculpture and some noteworthy paintings, including works by old Dutch masters.

Ceramic vessel from Museo Canario

🏛 Centro Atlántico de Arte Moderno (CAAM)

Los Balcones, 8–10.
📞 928 311 824. ⭕ 10am–5pm Mon–Fri; 10am–2pm Sat–Sun. 🈳

CAAM organizes exhibitions, mainly of avant-garde art. It also has its own collection of works by artists influential in shaping 20th-century Canary art. CAAM provides a venue for academic symposia on the subject of modern art and has an extensive library, including videos. In stark contrast to the 18th-century façade of this former hotel, the modern interior, designed by Francisco Sainz de Oiza and Martín Chirino, is light and airy.

NÉSTOR MARTÍN FERNÁNDEZ DE LA TORRE

Néstor Martín Fernández de la Torre (1887–1938) was one of the most original artists to come from the Canary Islands. Born in Las Palmas, he studied in Paris where he became familiar with the work of Pre-Raphaelite, Symbolist and Secessionist artists. In 1910, he represented Spain in the World Exhibition in Brussels. He produced paintings, stage designs, theatre and opera costumes and interior designs, but was known principally for his murals. In 1934, he settled permanently in Gran Canaria, and devoted the last years of his life to developing and publicizing Canary art forms.

Painting by Néstor in Museo Néstor *(see p50)*

Exploring in Triana

To the north of the motorway that encloses the area of La Vegueta lies Triana – the commercial district of town, marked to the north by **Bravo Murillo** street along which runs the old city wall. The street leads to the ruins of the old castle – **Castillo de Mata**. The centre of this regularly shaped area is cut across by the Boulevard **Calle Mayor de Triana**. The ground floors of its Modernist houses are occupied by shops. Evidence of bloody battles fought with pirates can be seen in **San Francisco Church**, destroyed during an attack by Dutch pirates, led by Peter van der Does, in 1599 and subsequently restored in the 17th century. Opposite the church stands the bust of Christopher Columbus. Unveiled in 1892, this is one of many landmarks symbolizing the town's links with great geographic discoveries.

Tiled café in the Modernist kiosk in Parque San Telmo

🎭 Teatro Pérez Galdós

C/Lentini, 1. 🔲 928 322 008.
In the south of Triana, almost opposite Mercado Público, stands a theatre named after the respected writer Benito Pérez Galdós (1843–1920).

Built in 1919, this structure is the work of Miguel Martín Fernández de la Torre. The opulent interior decorations and the auditorium for 1,400 spectators were designed by his brother, Néstor Martín Fernández de la Torre. Today this is the best theatre in Las Palmas and one of the best in the Canary Islands.

🏛 Casa Museo Pérez Galdós

C/Cano, 6. 🔲 928 366 976. FAX 928 373 734. ◯ 9am–9pm, Mon–Fri; 9am–6pm Sat; 10am–3pm Sun.
The Museum of Benito Pérez Galdós, the most distinguished writer from the Canary Islands, occupies the house in which he was born and where he lived until 1862. This five-storey building has a small patio adorned with a statue of the writer. The museum, which opened in 1964, still has the original interior décor. It contains objects associated with the writer's life, as well as photographs of many actors who appeared in his plays.

♿ Gabinete Literario

Plaza Cairasco.
This building, which was reconstructed in the Modernist style, was built in 1842 as a theatre. In 1894 it was turned into a club. Now it houses, among other things, a library and a restaurant.

🍁 Parque San Telmo

San Telmo Park is reached via the **Calle Mayor Triana** Passage. At the edge of the park stands the small, 17th-century **San Telmo Chapel**, devoted to this patron saint of fishermen. On the opposite side is a Modernist **kiosk**, built in 1923 and decorated with ceramic tiles. Standing on the side of the park is the **Gobierno Militar** building where, on 18 July 1936, General Franco declared his opposition to the Republican government, signalling the start of the Spanish Civil War.

Patio of Casa Museo Pérez Galdós in Triana, with the writer's statue

Exploring Ciudad Jardín
Ciudad Jardín is an oasis of peace in the bustling city of Las Palmas. This leafy residential district was created in the early 20th century by British residents, who dominated the economic life of the town at that time.

This "Garden Town", with its regular layout, now has many embassies and beautiful houses set in small gardens. These buildings display a variety of architectural styles. The district's main feature is the large Parque Doramas with its interesting statues.

❦ Parque Doramas
This beautifully landscaped park, featuring water cascades and a municipal swimming pool, is named after the Guanche chieftain Doramas, who, in the late 15th century, put up a fierce resistance to the Spanish invaders. His struggles are symbolized by the monument depicting Guanches tumbling over a precipice to escape capture.

⏣ Hotel Santa Catalina
C/Leon y Castillo, 227.
☎ *928 243 040.* **FAX** *928 242 764.*
W *www.hotelsantacatalina.com*
Set among the sub-tropical greenery of the Parque Doramas stands the Santa Catalina Hotel. Originally built

The exclusive Hotel Santa Catalina, in Ciudad Jardín

in 1890 for the British employees of the Grand Canary Island Company *(see p33)*, the building was redesigned by Canary artist Néstor Martin Fernandez de la Torre between 1947 and 1952.

Royalty and celebrities have stayed in this grand hotel, but the lovely views of the park from the bar can be enjoyed by non-resident visitors.

⏣ Pueblo Canario
Parque Doramas.
The park's attractions include Pueblo Canario – a model Canary village with gates, turrets and an atrium. It was designed in 1937 by the Canary artist Néstor Martín Fernández de la Torre *(see p48).* The large courtyard, which is surrounded by shops selling local handicrafts, serves as a venue for folk dance shows.

🏛 Museo Néstor
Pueblo Canario.
☎ *928 245 135.*
W *www.museonestor.com*
🕐 *10am–8pm Tue–Sat;*
10:30am–2:30pm Sun,
public holidays. 📷
Opened in 1958, the museum exhibits works by Néstor, including sketches, still lifes and erotic and symbolic paintings. One of the museum's highlights is the dome of the rotunda, which is decorated with eight murals illustrating Torre's *Poema del Mar* (Sea Poem).

Exploring Santa Catalina
The narrow streets of this district are filled with Indian shops, offering electronic goods, alcohol, tobacco products, jewellery and clothes. Trade blossomed when the Canary Islands were a duty-free zone. Shopping here is not quite as profitable these days, but it is still acceptable to haggle and get some bargains.

Santa Catalina has many hotels, most of which seem to face north, towards the long, golden sands of the popular Las Canteras beach.

🚢 Muelle Santa Catalina
On the south side of Avenida Marítima del Norte is the ferry terminal, which provides ferry and hydrofoil services to Tenerife and the other islands. This modern building can be seen from far away.

🏖 Playa de Alcaravaneras
South of the ferry terminal, within the district of Alcaravaneras, is the 1 km (0.5 mile) golden sand Alcalavaneras beach. This is the second longest of the Las Palmas beaches, after Las Canteras. The modern yacht marina of the **Real Club Náutico**, south of the beach, is packed with glamorous ocean-going boats.

❦ Parque Santa Catalina
At the heart of the district is Santa Catalina Park, which has played an important role in the development of the town's mass tourism. During the 1960s it was the most popular meeting place for visitors to Las Palmas. Today

Monument to the Guanches, in Parque Doramas

the park is the centre of the city's nightlife, with numerous restaurants, bars, clubs and discotheques filled until the small hours by fun-loving guests. Horse-drawn cabs line up in the park, ready to serve as taxis or take tourists on a sightseeing tour. There is also a tourist information office here.

At carnival time, a large stage is erected here and Santa Catalina Park becomes the focal point in Las Palmas for this great celebration.

Denizens of Las Palmas playing chess in Parque Santa Catalina

Exploring Playa de las Canteras

Playa de las Canteras is a mixed district of hotels and offices. Scores of hotels and shops line the seaside promenade, Paseo de las Canteras, where there are also a great many bars and restaurants. This district has one of the town's biggest shopping centres – Las Arenas.

🎵 Auditorio Alfredo Kraus

Playa de las Canteras, s/n.
📞 928 491 770.
🖥 auditorio-alfredokraus. com

Auditorio Alfredo Kraus has been hailed as a masterpiece of modern architecture. Built in 1997, it was designed by Oscar Tusquet and Canary sculptor Juan Bordes. It serves as a venue for operas, concerts and an international music festival. The auditorium, named after an outstanding Canary tenor – Alfredo Kraus – also serves as a conference centre.

🏖 Playa de Las Canteras

This stretch of yellowish-brown sand is almost 4 km (3 miles) long and in places 100 metres (300 yds) wide. This is the best beach in Las Palmas. It is well-served by cafés and restaurants, and there are sun loungers for hire. La Barra, a natural rock barrier protecting the beach against strong surf, makes bathing possible, even in rough conditions.

Exploring La Isleta

Situated on a small, round peninsula, La Isleta is a residential quarter built on steep terrain, featuring narrow streets and renowned for its small local shops, bars and street vendors offering dried fish. The peninsula is separated from the modern

Statue on the paseo, Playa de las Canteras

part of Las Palmas by a narrow inlet. At the centre of La Isleta is Plaza Manuel Becerra – a lively square, bordered on one side by the harbour gate and on the other side by a lighthouse. There is also an important naval base here and there are some no-go areas.

⚓ Harbour

Las Palmas harbour boasts a long and glorious history and is an important factor in the prosperity of Gran Canaria. Around 1,000 ships use the harbour each month. The traffic was even heavier when the Canary Islands enjoyed duty-free status and the harbour was one of the most important in the world.

The harbour area includes a marina, which is the starting point for the annual Canary Islands to Barbados race.

⛴ Castillo de la Luz

C/Juan Rejón, s/n. 📞 928 464 757.
🕐 10am–1pm, 6–9pm Mon–Fri; 10am–2pm Sat–Sun. ⬤ between exhibitions.

On the south shore of La Isleta, near the harbour, stands Castillo de la Luz – the Castle of Light. This well-preserved fortress dates from the 16th-century, and was built to guard the town of Las Palmas against pirates. It was restored in 1990, and is now used as a venue for art exhibitions.

Playa de las Canteras – the most beautiful beach in Las Palmas

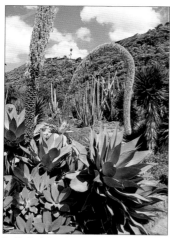

Jardín Botánico Canario, near Tarifa Alta

Tafira Alta ❷

🏠 *3,000.* 🛈 *Jardín Canario.* 📞 *928 353 604.* 🎭 *San Francisco (Oct).*

Set among the hills is the small town of Tafira Alta, famous for its beautiful residences surrounded by gardens. These colourful villas, featuring a variety of architectural forms and details, have maintained the original colonial atmosphere of the place. Many houses show the influence of Moorish or Bauhaus style. No wonder then, that Tarifa Alta is a favourite with Las Palmas's financial elite and with wealthy foreigners.

At the beginning of the 20th century, the British built several elegant hotels here, including **Los Frailes**. This was used as a meeting place by General Franco's supporters as they plotted to overthrow Spain's Republican government in 1936.

Environs: The Botanical Gardens, Jardín Botánico Canario Viera y Clavijo, situated on the outskirts of town, are named after José Viera y Clavijo (1731–1813), the author of the *Canary Islands Dictionary of Plants*. The gardens were created in 1952 by a Swede, Eric Sventenius (1910–73), who remained their director until his death. Set on terraces and growing in their natural environment are plants from all the islands in the archipelago. They include species of the native Canary palm, Canary pine and heathers. Also featured are plants from other regions including the Azores, Madeira and the Cape Verde Islands as well as two thousand cacti, from all corners of the world.

🌸 **Jardín Botánico Canario**
🕘 *9am–6pm daily.*

Caldera de Bandama ❸

It is worth travelling the 6-km (4-mile) distance from Tafira, half of which is over a narrow mountain road, in order to reach the peak of the volcano Pico de Bandama. This relatively low mountain (570 m/1,866 ft) provides one of the best viewpoints on Gran Canaria. Mirador de Bandama offers a magnificent view over the whole of Las Palmas and the mountainous centre of the island. Below is the vast volcanic caldera of Bandama, 1,000 m (3,300 ft) in diameter and 200 m (650 ft) deep. It is named after a Dutch merchant, Daniel von Damme. In the 16th century, von Damme, together with his wife Juana Vera, who was born in Gran Canaria, grew vines inside the crater. Today the area is overgrown with orange and fig trees and palms. Eucalyptus and agaves grow on the slopes, among shrubs and bushes.

A golf course, just south of Pico de Bandama, was set up by English residents of the island in 1891. It is the oldest golf course in Spain.

Santa Brígida ❹

🏠 *13,000.* 🚌 🚆 *Sat–Sun.* 🎭 *Corpus Christi (Jun).*

This prosperous old town lies on the slopes of a gully covered with cypress and tall palms. Its picturesque narrow streets are lined with eucalyptus trees and flower-filled balconies. As a result of its proximity to Las Palmas, Santa Brígida is often visited by the capital's inhabitants.

The slopes of the neighbouring mountain are clothed with vineyards producing Vino del Monte – the best red wine on the island. The terrace in front of **Santa Brígida Parish Church** provides a good view over the surrounding palm groves. This triple-nave, Neo-Gothic basilica was built in 1904 on the site of a chapel constructed in 1520 by Isabel Guerra, the granddaughter of Pedro Guerra – a conquistador and one of the conquerors of Gran Canaria. The chapel was subsequently replaced by a church built in 1580. This, in turn, was almost destroyed by fire in the late 19th century. The only part that escaped destruction was the tower, built in 1756 .

Caldera de Bandama, almost 1 km (0.5 mile) in diameter

Casa Museo de Cho-Zacarías in Vega de San Mateo

Vega de San Mateo ❺

🏠 7,000. 🚍 Sat, Sun.
🎉 San Mateo (21Sep).

THIS SMALL TOWN, situated in a fertile, green valley, is known for its large agricultural market, held every Sunday. As well as fruits, vegetables and numerous types of cheese, the local farmers also bring goats, pigs and cows for sale.

In the church of San Mateo stands a 17th-century statue of Saint Matthew – the town's patron saint. **Casa Museo de Cho-Zacarías** in the town centre is an ethnographic museum devoted to the island's past. It is housed in five peasant cottages, one of which dates back to the 16th century. As well as furniture the collection includes historic agricultural implements.

🏛 **Casa Museo de Cho-Zacarías**
📞 928 660 627.
🕐 10am–1pm Mon–Sat.

Teror ❻

🏠 13,000. 🚌 ℹ Plaza de Sintes, 1.
📞 928 630 143. 🚍 Sun.
🎉 Fiesta del Agua (last Sun in Jul), Virgen del Pino (8 Sep).

SINCE HER FIRST appearance among tree branches in 1481, Nuestra Señora del Pino (Our Lady of the Pines) has played an important role in the history and everyday life

of Gran Canaria. In 1914, Pope Pius XII proclaimed her the patron saint of the island. Teror, with its sanctuary, became the religious capital of the island. Every year, on 8 September, the town is visited by many pilgrims, who travel here from all over Gran Canaria.

Large historic houses line the town's main square, **Plaza de Nuestra Señora del Pino**, and the **Calle Real de la Plaza**. Some of these mansions date from the 16th century and have lavishly carved wooden and stone balconies.

The basilica of **Nuestra Señora del Pino**, completed in 1767, was the third church to be built on this site. Only

the tower remains from the earlier church, and dates from 1708. Its octagonal shape and striking mix of Moorish and Baroque elements make the tower a distinctive landmark.

The main feature of the large, triple-nave interior is the vast, Baroque altar with its 15th-century, carved figure of the Virgin. The Virgen (known as both of the pine and of the snow) is the patron saint of the island and the reason for one of the biggest fiestas in the Canary Islands (see p25). Other attractions include the Treasure Room, which contains precious gifts, donated at past festivals, to celebrate the saint.

Not far from the church is **Plaza Doña María Teresa de Bolívar**, named after María Teresa, the wife of Simón Bolívar's fight for independence, whose great grandfather was born in Teror. The **Casa Museo de los Patrones de la Virgen**, built on the site of his former home, is a museum displaying old photographs, weapons and furniture, including the bed slept in by King Alfonso XIII during a 1906 visit.

Central part of the church façade in Teror

🏛 **Casa Museo de los Patrones de la Virgen**
Plaza Nuestra Señora del Pino, 8.
🕐 11am–6:30pm Mon–Sat, 10:30am–2pm Sun.

Drawing room in Casa Museo de los Patrones de la Virgen in Teror

Arucas

🏛 30,000. 🚌 ℹ Plaza de la
Constitución, 2. ☎ 928 623 136.
🍽 Mon–Sat. 🎭 Corpus Christi (Jun).

W HEN APPROACHING Arucas,
the first sight you see is
the towers of the Neo-Gothic
Parish Church of San Juan.
The church, mistakenly called
a "cathedral", was designed by
Manual Vega March and built
between 1909 and 1977. As
well as the fine stained-glass
windows and retable, the
interior features the sculpture
of Cristo Yacente (the Resting
Christ), which is the work of a
local sculptor, Manuel Rasmos.

The old **town hall** in Plaza
de la Constitución, designed
by José A. López de
Echegarret, was built in 1875
and then rebuilt in 1932. On
the opposite side of the
square is the leafy **town
park**, which boasts many
species of rare tropical trees,
including the soapbark tree
(Quillaja saponaria).

Encircling the park, **Calle
de la Heredad** features one
of the town's most beautiful
buildings, **Heredad de Aguas
de Arucas y Firgas**, which
was built in 1908 and now
houses the Water Board. In
the second half of the 19th
century and the early years of
the 20th century, the
Board initiated the
construction of an
irrigation system and
the town itself

Ceramic ornaments in Paseo de Gran Canaria, Firgas

acquired its present shape.
The Canary Islands' largest
rum factory was built in
Arucas in 1884. The factory
has a museum devoted to the
history and distillation method
of this drink. Near the factory
entrance stands an early 18th-
century chapel – **La Ermita
de San Pedro**.

ENVIRONS: About
1.5 km (1 mile)
north of Arucas is
**Montaña de
Arucas**. At the
highest point
of the town
is a restaurant
with a viewing
platform, with
views over
town and the
entire island.

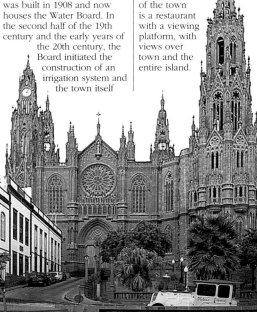

Neo-Gothic Parish Church of San Juan, Arucas

Firgas

🏛 5,500. 🚌 🎭 San Luis (21 Jun).

F IRGAS IS FAMOUS for its
production of sparkling
mineral water. The water is
drawn from a spring some
5 km (3 miles) away, in
Barranco de la Virgen, and
200,000 bottles a day are
produced. Firgas water is
very popular throughout
the islands, where there is
a shortage of fresh water.

A feature of Firgas, which
celebrated its five hundredth
anniversary in 1988, is the
Paseo de Gran Canaria, where
cascades of water flow along
passages that were laid out in
1995. On either side of the
passage, by the walls of
surrounding houses, are
benches whose backrests are
decorated with landscapes or
historic symbols of Gran
Canaria. The white walls of
the houses feature colourful
town crests. The further
section of the passage, above
Plaza de San Roque, is
filled with giant slabs with
ceramic maps and views of
the individual islands. These
provide an unusual lesson in
the geography of the Canary
Islands. Still further along the
passage there is a fine display
of the flags of all the islands
fluttering in the breeze.

The historic 15th-century
Molino de Gofio and the
19th-century fountain were
restored in 1988. The whole
town is decorated with
modern sculptures, including
an amusing statue of a
peasant with a pink cow.

Moya ❾

🏛 7,500. 🚌 🚆 Sun. 🎭 Virgen de la Candelaria (2 Feb), San Antonio (13 Jun).

TUCKED AWAY FROM the main tourist attractions, the road to this small town meanders through volcanic valleys, with countless turns and bends. The place is worth visiting for its vast, Neo-Romanesque church, dating from the first half of the 20th century. The church is imposing with two towers and a position at the edge of the **Barranco de Moya** precipice – a gully crisscrossed with wild crevasses.

Moya is the birthplace of Tomás Morales – a modernist Canary poet. The house in which he was born and lived was converted into a museum, **Casa-Museo Tomás Morales**, in 1976. There is a permanent exhibition dedicated to the poet which includes photographs, manuscripts and first editions of his works displayed in rooms decorated in period style. The museum also organizes exhibitions of contemporary art.

By the entrance to the nearby catacomb cemetery, typical of the Canary Islands, stands a large stone cross – a monument to the victims of the 1936 Spanish Civil War.

🏛 **Casa-Museo Tomás Morales**
Plaza de Tomás Morales.
📞 928 620 217. ⏰ 9am–2pm, 4–8pm Mon–Fri; 10am–2pm, 5–8pm Sat; 10am–2pm Sun.

TOMÁS MORALES (1884–1921)

Tomás Morales is hailed as one of the Canary Islands' most outstanding poets. Although he completed medical studies at the University in 1909 and practised in Agaete and Las Palmas, his true passion was poetry. He started writing poems at the age of 15 and had his first works published in 1902. In 1908 his first book, *Poems of Glory, Love and Sea* appeared, and two years later Las Palmas Theatre staged his *Dinner at Simon's House* – a dramatic prose poem. His strong identification with his homeland is reflected in his work – a complex brew of feelings that combine a love of the sea, loneliness, warmth and eclecticism. His great poem *Ode to Atlantic*, celebrates man, ship and ocean.

Bust of Morales in front of the museum in Moya

Santa María de Guía de Gran Canaria ❿

🏛 12,300. 🚌 🎭 Fiesta del Queso de Flor (May), Nuestra Señora de Guía (15 Aug), La Rama de las Marías (3rd Sun in Sep).

THE ONLY noteworthy historic building in this town is the Church of **Santa María de Guía**, built on the site of a chapel erected in 1483–1509. Some parts of this triple-nave church date back to the 17th century; the façade was completed only in the middle of the following century.

Guía is the birthplace of José Luján Pérez (1756–1815), who was the most popular of the Canary Islands' sculptors during his lifetime. His works, such as the statue of Nuestra Señora de las Mercedes or St Sebastián, adorn the interior of the local church. However, Guía is best known for its cheese – *queso de flor*. It is made of sheep's milk, with added artichoke juice, which gives the cheese its unusual, distinctive flavour and allows it to remain moist even when stored for a long time.

ENVIRONS: Some 5 km (3 miles) east of Guía is **Cenobio de Valerón**, a group of about 300 caves set into a cliff at various levels. The caves were used for grain storage and for religious services. Guanche individuals were selected to spend several years in solitude in these caves, giving themselves to the service of the god Abor. Their prayers were to ensure the god's protection for the island's people.

🏛 **Cenobio de Valerón**
⏰ 10am–5pm Wed–Sun.

Breathtaking view of Barranco de Moya

How Rum is Made

Rum, a by-product of sugar production, is a drink normally associated with the Caribbean, where its most famous producers are Jamaica, Cuba, Haiti and Martinique. However, the legacy of the Canary Islands' sugar plantations *(see p32)* is a respected and thriving rum industry. The local rum is generally valued for its outstanding flavour and

Canary Islands rum served in a small glass

its warming and even medicinal properties. Its alcohol content can vary from 40 to 80 per cent. It is the main ingredient of another famous beverage, grog, which is 50 per cent rum, as well as of cocktails such as Daiquiri and Cuba Libre, which use rum. One of the Canary Islands' specialities is *ron miel* – a mead rum. Rum is also used in confectionery.

1 Rum is made from sugar cane, which is processed in order to obtain sugar syrup and molasses – both are used in the later stages of production. As there are no big sugar-cane plantations on the islands, local rum is produced mainly from imported semi-finished products.

2 Inside these large vessels, sugar juices or molasses undergo a fermentation process. Strong rums are produced by combining molasses with the scum collected from the boiling juices and the brew known as "dunder". The alcohol obtained by fermentation subsequently undergoes a distillation process.

3 To ensure a refined flavour, the rum is left to mature in traditional oak barrels – a process that can last anything between three and ten years. The room in which the barrels are stored must be maintained at a constant temperature and humidity.

5 The Canary Islands' rums are well known even outside of the archipelago. Particularly highly regarded is the rum from La Palma – the best brand is believed to be Ron de la Aldea. Also popular are mead rums, whose ingredients include palm juice. The resulting orange-coloured beverage is weaker than rum and its unique flavour resembles neither rum nor mead.

4 Bottling and labelling are the final stages of rum production. This is a fully automatic process, which takes place in perfectly sterile conditions, with no people present. The bottles are appropriately labelled, showing the brand and provenance of the product.

Vast banana plantations around Gáldar

Gáldar ⓫

🏠 22,000. 🚌 🎭 *San Isidro (15 May), La Rama (20 Aug).*

AT THE FOOT of Pico de Gáldar volcano stands Gáldar – a sizeable town that was once the centre of Guanche civilization. There are no traces left of the ancient court of their ruler *(Guanarteme)* since, along with a small Spanish fort, it was destroyed to make way for the construction of **Santiago de los Caballeros Church**. This vast Neo-Classic church has three naves and was designed by Antonio José Eduardo. The construction works started in 1778 and were not completed until the mid-19th century.

Inside the church is the *pila verde* – a green font brought from Andalusia in the late 15th century and, since the island's conquest, used for baptizing the local population. Other noteworthy features are the statues of Christ and the Virgin Mary – both the work of Luján Pérez.

On the square, opposite the town hall, grows the oldest dragon tree *(see p14)* in Gran Canaria, planted in 1719.

The star attraction of Gáldar is the **Cueva Pintada**. Discovered in 1873, the cave is decorated with rock paintings consisting of geometric patterns. Following conservation works, carried out between 1970 and 1974, the cave was closed in order to prevent the paintings from being destroyed by the increased humidity. Building

at the site has been creating a new archaeological park, which will feature a museum, library and restaurant when it opens in 2003. A replica of the cave can be seen at the Museo Canario in Las Palmas *(see p48)*.

ENVIRONS: Just 2 km (1.5 miles) north of Gáldar is **Tumulo de la Guancha**. Discovered in 1936 during agricultural works, this Guanche cemetery dates from the late 11th century and consists of 30 round tombs, built of vast lava blocks. These were the burial places of members of the Andamanas royal family who ruled this part of the island.

At 6 km (4 miles) west, Sardina is at first glance an unremarkable fishing village. Nestled between high cliffs and a sandy beach, it tempts swimmers with its crystal-clear water and golden sands, as well as its excellent seafood.

Agaete ⓬

🏠 5,700. 🚌 🚹 *Antonio de Armas, 1.* 📞 *928 898 002.* 🎭 *Bajada de las Ramas (4–7 Aug).*

AGAETE LIES ON the north-west coast of the island, at the end of a steep ravine – **Barranco de Agaete**. Plantations of banana, papaya, avocado and mango flourish on the steep slopes. The small town of Agaete, with

Dedo de Dios, Puerto de las Nieves

its narrow streets and whitewashed houses surrounded by lush greenery, has become popular with artists and art-lovers, who have converted local houses and garages into art galleries.

Despite being an old town, which celebrated its five-hundredth anniversary in 1981, Agaete has few historic sites. The oldest is the parish church, which was built in the second half of the 19th century. There is also a charming, small botanical garden, **Huerto de las Flores**, which features many species of Canary and sub-tropical flora

Punta Sardina lighthouse

ENVIRONS: Some 2 km (1.5 miles) to the west is a small harbour, **Puerto de las Nieves**, with a terminal for ferries to Santa Cruz de Tenerife. This small, picturesque fishing village, nestling against tall cliffs, has become increasingly popular with tourists. Guests are drawn not only by its craft shops, galleries and seafood restaurants, but also by the Dedo de Dios – God's Finger – a photogenic 30-m (100-ft) solitary basalt rock rising from the sea and visible from the harbour jetty. Apartment blocks have sprung up around the port.

Puerto de las Nieves' rich history can be seen in the opulent furnishings of the Ermita de las Nieves, a chapel, built in the 16th century. It contains a display of model sailing ships and a triptych devoted to the Virgin Mary, painted by the outstanding Flemish artist Joos van Cleve (1485–1540). During the Fiesta de la Rama (Branch Festival) in August, the chapel's altar is carried in a ceremonial procession to the nearby parish church in Agaete.

🌸 **Huerto de las Flores**
C/Huertes. 🕐 *10am–1pm, 4–7pm Mon–Sat.*

Cactualdea – cactus park in San Nicolás de Tolentino

San Nicolás de Tolentino ⑬

🏃 11,000. 🚍 🎭 Bajada de la Rama (10 Sep), El Charco (11 Sep).

A FERTILE, GREEN valley, criss-crossed with ravines, is the setting for this small town. It is surrounded by plantations of banana, orange, avocado, papaya and mango and the slopes are overgrown with cacti and bamboo. The only building worth visiting is the **San Nicolás Church**, built in 1972 along traditional lines, featuring sculptures by Luján Pérez. It was built on the site of an old chapel dating from the early 18th century.

A popular tourist attraction is **Cactualdea** – a park with thousands of cacti imported from Madagascar, Mexico, Bolivia and Guatemala; other plants include palms, dragon trees *(see p14)* and aloe. Other features of interest include a large amphitheatre, used for wrestling matches, and a Guanche Cave.

ENVIRONS: Some 9 km (6 miles) to the north is the **Mirador del Balcón** – a viewpoint poised on the edge of rugged cliffs, rising 500 m (1,650 ft) above the sea. It provides views over north-eastern Gran Canaria.

♣ **Cactualdea**
📞 928 891 228. ⏰ 10am–6pm daily. 🖼️

Puerto de Mogán ⑭

🏃 680. ℹ️ C/General Franco. 📞 928 569 100. 🚍 ⛴️ Fri. 🎭 Virgen del Carmen (16 Jul).

U NLIKE THE BUSTLING resorts on the south of Gran Canaria, such as Playa del Inglés and Maspalomas, Puerto de Mogán is the ideal spot for visitors longing for

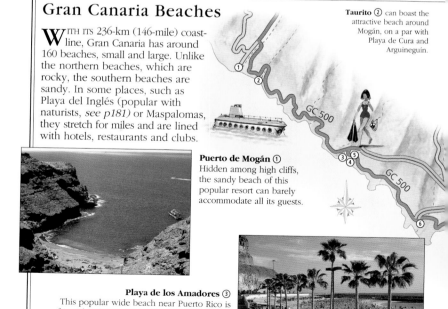

Gran Canaria Beaches

W ITH ITS 236-km (146-mile) coast-line, Gran Canaria has around 160 beaches, small and large. Unlike the northern beaches, which are rocky, the southern beaches are sandy. In some places, such as Playa del Inglés (popular with naturists, *see p181*) or Maspalomas, they stretch for miles and are lined with hotels, restaurants and clubs.

Taurito ② can boast the attractive beach around Mogán, on a par with Playa de Cura and Arguineguín.

Puerto de Mogán ①
Hidden among high cliffs, the sandy beach of this popular resort can barely accommodate all its guests.

Playa de los Amadores ③
This popular wide beach near Puerto Rico is fringed with beautiful palm trees and a wide, elegant promenade.

some peace and quiet. This picturesque town and yachting marina lie at the end of the green Mogán Valley, at the foot of a rocky plateau. The old and slightly scruffy fishing port and town lies adjacent to and behind the attractive, purpose-built marina and resort complex. The resort consists of a village-like complex of colourful, flower-decked apartments, prettily designed in Mediterranean style, lining narrow pedestrianized streets. The waterfront is lined with bars, shops and restaurants.

For swimming fans, there is a man-made rocky beach that shelters between the cliffs and is filled with several layers of sand that was imported from Africa.

There is a range of tourist trips available from here. A little, yellow submarine offers tourists the opportunity to get a glimpse of the rich underwater life of the Atlantic. Small replicas of old sailing ships ferry passengers to the beaches of Puerto Rico and

Yellow submarine in Puerto de Mogán harbour

Maspalomas several times a day. There are also deep-sea fishing trips to catch tuna and marlin. The renowned "Blue Marlin" angling competition is held here every July.

ENVIRONS: Around 8 km (5 miles) north of Puerto de

Mogán, in a fertile valley planted with such exotic crops as pawpaw and avocado, lies **Mogán**. This picturesque town is the capital of the district. There is a choice of good restaurants here, including Acayama on the edge of town, one of the best on the island.

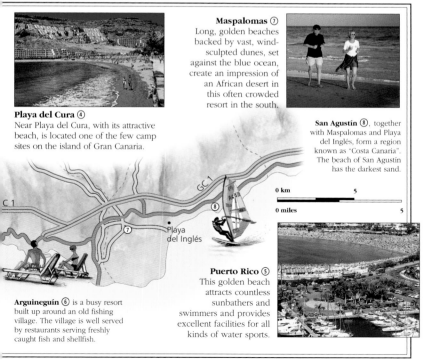

Maspalomas ⑦
Long, golden beaches backed by vast, wind-sculpted dunes, set against the blue ocean, create an impression of an African desert in this often crowded resort in the south.

Playa del Cura ④
Near Playa del Cura, with its attractive beach, is located one of the few camp sites on the island of Gran Canaria.

San Agustín ⑧, together with Maspalomas and Playa del Inglés, form a region known as "Costa Canaria". The beach of San Agustín has the darkest sand.

Arguineguín ⑥ is a busy resort built up around an old fishing village. The village is well served by restaurants serving freshly caught fish and shellfish.

Puerto Rico ⑤
This golden beach attracts countless sunbathers and swimmers and provides excellent facilities for all kinds of water sports.

0 km   5
0 miles   5

Playa del Inglés

Puerto Rico – one of Gran Canaria's most popular resorts

Puerto Rico **⓯**

🏊 1,500. **🛈** Avda. de Mogán.
📞 928 560 029.
🎎 María de Auxiliadora (May).

PUERTO RICO LIES on the coast, at the mouth of a large valley. This former fishing port has, in recent years, developed into a popular resort, thanks to its reputation as the sunniest place in Spain. Scores, if not hundreds, of hotels and apartments have been built on the terraces of the steeply descending slopes.

One of the best features of this town, which is swamped in greenery, is its small but picturesque beach, covered with sand imported from the Sahara. Other attractions include golf courses and a water park, featuring all kinds of amusements. Puerto Rico's numerous attractions range from watersports such as water-skiing, sailing, diving and windsurfing to leisure excursions such as glass-bottomed boats and open sea cruises for dolphin-watching. This helps to compensate for the fact that this is a rather over-built resort with remarkably limited amounts of sand for the numbers of visitors it receives.

Another very popular activity is sport-fishing for marlin, shark, eel and ray. Puerto Rico claims many world records in this area: the world's largest blue marlin, caught in 1997, weighed in at 488 kg (1,075 lb).

Maspalomas **⓰**

🏊 36,000. 🚌 **🛈** Avda. de España.
📞 928 140 664. 🕑 Wed, Sat.
🎎 San Bartolomé (24 Aug).

THE BIGGEST RESORT in Gran Canaria has more than 500 hotels, apartment blocks and chalets, capable of accommo-dating 300,000 guests at a time. The town is pulsating with life both day and night. Tourists flock here, attracted by miles of sandy beaches, as well as hundreds of restaurants, bars, discotheques and shops.

The resort is popular with surfers and windsurfers, as well as deep-sea fishing and diving enthusiasts. For those who enjoy aquatic fun and games, the resort also offers **Aquasur** – the biggest water-park in the Canary Islands, with 29 slides. Another big attraction is **Holiday World** – an amusement park occupying 14,000 sq m (3.5 acres) and featuring a traditional ferris wheel, 27 m (88 ft) high.

This large, modern resort, criss-crossed with numerous palm-lined boulevards, has an excellent golf course – the biggest on the island – while spiritual needs are served by the ecumenical church – **Templo Ecuménico**.

Although Maspalomas gives the impression of being a single entity, it is in fact a conglomeration of three separate resorts, reached by three different exits from the south-coast motorway.

The furthest east is **San Agustín**. This quiet, tourist town, full of greenery, with dark sand beaches, is aimed at an upmarket clientele, rather than at mass tourism. It has a number of luxurious hotels, exclusive clubs, a casino and scenic promenades.

In the middle of the Maspalomas coastline is **Playa del Inglés**. This is the most crowded and liveliest resort, with Yumbo, a multi-storey shopping/restaurant centre, in the middle of town.

To the south of Playa del Inglés are the **Dunas de Maspalomas** – a vast, 4-sq km (1.5-sq mile) expanse of dunes and now a national park with a salt-water lake and palm grove, which can only be explored on foot or by camel. The dunes provide a habitat for lizards, rabbits and naturists. (This is also an area used by cruising gay men.) The nearby lagoon provides numerous migrant birds with a stop en route between Europe and Africa.

The spectacular dunes of Maspalomas

Colourful parrots in Palmitos Parque

ENVIRONS: Some 10 km (6 miles) north of Maspalomas, set in a mountain valley, is **Palmitos Parque**. Amid its lush, tropical vegetation live 1,500 birds, including birds of paradise from New Guinea, miniature humming birds and toucans, with their colourful beaks. Bird shows involving trained parrots, eagles and falcons entertain visitors at intervals. Other attractions include the Casa de las Orquideas, which houses around 1,000 orchids. The huge aquarium, with its vast tanks of water, has a large variety of fish from all over the world, including the Canary Islands' sea, Indian Ocean and South American waters. A further attraction of the park is the butterfly house – the largest of its kind in Europe. The park also boasts white-handed gibbons, whose natural habitats are the Malayan Peninsula and Burma, and who have been bred successfully here: the first time in captivity.

Just 6 km (4 miles) to the north is **Mundo Aborigen** – a reconstruction of an ancient Canary village. Set on a gentle slope, with a splendid view over the Barranco de Fataga, it consists of several crofts. Life-sized Guanche figures and recorded domestic animal noises give the setting some realism. A marked trail leads to a series of lifelike scenes including: a butcher gutting a goat; a doctor operating on a patient; wrestlers fighting in a small stadium. Nearby a farmer is shown sowing a field, while

the local executioner can be seen smashing a convict's head with a rock. A sentry, poised at the highest point above the village, keeps watch over the surrounding area.

Some 10 km (6 miles) northeast, at the end of a rocky valley, is the small theme park **Sioux City**, which represents a ragbag of familiar associations with American culture. At the entrance, next to a wooden cart containing models of the first settlers travelling west, we come across "Cadillac Café" with a genuine 1960s American car.

Visitors drinking in the saloon can enjoy dramatic interruptions from actors staging fights. Apart from such traditional fun there is also the "foam party" – a discotheque where participants throw foam at each other. The narrow streets of Sioux City provide the setting for scenes from westerns, including mock fistfights, gunfights and bank robberies. The air is filled with country and western music.

✈ Palmitos Parque
Barranco de los Palmitos. **(** *928 140 276.* **◯** *10am–6pm daily.* ◐
🏛 Mundo Aborigen
Macizo de Amurga. **(** *928 172 295.* **◯** *9am–6pm daily.* ◐
🏛 Sioux City
Cañon del Águila. **(** *928 762 573.* **◯** *10am–5pm Tue–Sun.* ◐

San Bartolomé de Tirajana ⓱

🚶 *24,000.* 🚌 🎭 *Carnival (Feb), Santiago (25 Jul).*

FOUNDED IN the 16th century by the Spanish, this picturesque little town was once a shepherd settlement. Situated in the lush green valley of Tirajana, this district is known for its orchards of almonds, plums, peaches and cherries, which are used in the production of vodkas and liqueurs. The local speciality is cherry liqueur, *guindilla.*

The first chapel in San Bartolomé was built in the 16th century. In 1690, work started on its site to build a much grander, triple-nave parish church, which was not, in fact, consecrated until 1922. Its noteworthy features include the Mudéjar-style wooden vaults and carved statues of the saints. It is also worth visiting the old cemetery, set on a hill, where – contrary to the Spanish tradition – the dead were buried in the soil rather then being entombed in the cemetery wall.

Statue of Indian at Sioux City

ENVIRONS: Some 8 km (5 miles) to the south of San Bartolomé, in a beautiful setting of tall cliffs, palms and fruit trees, is **Fataga** – a mountain village with old houses and the 1880 church of San José. Next to the church are reservoirs – Embalse de Tirajana and Embalse de Fataga – both of which are excellent goals for walkers.

Children's water slide at the Aquasur water park, Maspalomas

Around Pico de las Nieves ⑱

AN ALL-DAY TOUR through the mountains of Gran Canaria can start from any point. The diverse character of the island's landscape makes it an unforgettable experience. The scenic road follows a serpentine course as it climbs mountain slopes, and passes through enchanting villages and deep ravines. Lush sub-tropical vegetation, including exotic fruit trees and terraced fields, can be seen along the way. There are also numerous viewpoints en route that offer spectacular panoramas, even to the peak of Mount Teide on Tenerife. Some of the less accessible places can be reached by minor roads and tracks.

Artenara ⑦
One of the caves in this village houses a small chapel, another an unusual restaurant – Mesón de la Silla.

Caldera Pinos de Gáldar ⑥
On the road leading to Artenara, surrounded by the conifer forests of Pinos de Gáldar, stands a picturesque cathedral. From here you can see the whole northern coast of the island.

Tejeda ⑧
This quiet little town, occupying a particularly scenic location on the mountain slopes, provides a good stopping place for lunch when touring the area.

Roque Bentaiga ⑨
Along with nearby Roque Nublo, this basalt rock, rising to 1,412 m (4,632 ft) above sea level, was regarded as a holy place by the Guanches, who left rock inscriptions, granaries and ceremonial sites in this area.

SAN NICOLÁS DE TOLENTINO

GC 21

GC 60

MOGÁN

MASPALOMAS

| 0 km | 2 |
| 0 miles | 2 |

KEY

▬ Suggested route

▬ Scenic route

═ Other roads

☀ Viewpoint

Roque Nublo ⑩
This 60-m (195-ft) tall basalt monolith tops a 1,700 m (5,578 ft) peak. Thought to have been held sacred by the Guanches, this finger of rock was formed by erosion, and is often shrouded in clouds.

Cruz de Tejeda ⑤

Carved in stone, this cross – from which the area takes its name – marks the central point of Gran Canaria. The view from this point on the mountain pass (altitude 1,450 m/4,757 ft) was described as a "petrified storm" by artist Miguel de Unamuno.

TEROR

Ariñez

GC 400

GC 15

LAS PALMAS DE GRAN CANARIA

⑤

④

GC 150

GC 130

② GC 600

③

GC 60

San Bartolomé de Tirajana ①

The town is surrounded by a lush valley of orchards. The fruit from plum, cherry and peach trees is used to make fine vodka and liqueurs.

SANTA LUCÍA

MASPALOMAS

> **TIPS FOR TOURISTS**
>
> **Starting point:** San Bartolomé de Tirajana.
> **Length:** 80 km (50 miles).
> **Stopping places:** The best place to stop for lunch is the parador at Cruz de Tejeda, which has an excellent restaurant. There are also restaurants in Artenara and San Bartolomé de Tirajana.

La Degollada de Becerra ④
This viewpoint offers a spectacular view to the west and of the Roque Bentiga peak.

Pico de las Nieves ③

Also known as Pozo de las Nieves (the Well of Snow), this is the highest peak on Gran Canaria at 1,949 m/6,394 ft. It is often cold and misty here, with occasional snowfall in winter. At the top stands a military radio station.

Presa de los Hornos ②
The best view of the highest reservoir on the island can be seen near the summit of Roque Nublo *(see p62).*

Santa Lucía ⑲

LOCATED IN THE high country,
this tiny village stands 700
m (2,300 ft) above sea level,
in the upper reaches of the
fertile palm valley of Santa
Lucía de Tirajana. Standing on
top of the hill is the **Church
of Santa Lucía**, which was
built in 1898 on the site of a
former 17th-century chapel.

Various archaeological
finds, unearthed on the slopes
of the surrounding hills and
dating from the time of the
Guanches, can now be seen
in the local **Museo del
Castillo de la Fortaleza**.
This ethnography/archaeology
museum is housed in a
recently built pseudo-castle
with turrets and battlements.
The museum also features a
reconstructed bedroom,
typical of those in a 17th-
century Canary home, and
displays of pottery (including
a 3rd-century amphora), fish,
leather goods, basket-work,
skeletons and other exhibits.

ENVIRONS: A scenic road leads
5 km (3 miles) south to the
viewpoint of Mirador de
Guriete, with its spectacular
views of the area.

🏛 **Museo del Castillo
de la Fortaleza**
📞 *928 798 310.*
🕐 *10:30am–5:30pm Mon–Fri,
11:30am–5:30pm Sat & Sun.* 🖼

Agüimes ⑳

THE OLD PART of this small
town, with its narrow
streets and beautiful houses,
is overshadowed by the two
huge towers of **San
Sebastián Church**, standing
in the Plaza del Rosario. The
basilica has three naves and
a barrel vault, and was constructed between 1796 and
1808. Along with the
cathedral in Las Palmas de
Gran Canaria, this is one of
the best examples of the
Canary Islands' Neo-Classical

Picturesque narrow streets of Agüimes

architecture. The vast dome
lends an oriental touch to the
building. The statues of saints
inside the church are the
work of a Canary sculptor –
Luján Perez (1756–1815).

Another attraction of
Agüimes is the **Parque de
los Cocodrilos**. This mini-
zoo puts on shows of trained
crocodiles and parrots.

The town comes to life
every September during the
Encuentro Internacional Tres
Continentes, an international
festival of theatre. Groups
from Europe, Africa and South
America come to participate
in this lively event.

🐊 **Parque de los
Cocodrilos**
Ctra. de los Corralillos. 📞 *928 781
723.* 🕐 *10am–6pm Sun–Fri.* 🖼

Ingenio ㉑

SITUATED IN THE eastern
region, near Barranco
Guayadeque, this small town
is one of the oldest on Gran
Canaria. It owes its name to
the local sugar-cane industry
that flourished here in the
17th century (*ingenio* means
sugar mill). Later, the region
turned towards rum production but now it is a largely
agricultural area, its main
crop being tomatoes. Ingenio

is, however, best
known for its
embroidery. There is a
School of Embroidery
housed in the **Museo
de Piedras y
Artesanía** – a white,
bougainvillea-covered
building with deco-
rative turrets. The
museum also houses
a collection of rocks
and minerals, agricul-
tural tools, pottery and
basketwork.

The imposing
**Church of Nuestra
Señora de la
Candelaria** looms
over an attractive
square, bordered by
pretty houses with
wooden balconies.

ENVIRONS: On the slope of a
mountain, half-way along the
road between Ingenio and
Telde, is an archaeological
site discovered in the 19th
century. It consists of four
caves, including **Cuatro
Puertas**, with four openings
(hence the name), which
used to be the home
of Telde rulers, or the site of
sacrifices. The other three
caves, which face the sea,
were used by the Guanches
to bury the embalmed bodies
of their dead.

🏛 **Museo de Piedras
y Artesanía**
Camino Real de Gando, 1. 📞 *928
781 124.* 🕐 *8am–6:30pm Mon–Sat,
8–10am Sun.* 🖼

**Entrance to Museo de Piedras y
Artesanía in Ingenio**

Green and white painted houses in Plaza de San Juan – the main square in Telde

Barranco de Guayadeque ㉒

2 km (1.5 miles) north of Ingenio.

A SCENIC, WINDING road runs 7 km (4 miles) along the bottom of the Guayadeque Canyon, whose name in the Guanche language means "place of the flowing waters". The stream flowing along the canyon supplies water to the neighbouring towns of Ingenio and Agüimes.

Guayadeque is overgrown with cacti, agaves, palms and Canary pines, in addition to about 80 species native to the Canary Islands. In spring, the parched, rough terrain of the canyon is softened by blossoming almond trees.

This region is one of the most important prehistoric burial grounds, where the dead, often wrapped in animal skins, were interred in inaccessible caves. Many of these graves were plundered in the 19th century by the local population, who sold the mummies to the Museo Canario in Las Palmas. Local caves were also used by the Guanches as dwelling places, food stores and as sites used for fertility rituals.

Barranco de Guayadeque is popular with modern-day people who, following in the footsteps of the Guanches, have made their homes in the caves. This small troglodyte population has a chapel carved into the rock to meet their spiritual needs, while more earthly delights are provided by cave bars serving the strong local wine, bread and Temisas olives in green mojo sauce *(see pp166–7)*.

Guayadeque is also popular for Sunday picnics. The road running along the canyon ends at Montañade las Tierras restaurant. Further on, the route is impassable for cars and ends up with a narrow footpath. During the summer, the sun's rays on the rocks dazzle spectators. In winter, the place can be cold, and clouds often cover the high ridges of the canyon.

Peaks shrouded in clouds above Barranco de Guayadeque

Telde ㉓

92,700.   San Juan (24 Jun).

D URING PRE-COLONIAL times, Telde was the seat of the local king of the Guanches. Following the conquest of the island, it became known as a port for loading sugar cane.

Towards the end of the 15th century, the Spanish built a small chapel here. In 1519, work commenced on the site to build the present **Church of San Juan Bautista**. The highlights of this large basilica are the Mannerist altar and a Flemish triptych dating from the first half of the 16th century.

From **Plaza de San Juan**, in which the church stands, runs **Inés Cemida**, a street connecting San Juan with another historic part of town – San Francisco. Here, the two-storey buildings are similarly painted in white and green. The narrow streets are lined with houses adorned with balconies of wrought iron and timber.

FERNANDO DE LEÓN Y CASTILLO (1842–1918)

León y Castillo, an engineer and diplomat born in Telde, played an important role in the regeneration of Gran Canaria. It is to him that the island owes the development of the Las Palmas harbour, gaining the island equal status with Tenerife. Opposed to Tenerife's domination, he was an advocate of the archipelago's division into two provinces. In 1881, he became Minister of Foreign Affairs, and also served as Spanish ambassador to France. In recognition, he was awarded the title of Marqués del Muni.

Bust of León y Castillo, in Telde

FUERTEVENTURA

FUERTEVENTURA IS BLESSED *by sun and sand in equal measure. Much of its interior, consisting of arid dunes and rocky mountain ridges, is reminiscent of the western Sahara, which lies only 100 km (62 miles) to the east. Most of the island's tourists stick to the coast where the fine sandy beaches are irresistible to sun worshippers, and strong winds provide ideal conditions for surfing.*

With a distance of 97 km (60 miles) between Punta de la Tinosa, in the north, and Punta de Jandía, in the south, Fuerteventura is the longest and the second largest of the Canary Islands. Yet despite its size, it is one of the most sparsely populated, and its 40,000 or so inhabitants are outnumbered by the many goats that scratch a meal from the island's dry scrub.

Goats – both a symbol of the island and part of its landscape

An island known as Forte Ventura first appeared on a map drawn by the cartographer Angelino Dulceta in 1339. Between 1402–05 it was taken by conquistadors, led by Jean de Béthencourt and Gadifer de la Salle. The village that grew up around the camp of Jean de Béthencourt, Santa María de Betancuria, subsequently became the island's capital. Territorial expansion in the mid-17th century extended to the region of El Cotillo and included the seat of the former kingdom of Maxorata. Volcanic eruptions and sand carried from the Sahara desert, as well as frequent droughts during the 18th and 19th centuries, caused the collapse of Fuerteventura's agriculture, once called the granary of the Canaries, and today most of the island's revenue comes from tourism.

The climate is harsher here than on the other islands thanks in part to a cooler prevailing wind called *gota fría*. The annual temperature stays more or less constant at around 19° C (66° F).

The arid climate and deforestation are responsible for the limited vegetation found here. An almost total absence of rain means that drinking water must be obtained either by desalination or shipped over from the mainland.

Miles of unspoiled golden beaches south of Corralejo

◁ **The steep shores of the gulf near Ajuy**

Exploring Fuerteventura

FUERTEVENTURA WAS discovered by tourists later than the other islands in the region and as a consequence the local tourist industry is still in its infancy. The number of visitors is increasing, however, as news gradually spreads of the island's scenic landscape, and the peace and quiet to be found here. The vast stretches of white beach are a particular draw to sun worshippers – the more accessible ones are found in the northern part of the island, near Corralejo, the wilder ones around Cofete. The shores of Jandía provide perfect conditions for surfing and windsurfing, while rich underwater life is a tempting attraction for divers. Fuerteventura is also an excellent area for walking and cycling. Those interested in history will find many interesting places to visit, including Betancuria and Pájara.

LOCATOR MAP

Mountain view on the road from Pájara to La Pared

SIGHTS AT A GLANCE

Ajuy **10**
Antigua **8**
Betancuria **9**
Caleta de Fustes **19**
Cofete **16**
Corralejo **3**
Costa Calma **13**
El Cotillo **5**
Gran Tarajal **17**
Isla de los Lobos **4**
La Oliva **6**

La Pared **12**
Malpaís Chico and Malpaís Grande **18**
Morro Jable **14**
Pájara **11**
Parque Natural de las Dunas de Corralejo **2**
Península de Jandía **15**
Puerto del Rosario **1**
Tefía **7**

Herds of goats, the main livestock on Fuerteventura

10 AJUY

PÁJ

TESEJERA

LA PARED **12**

TARAJA

LA LAJIT

COSTA CALMA **13**

COFETE **16**

15 PENÍNSULA DE JANDÍA

14 MORRO JABLE

0 km 5

0 miles 5

ISLA DE
LOS LOBOS

CORRALEJO 3

EL COTILLO 5   LAJARES

PARQUE NATURAL
DE LAS DUNAS
DE CORRALEJO

FV 101

LA OLIVA 6

TINDAYA   FV 10

FV 1

TETIR

TEFÍA 7   FV 10

CASILLAS
DEL ÁNGEL

FV 30   FV 20   PUERTO
DEL ROSARIO 1

LA AMPUYENTA

TANCURIA 9

ANTIGUA 8   CALETA DE
FUSTES 19

EGA
E RÍO PALMAS   FV 50   FV 2

FV 20

MALPAÍS CHICO 18
AND MALPAÍS GRANDE

TUINEJE   FV 2

FV 20

FV 2   LAS PLAYAS

GRAN TARAJAL 17

The lush garden of Casa de Santa
María, in Betancuria

GETTING THERE

Fuerteventura has direct air
links with Lanzarote, Gran
Canaria and Tenerife, and
connects via Tenerife to the
western islands. There are also
flights from mainland Spanish
cities as well as a number of
European centres. Regular ferry
links connect Puerto del
Rosario with Arrecife (Lanzarote)
and Las Palmas de Gran Canaria,
and Corralejo with Playa Blanca
(Lanzarote). A hydrofoil runs
from Morro Jable to Las Palmas
de Gran Canaria. The local
transport is limited.

SEE ALSO

- **Where to Stay** pp158–9.
- **Where to Eat** pp170–71.

KEY

- ▬ Motorway/Highway
- ▬ Major road
- ▬ Other road
- ▬ Scenic route
- ✈ Airport
- ⚓ Ferry harbour
- ☼ Viewpoint

Scenic approach road leading to the centre of La Pared

Drawing room of Casa Museo de Unamuno, Puerto del Rosario

Puerto del Rosario ❶

🏃 14,000. ✈ 🚌 ⛴
ℹ C/1Mayo, 37, 928 530 844.
🎭 Nuestra Señora del Rosario (7 Oct).

PUERTO DEL ROSARIO, the current administrative centre of Fuerteventura, was established in 1797 as a port for locally produced soda and grain. The port began to grow in the mid-19th century and by 1860 had become the capital of the island. Until 1957, the town, whose name means Port of Roses, was Puerto de Cabras – Port of Goats – in reference to the watering hole in the nearby canyon.

Today the port has a thriving cargo and passenger harbour, with ferries sailing to Gran Canaria and Lanzarote. It also has a yachting marina. Not far from the town – which is the largest on Fuerteventura and inhabited by more than half of the island's population – is an international airport.

Another feature of Puerto del Rosario is the huge barracks of the Spanish Foreign Legion. In 1975, when the Spaniards finally left the western Sahara, 3,000 legionnaires were transferred here – numbers have since dwindled and there are now fewer than 1,000.

While in Puerto del Rosario, it is worth taking time to visit the church of **Nuestra Señora del Rosario**, with its classical façade. Standing opposite it is **Casa Museo de Unamuno**, which will interest lovers of Spanish literature, as it was the home of the writer and philosopher Miguel de Unamuno during his exile. Part of the house is furnished with period pieces including the original desk used by the writer, and it represents a typical interior from his times.

🏛 Casa Museo de Unamuno
C/del Rosario 11. 📞 928 862 300.
🕐 9am–1pm and 5–7pm Mon–Fri;
9am–1pm Sat.

ENVIRONS: Just 12 km (7 miles) to the north is a small village, **Cassilas del Angel**, with pretty houses. The beautiful church of Santa Ana (Saint Anne), dates from 1781 and has a black, volcanic-stone façade.

Parque Natural de las Dunas ❷

IN THE NORTHEAST corner of the island is the Parque Natural de las Dunas de Corralejo, which stretches south right up to the base of the Montaña Roja volcano

Goats picking at the scrub in the Parque Natural de las Dunas

(312 m/1,023 ft). Occupying 27 sq km (10 sq miles), this wide belt of seemingly endless, shifting sands encroaches on the road between Puerto del Rosario and Corralejo and descends to the ocean.

Reminiscent of the Sahara desert, the Parque Natural de las Dunas de Corralejo is almost totally devoid of any vestiges of civilization. Even when the tourist season is at its height there is plenty of solitude and open space to be found here (don't forget to take a hat). The only signs of life are the stone walls built as windbreaks on the sandy hills. The area was declared a National Park in 1987.

Sand-sculpture of a dragon on a beach, Corralejo

Corralejo ❸

🏃 4,000. ⛴ ℹ Plaza Pública de Corralejo, 928 866 235. 🛒 Mon, Tue, Thu, Fri. 🎭 Carnival (Mar), Nuestra Señora del Carmen (16 Jul).

THIS NORTHERNMOST town of Fuerteventura has a passenger harbour, with ferries sailing several times a day to Playa Blanca in Lanzarote. Small cruising boats also take tourists to the neighbouring island of Los Lobos. Weather-beaten fishing boats moored at the quayside and several fish restaurants add a touch of charm to this old fishing village.

Corralejo was only recently developed for tourism but has rapidly become the island's second most important vacation centre, after the Jandía peninsula. Visitors come here not so much for the town but for its setting, with striking views of Lanzarote and Los Lobos and the wonderful beaches to the south of the centre. Excellent conditions for surfing and windsurfing are another

Jet-skis and sailing school in Corralejo harbour

MIGUEL DE UNAMUNO (1864–1936)

Miguel de Unamuno, the "Philosopher from Salamanca", played a major part in the rebirth of Spanish literature and in the intellectual life of Spain in the early 20th century. He was the rector of Salamanca University from 1900. Having spoken out against the dictatorship of Primo de Rivera he was forced into exile in the Canary Islands for a few months. His opposition to Franco led to his being put under house arrest. In his work, he advocated the view that philosophy should express the tragedy of the human dilemma. Declaring himself a defender of "pure Spanishness", his *Spanish Travels and Scenes* (1922) is a testament to the author's love for his homeland.

Miguel de Unamuno, outspoken and defiant

attraction. Thanks to a year-round stiff breeze, the El Río strait between Corralejo and Lanzarote is an ideal place for water sports. The clear water teems with a rich variety of fish. Angling, diving and glass-bottomed boat trips are very popular.

The only interesting sight in town is its modern church in **Plaza de la Iglesia**. The town's main attraction is sand-sculpting – on a small beach by the harbour, giant dragons and camels can be conjured up before your eyes.

Isla de los Lobos ❹

🔲

THIS SMALL VOLCANIC island, occupying only 4.4 sq km (1.7 sq miles) is situated in the El Río strait, midway between Fuerteventura and Lanzarote. It can be reached by small cruising boat from Corralejo or by glass-bottomed motor-yacht. The island of Los Lobos is very young, little more than 6,000–8,000 years old, and owes its name to the seals – *lobos marinos* – which once made their home on its sandy shores.

According to the history books, the French adventurer de la Salle dropped anchor by the island of Los Lobos in 1402. He and his crew were saved from starvation by seal meat. In the early 15th century, Jean de Béthencourt built a hermitage on the island. Later on, the island served as a base for pirates raiding the neighbouring islands of the archipelago. It was also a centre of the slave trade.

Until 1968, the only permanent residents of the island were the lighthouse keeper and his family. Thanks to the fact that the island remained uninhabited for so long, it has retained its original ecosystem. The natural botanical garden on the slopes of the Montaña Lobos is used as a resting place by migrating birds.

The whole of the island of Los Lobos is a nature reserve, and development of its tourist trade has been slow and sensitive as a result. There are no more than a handful of small pensions on the island. The sandy coves offer ideal conditions for swimming and relaxing, while angling is limited to a few allocated spots. There is a good marked walking trail around the island; it starts and ends in Casas del Puertito – a small hamlet with a harbour.

Isla de los Lobos, a fine destination for barbecues, swimming and hiking trips

Fishing harbour in El Cotillo, with the mighty Fortaleza del Tostón guarding its entrance

El Cotillo ❺

🚌 ℹ️ *928 866 235.* 🎉 *Nuestra Señora del Buen Viaje (3rd Sun in Aug).*

THE EARLY DAYS of this small fishing town are associated with the Guanches. This was once the seat of the tribal chiefs of Maxorata – the ancient kingdom that encompassed the northern part of Fuerteventura.

The round fortified tower – **Fortaleza del Tostón** – dates from more recent times. A small fort, it was built in 1797 as a defence against British and Arab pirates. Thanks to restoration work it is now well preserved. Approached via stone steps with a drawbridge, this is a two-storey structure. Originally the upper floor housed a water tank, while the lower level was used as soldiers' quarters.

The small harbour features a **giant rock** rising out of the water. Although highly picturesque, it makes it hard for the fishermen to steer in and out during rough weather. Other attractions of El Cotillo are its scenic coves and nearby sandy beaches.

La Oliva ❻

👥 *2,300.* 🚌 ℹ️ *928 866 235.* 🎉 *Nuestra Señora de la Candelaria (2 Feb), Nuestra Señora del Rosario (Oct).*

SITUATED AT THE northern end of Fuerteventura, La Oliva is one of the prettiest villages on the island and a popular excursion destination.

It stands in the shadow of Montaña de Escantraga (529 m/1730 ft). The first European settlers arrived here in the early 14th century. In 1709, the newly established military governor of the island (the "Colonel") chose La Oliva as his seat. The town soon became the military capital of the island and, along with Betancuria, a centre of Fuerteventura's political life.

The military headquarters were at the **Casa de los Coroneles**. The "House of Colonels", built in the 18th century, is a large austere edifice featuring two low towers at the corners and numerous windows: it is said to have one window for each day of the year though this is inaccurate. The nearby **Casa del Capellán** (Chaplain's House) is a modest single-storey building with an ornately decorated portal and window frames.

Sculpture, Centro de Arte Canario

In the town centre stands the **Iglesia de Nuestra Señora de la Candelaria**. The white walls of this attractive church, which dates from 1711, stand in stark contrast to its square belfry, built of black volcanic stone. The interior of the church is decorated with numerous fine sculptures and paintings by Juan de Miranda. The **Centro de Arte Canario**, displaying the works of local artists, and the **Museo del Grano** – with an exhibition on grain production in an early 19th-century granary, are both worth a visit.

🏛️ **Centro de Arte Canario**
📞 *928 868 233.* ⏰ *Summer: 10am–6pm Mon–Sat; Winter: 10am–5pm Mon–Sat.*
⏺️ *Sun.*
🏛️ **Museo del Grano La Cilla**
⏰ *10am–6pm daily.* 📷

The triple-naved Iglesia de Nuestra Señora de la Candelaria, La Oliva

Tefía ❼

🖼 230.

THIS VILLAGE, which lies on the road from La Oliva to Betancuria, has an interesting open-air museum – the **Ecomuseo de la Alcogida** – featuring seven reconstructed houses typical of traditional Fuerteventura architecture. The exhibition illustrates the former life of the islanders, their occupations relating to farming and crafts, and also explains the process of the houses' reconstruction.

Reconstructed farm buildings in the Ecomuseo de la Alcogida, Tefía

🏛 **Ecomuseo de la Alcogida**
📞 928 175 434.
🕓 9:30am–5:30pm Tue–Fri, Sun.

ENVIRONS: Some 12 km (7 miles) northeast is the small town of **Tetir**. It's worth visiting for its traditional houses with balconies and the local church, Santo Domingo de Guzmán (1745). The square in front of the church features a bust of Juán Rodríguez y Gonzáles (1825–93), the founder of the Banco de Canarias, who was born here.

A further 8 km (5 miles) north, on the slopes of **Montaña Quemada**, stands a monument to Miguel de Unamuno. Made of sandstone and over 2 m (7 ft) tall, it was carved in 1970 by Juan Borges Lineres.

Antigua ❽

🚌 🖼 Nuestra Señora de Pino (8 Sep).

ANTIGUA, in the centre of Fuerteventura at the foot of the mountains, is – true to its name – one of the oldest towns on the island. It was established in 1485 by the settlers arriving from Andalusia and Normandy, who began cultivating the soil and breeding animals. Many windmills erected at the time were used to irrigate the fields. In 1812, Antigua was granted municipal rights and from 1835 it was the capital of the island.

Its more interesting features include the small, single-nave church of **Nuestra Señora de Antigua** (1785), which has wooden vaults and a high altar incorporating folk motifs.

The **Centro de Artesanía Molinos de Antigua**, situated on the town's outskirts and surrounded by a low wall, is a museum village, built under the supervision of César Manrique, which includes a craft centre, a reconstructed

Façade of the late 18th-century church, Antigua

windmill, and a gallery and exhibition halls devoted to ethnography and archaeology.

🏛 **Centro de Artesanía Molinos de Antigua**
📞 928 878 041.
🕓 9:30am–5:30pm Tue–Fri, Sun. 🖼

ENVIRONS: Travel 8 km (5 miles) to the north for **La Ampuyenta**, a small village with a 17th-century chapel, San Pedro de Alcántara. This picturesque sanctuary is surrounded by a fortification erected by Norman settlers.

Some 9 km (6 miles) south is the village of **Tiscamanita**, with the 17th-century chapel of San Marcos. The main draw here is the **Centro de Interpretación de los Molinos**, where visitors can learn something about the island's many windmills.

🏛 **Centro de Interpretación de los Molinos**
🕓 9:30am–5:30pm Tue–Fri, Sun. 🖼

JEAN DE BÉTHENCOURT (C.1360–1422)

On 1 May 1402, Jean de Béthencourt, together with Gadifer de la Salle, set sail from La Rochelle in France, at the head of a small expedition intent on conquering the Canary Islands. He left some of his men on Lanzarote and sailed to Spain to seek support. He returned not only with ships, soldiers and money, but also with a title – he was now the lord of four of the islands: Fuerteventura, Lanzarote, El Hierro and La Gomera. The furious de la Salle immediately returned to France. Béthencourt, having handed over the power to his nephew, Maciot de Béthencourt, also returned to France in 1406. He died at his castle in Normandy in 1422.

Jean de Béthencourt, Norman conqueror

Betancuria's lush vegetation, a contrast to the stark mountains beyond

Betancuria ❾

🏯 600. 🚌 ℹ️ C/Amador Rodríguez, 6, 928 878 092.
🎎 San Buenaventura (14 Jul).

NESTLING IN A volcanic crater sheltered from the winds, Betancuria lies in the central region of the island, where the rugged peaks of extinct volcanoes punctuate the wide, fertile valleys. Practically all of this area is within the Parque Natural de Betancuria. The highest peak, Pico de Betancuria, offers a splendid vantage point.

The town was founded in 1404 and was given its full name, Villa de Santa María de Betancuria, by Jean de Béthencourt. The Norman made the town the island's capital and it remained so until 1834. Betancuria's inland position was intended to protect it against pirate raids. However, in 1593, the Berber pirate Xabán de Arráez pillaged it mercilessly, destroying virtually every building and taking 600 of its inhabitants captive.

Today, Betancuria is the prettiest village on Fuerteventura. At its centre stands the **Iglesia de Santa María**. The first church built on this site in 1404 was elevated to the status of a cathedral and bishopric by Pope Martin III in 1425, but no bishop ever arrived to take up the post. In 1593, the church was burned by Arráez; it was rebuilt in 1620. Noteworthy features of its interior include the Baroque altar, the original stone floor set in a wooden frame, the carved stalls and the coffered

ceiling. The space behind the choir contains a vast painting, *Nava de La Iglesia*, depicting the church as a ship, painted by Nicolas Medina in 1730.

On the northern outskirts of the village is the Franciscan abbey of **San Buenaventura** – the oldest abbey on the island. Its roof collapsed in the mid-19th century and what remains today are merely scenic ruins. Next to the abbey stands **Pozo del Diablo** – Devil's Pit. According to legend, Satan was chained to this rock and forced to carry stones used in the building of the abbey.

Betancuria has two small museums. The **Museo de Arte Sacro**, established in a former parish house, has a collection of sacred art and photographs showing almost every church on the Canary Islands. The **Museo Arqueológico** has a collection dating from the time of the Guanches, as well as antique items of everyday use. Visitors to the restored 16th-

century town house of Casa de Santa Maria can pick up a few souvenirs from the craft shop.

🏛 **Museo de Arte Sacro**
Alcalde Carmelo Silvera, s/n.
📞 928 878 003. 🕐 11am–4pm Mon–Fri, 11am–2pm Sat. ⬤ Sun
🏛 **Museo Arqueológico**
Roberto Roldán, 12–14.
📞 928 878 241. 🕐 11am–5pm Tue–Sat, 11am–2pm Sun.

ENVIRONS: Some 2 km (1 mile) north of Betancuria, Mirador de Morro Velosa offers a fine view over the island's dramatic lunar-like landscape.

Ajuy ❿

30 km (19 miles) southwest of Betancuria.

AJUY PERCHES ON the shores of a small bay and is surrounded by steep cliffs. Jean de Béthencourt, accompanied by Gadifer de la Salle, landed here in 1402 and embarked on the conquest of the island. For many years the bay served as a harbour for settlers arriving in Betancuria.

Today Ajuy is a quiet fishing village. The fishing season lasts from May until October and during this time the simple beach-side restaurants serve up the day's catch. Numerous caves, such as the Arco de Jurao, can be explored.

With its rocky seabed, vast underwater caves and shoals of darting fish, Ajuy is a paradise for scuba divers.

Waves battering the steep cliffs around Ajuy

Old irrigation equipment, Pájara

Pájara ⓫

 Virgen del Carmen (16 Jul).

To the south of Betancuria lies the small town of Pájara, linked with the island's capital by a scenic road. This is one of the oldest settlements on Fuerteventura. It was founded by fishermen and goatherders who settled here in the 16th century.

Historic attractions include the church of **Nuestra Señora de la Regla**. Built in 1684, the church is worth seeing for its Latin American influences. The stone reliefs above the main portal depict stylized images of fish, lions, birds and snakes devouring

Portal of the church in Pájara

their own tails. The origin of these motifs, said to be inspired by Aztec art, is unknown. The church's interior features two wooden altars, including a smiling figure of the Madonna and Child, and one of Our Lady of Sorrows (Nuestra Señora de los Dolores), the patron saint of the island.

ENVIRONS: Some 11 km (7 miles) northeast lies **Vega de Río Palmas**. Here, perched among high rocks is the hermitage of Nuestra Señora de la Peña which features another image of Our Lady of Sorrows. Each year on the third Sunday in May a feast is held here in her honour. The church (1666) contains statues of saints, believed to have been brought here by Béthencourt for the first church built in Betancuria.

La Pared ⓬

About 21 km (13 miles) south of Pájara.

This small tourist town has undergone a fair degree of development and includes an elegant hotel. It is worth visiting both for its historical associations and for its landscape.

Before the Spanish conquest, a land wall running around here *(la pared)* marked the boundary between two rival Guanche kingdoms: Maxorata and Jandía. Much of the wall may have been dismantled to use as building material; today no trace of it remains.

La Pared has the most extensive dunes to be found anywhere in Fuerteventura and separates the Jandía peninsula from the remaining part of the island. It also forms a natural border between two beaches of completely different sand colour. The southern Playa del Vejo Rey has golden sand. To the north, Playa de la Pared consists of black sand.

A trek of several hours along some interesting volcanic formations leads to a ravine at the foot of the Risco del Pasco mountain, where it joins the road leading to Morro Jable.

Costa Calma ⓭

Costa calma is an upmarket modern resort distinguished by its tasteful architecture. It lies at the northern end of Playa del Sotavento, which is the longest and most scenic beach on the island, with excellent conditions for windsurfing.

The first private homes appeared here in the late 1960s and the first hotel was built in 1977. The rapid growth of Costa Calma contributed to the construction of an asphalt road connecting Puerto del Rosario with Morro Jable. The building of a sea-water desalination plant followed in 1986. Large-scale construction works began in the mid-1990s to provide tourist facilities, including hotels, restaurants and shops.

ENVIRONS: The small village of **La Lajita** lies 6 km (4 miles) north. Visitors come here for the **Zoo Parque de los Camellos**, home to 200 species of exotic birds and mammals from around the world. A local garden centre sells specimens of tropical and subtropical flora, as well as native plants. Other attractions include half-hour camel rides and parrot shows.

Zoo Parque de los Camellos
928 161 135.
9am–6pm daily.

An eerie lunar landscape, the mountainous region north of La Pared

Virtually uninhabited northern coast, the Península de Jandía

Morro Jable 🄮

🏚 6,000. 🚢 🛥

Set amid long sandy beaches, on the southern end of Fuerteventura, Morro Jable is an old fishing village with narrow streets and lively taverns, which serve dishes of freshly caught seafood. Once a sleepy little place, the village has grown in recent years to become the biggest resort on the island.

The modern part of town is geared for tourists and includes countless hotels and apartments, shopping malls, restaurants and bars. Hydrofoils and ferries sail from the local harbour to Las Palmas on Gran Canaria, while the marina is full of yachts. Morro Jable is also a good starting point for hikes on the Península de Jandía.

Península de Jandía 🄯

The Jandía peninsula is surrounded by miles of scenic beaches with fine white sand. The longest beaches with the highest waves to be found on the island, they are particularly attractive to surfers, while the secluded beach of Barlovento, on the northwestern shore, is popular with scuba divers.

The area around Puerto de la Cruz, near Punta de Jandía – the southwestern headland

of the island with rocky shores and a solitary lighthouse – has in recent years become a Mecca for caravanning holiday-makers. In this remote region, it is possible to escape from most of the noise and bustle of mass tourism.

A considerable part of the peninsula, with its rugged hills, is a conservation area and forms part of the **Parque Natural de Jandía**. Covering 140 sq km (55 sq miles), it features many species native to the island. In the remote mountain valleys, it is still possible to see wild goats and donkeys.

During World War II, this was a closed area and belonged to the German industrialist Gustav Winter. Rumour has it that he ran a secret submarine base in southwest Fuerteventura during the war and stories about spies and buried Nazi treasure persist to this day.

Cofete 🄰

🏚 20.

Judging by the surroundings of this small, windswept village, Fuerteventura appears to be a desert island. Only a roughly surfaced road connects it with Morro Jable. At the height of Playa de Juan Gómez, the road forks: one road leads to the southwestern end of the island; the other winds up at Cofete. Cofete is the end of the line and marks the starting point for hiking trails along the ridge of Gran Valle and the pass between the peaks of Pico de Zarza and Fraile.

Beyond the village, perched below the Degollada de Cofete, is Gustav Winter's imposing villa. Cofete features the only restaurant found on the northern shore. A 2-km (1-mile) trail leads to the coast, and the Playa de Cofete, and further on, to Barlovento.

Gustav Winter's villa, on land given to him by General Franco

Windmills

WINDMILLS OF ALL types, driven by the steady trade winds, form an important element of the Canary Islands' landscape. Introduced in the 17th century, they came to replace the horse-driven mills – *tahonas*. The oldest type of windmill is the *molino*. Built of local stone, plastered in white, with a round body and conical roof, the *molino* has four to six sails. The 19th century saw the arrival of a second type of windmill – the *molina*. This differed from the previous design in the way its structure was exposed. Modern turbines were later introduced for use in desalination plants. In recent years an increasing number of wind farms have been popping up all over the island. These are used for generating electricity.

Wind turbines – *the latest generation of powerful hi-tech wind farms is used to generate electricity for the island on an industrial scale.*

Old-style windmills *used in the generation of electricity, were also employed for pumping water in desalination plants.*

Sails, or wings, of the molino are made of strong slats.

Rigid sail panels

MOLINO
A typical feature of the islands' landscape, this kind of windmill is Spanish in origin. Such windmills were used to grind flour from wheat, barley and maize. The milling mechanism is mounted in the upper section.

Long rods turned the head of the windmill and were also used to stabilize the milling mechanism.

Grain was poured by hand onto the grindstone. The flour passed into a funnel-shaped dispenser from which it was sent by chute to sacks placed on a lower level.

Chute used for pouring flour into sacks

Entrance to the lower floor of the molino

The molino's grinding mechanism is simple: rotating sails turn a vast cogwheel, which connects directly with the grind wheel.

The molina's structure, unlike the molino, is visible on the outside and sits on top of the building that houses the grinding mechanism.

Gran Tarajal ⑰

📠 ℹ️ 928 162 723. 🎭 Fiesta de
San Diego de Alcalá (13 Nov).

T HIS FAIR-SIZED TOWN, the
second largest on
Fuerteventura, and an
important trade centre, is free
of much of the gloss typical
of modern resorts. Due to its
great strategic importance a
fort was built here at the time
of the island's invasion by
Jean de Béthencourt.

From the early 20th
century, the local port played
a more important role than
that of the island's capital
and even now it is used for
shipping merchandise from
the Península de Jandía
including tomatoes, fish
and cattle. For those who
enjoy swimming, Gran Tarajal
has a safe but drab beach
consisting of grey sand.

Apart from the single-nave
church of **Nuestra Señora de
la Candela**, built in 1900,
which can be found in the

**Waterfront at the harbour,
Las Playitas near Gran Tarajal**

town centre, there are
virtually no historical sights.

ENVIRONS: A detour 8 km (5
miles) to the east leads to a
small fishing village – **Las
Playitas**. The peaceful
atmosphere contrasts with
that of the crowded resorts.
Instead of vast hotels and
apartments, guests are invited
to stay in old fishermen's

cottages clad with
bougainvillaea and peppers,
and boasting fantastic sea
views. Local bars and
restaurants serve fresh fish
daily. Near the harbour is a
small stony beach. Some 6
km (4 miles) to the north is
Punta de la Entallada. This
is the point of Fuerteventura
closest to Africa and is
reached by a narrow, winding
road. On top of 300-metre
(1,000-ft) tall cliffs is a
lighthouse. Built in 1950, it
resembles a fortress. The site
offers a splendid view across
the mountainous part of the
island and the Atlantic.

Malpaís Chico
and Malpaís
Grande ⑱

T HE INHOSPITABLE REGIONS of
Malpaís Chico and Malpaís
Grande bear witness to the
island's volcanic past, and
occupy the central-eastern

Fuerteventura's Beaches

F UERTEVENTURA, one of the least
populated of the Canary Islands
relative to its size, features the
archipelago's most beautiful beaches,
which stretch for miles. The loveliest of
these are on the Península de Jandía,
where sunseekers will readily find peace
and quiet. There are almost 150 of these
remote beaches, of which some are
popular with nudists (see p181).

Cofete ②
It takes a determined effort to reach this
remote and windswept beach of white
sand near the village of Cofete.

Puerto de la Luz ③
This tiny fishing hamlet, situated
on the southwestern tip of the
island, is extremely remote.
Popular with windsurfers, it has
just one local restaurant, which
serves fresh seafood.

Playa de las Pilas ④
is a small but pretty
beach in a natural
and unspoilt setting.
The calm sea and
gentle winds attract
many visitors.

| 0 km | 3 |
| 0 miles | 3 |

part of Fuerteventura. It would be pointless to look for any traces of human activity here.

Don't look for any roads either. The bleak landscape is traversed by two hiking trails. One leads around Malpaís Chico, which was formed by lava flowing from the Caldera de Gaíra. The other, leading to Malpaís Grande, passes through the national park, declared a conservation zone in view of its unique geological features. Wildlife is scarce; one of the few creatures to inhabit this desert area is the Egyptian vulture.

Caleta de Fustes ⑲

🏃 2,600. 🚌 ℹ️ *Caleta Dorada, El Castillo, 928 163 286.*
📅 *Nuestra Señora del Carmen (16 Jul).*

CALETA DE FUSTES is one of the island's main vacation centres. Though not the most attractive resort, it is a quiet place. Located in the middle of the eastern coast, it is convenient for the airport. It features sprawling, low-built apartments, built around a horseshoe bay with a safe, sandy beach. Because of these factors, the resort is an excellent choice for visitors with small children.

At its centre is **Pueblo Majorero** – a modern, village-like complex of shops, bars and restaurants. One of the bungalow estates, the Barceló Club El Castillo, is built round the old **El Castillo** watchtower near the harbour. Built in 1741, it bears witness to the strategic importance of this place during the 18th century.

Tourist attractions include a good range of facilities for water sports including diving and windsurfing.

El Castillo, the watchtower in Caleta de Fustes

Playa de Barlovento ① is a remote beach popular with scuba divers, and can only be reached by off-road vehicles.

Costa Calma ⑦ is a fast-developing resort. The local beach borders Playa de Sotavento.

Playa de Sotavento ⑥
The 22-km (14-mile) belt of beaches is nicknamed "Rhapsody in Blue" due to the combination of wonderful beaches and azure, crystal-clear water.

Morro Jable ⑤
Located on the southern end of the Sotavento beaches, Morro Jable has a promenade running along the municipal beach with restaurants, bars and cafés.

LANZAROTE

THIS IS VOLCANO *country. Known as the Isla del Fuego, or Fire Island, most of Lanzarote's 795 sq km (300 sq miles) is covered with solidified lava in tones of black, pink, purple and ochre, and peppered with nearly 300 volcanic peaks. Many tourists stick to the coast, especially the northern shores. Others prefer to head inland to trek through Lanzarote's breathtaking lunar landscape.*

Much of the local architecture is in harmony with the island's unique landscape. The inhabitants continue to build in the traditional style and, as a result of strict planning controls, Lanzarote is almost totally free of high-rise buildings. This trend has been influenced by the artistic concepts of the late architect and artist César Manrique regarding the development of the island. In 1993, to support the local population in their efforts to preserve the natural landscape, UNESCO declared Lanzarote a Biosphere Reserve.

The island's name probably derives from the distorted name of the Genoese sailor Lanzarotto (or Lancelotto) Malocello, who first arrived here in 1312. In 1402, the island was conquered by Jean de Béthencourt.

The proximity of the African coast made the island prone to attacks by Algerian and Moroccan pirates, who often plundered the then capital, Teguise. In the 16th and 17th centuries, the island was also raided by English and French pirates. These attacks, combined with years of droughts and catastrophic volcanic eruptions, led at one time to the almost total depopulation of the island.

Timanfaya National Park logo

In the absence of any natural resources, the main occupations of the inhabitants were agriculture and fishing. Large plantations of prickly pear and vineyards still flourish. Other crops include tomatoes and sweet potato. In recent years, tourism has become the dominant industry, generating 80 per cent of the island's revenue. The development of agriculture and tourism has resulted in a severe water shortage. Until recently, drinking water was shipped in. Then, in 1964, the first desalination plant was opened and today almost every large estate has its own unit.

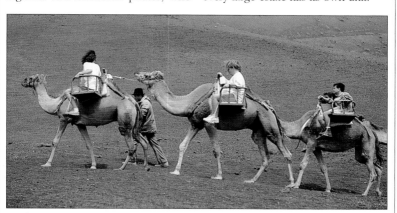

Camel caravan in Parque Nacional de Timanfaya

◁ **Typical vineyards in La Gería**

Exploring Lanzarote

ALTHOUGH LANZAROTE IS almost totally devoid of vegetation, many tourists, enchanted by the shapes and colours of its unique volcanic landscape, regard the island as the most picturesque in the archipelago. Camels, used in agriculture and tourism, are an intrinsic element of the landscape. Visitors also come here for the beaches. Lanzarote's northern shores are good for surfing; the waves are especially good at La Santa. The strange architectural designs of César Manrique, which merge with the natural landscape, are another of the island's attractions.

LOCATOR MAP

Fountain and church in the main square, San Bartolomé

SIGHTS AT A GLANCE

Mosaic in Tahiche's César Manrique Fundación

GETTING THERE

Lanzarote has air links with the other islands of the archipelago and with mainland Spain. Regular charter flights also bring in visitors from all over Europe. Frequent ferries connect Lanzarote with nearby Fuerteventura and Gran Canaria. The capital and other main towns have reasonable public transport. Not all places on the island are so well served, however. Many places, even those that are particularly attractive to tourists, cannot be reached by bus and it is advisable to make use of organized coach tours or to hire a car. Though the main roads are well-surfaced, some remote beaches require an all-terrain vehicle.

PARQUE NACIONAL DE TIMANFAYA ⓱

EL GOLFO ❿

SALINAS DE JANUBIO ⓴

YAIZA ⓲

㉒ *FEMÉ*

LZ-2

PLAYA BLANCA ㉑

Playa Papagayo near Playa Blanca

SEE ALSO

- *Where to Stay* pp159–160.
- *Where to Eat* pp171–2.

MONTAÑA CLARA

ISLA GRACIOSA
9

MIRADOR DEL RÍO **10** ÓRZOLA **8**

MALPAÍS
DE LA CORONA
7

5 JAMEOS
DEL AGUA

GUINATE **11**

6
CUEVA
DE LOS VERDES

HARÍA **12**

LA CALETA
DE FAMARA
14

LA SANTA ●

SÓO

LZ-1

TINAJO ●

LZ-10

4 GUATIZA

TIAGUA
15

13
TEGUISE

LZ-20

LZ-30

LZ-1

MOZAGA ●

3 TAHICHE

SAN BARTOLOMÉ **16**

2 COSTA TEGUISE

GC-740

LZ-1

L767

ERÍA

LZ-2

1
ARRECIFE

TÍAS ●

24
PUERTO DEL
CARMEN

KEY

▬	Motorway/Highway
▬	Main road
▬	Other road
▬	Scenic route
✈	Airport
⚓	Ferry port
☀	

0 km   5

0 miles   5

Picturesque house on the
ocean front, Arrieta

Charco de San Ginés, in Arrecife, with its small, picturesque fishermen's cottages

Arrecife ❶

🏘 35,000. ✈ 6 km (4 miles) west of Arrecife. 🚌 ℹ Calle Blas Cabrera Felipe, 3, 928 811 762. 🛥 Sat. 🎭 Carnival (Feb), San Ginés (Aug).

ARRECIFE HAS GENUINE Spanish character. With modern houses and a palm-lined promenade, it has been the capital of Lanzarote since 1852, as well as the island's main seaport and commercial centre.

The first harbour, protected by small islands and reefs, existed here as early as the 15th century. Two forts, the **Castillo de San Gabriel** (1574–99) and **Castillo de San José** (1771) were built to protect the island from seaborne raiders and have survived to this day.

The castle of St Gabriel, situated on a small island, is reached by a long drawbridge – Puente de las Bolas, or "Balls Bridge". Destroyed during a pirate attack in 1586, the castle was restored by Italian engineer Leonardo Torriani. Today it houses a small archaeological museum. As well as pottery, jewellery, coins and anchors it also contains a statuette of the wizard, El Brujo, which inspired César Manrique in his bold design for the logo for Timanfaya's national park.

The San José fortress, restored by Manrique, was turned into a modern art gallery in 1979. Four rooms of the **Museo Internacional de Arte Contemporáneo** are used for temporary exhibitions of the great masters, including Pablo Picasso, Joan Miró, Oscar Domingue or Manrique himself. Recitals of chamber and modern music are held in the concert hall. Manrique designed the spacious and stylish gallery as well as the castle restaurant.

Also worth visiting are the **Casa Augustín de la Hoz**, now a club, and **Casa de Los Arroyos**, dating back to 1749 and featuring a courtyard with wooden galleries and a well at its centre. This is now the home of the **Centro Científico Cultural**, housing a permanent exhibition devoted to the outstanding physicist Blas Cabrera Felipe (1878–1945), who was born in Arrecife and whose bronze statue stands on the square by Paseo Marítimo.

Quite different in character is the area around **Charco de San Ginés**, with its pretty fishermen's cottages overlooking a small lake that connects to the sea. The **Iglesia de San Ginés**, completed in 1665, is dedicated to the patron saint of Arrecife. This triple-naved church with timber vaults features late-Baroque statues of San Ginés and the Virgen del Rosario, which were brought from Cuba.

🏛 **Museo Arqueológico y Etnográfico**
C/Vargas, 1. 📞 928 802 884.
🕐 10am–1pm, 5–8pm Mon–Fri. 🎫
🏛 **Museo Internacional de Arte Contemporáneo**
Carretera de Puerto Naos.
📞 928 812 321. 🚫

Costa Teguise ❷

🏘 3,100. 🚌 ℹ Avenida de las Islas, 928 827 076.

THIS IS THE third largest resort on the island, after Puerto del Carmen and Playa Blanca. Just 9 km (6 miles) northeast of Arrecife, it is fairly new and dates back to 1977, when the five-star Gran Melia Salinas hotel was built here with the assistance of César Manrique.

Arrecife's Iglesia de San Ginés

This large resort with low-rise holiday developments of white bungalows has a golf course, a marina and a shopping centre. It also has some pleasant sandy beaches. The largest and most scenic of these is Playa de las Cucharas. Smart and modern, Costa Teguise once attracted an elite clientele (King Juan Carlos of Spain has a private villa here) though it is today fairly similar to other resorts on the island .

Constant breezes mean that the place is popular with windsurfers. Those preferring safer water sports can enjoy the water park located just outside town.

Monument at Playa de las Cucharas, Costa Teguise

Tahiche ❸

5 km (3 miles) north of Arrecife. 🚌

JUST OUTSIDE THE town, on the lava fields created by the 1730–36 volcanic eruptions, stands **Taro de Tahiche**. This house was built in 1968 by César Manrique, who lived here until 1988. Four years later he donated Taro de Tahiche to the **Fundación César Manrique**. Founded by himself and a circle of his friends, this organization aims to promote architecture that is in harmony with the natural environment.

In keeping with this aim, Manrique built his house amid the island's characteristic blue-black lava flows. The cubic forms above ground draw on the traditional style of the island, though the space is opened out with contemporary touches such as large

windows and wide terraces. Below ground, the design becomes more startling still. The lower floor features five volcanic "bubbles" – interconnected by tunnels. These vast compartments, 5 m (16 ft) in diameter, were formed by solidifying lava. Each of the "bubbles" has its own basalt staircase leading from the lower floor to the upper level. In one of the rooms, the upper and lower spaces are linked by a fig tree, which rises from the lower floor and into the drawing room above.

The house, which became the embodiment of the artist's dream to live near and in harmony with nature, now houses a modern art museum which has examples of Manrique's own works and project designs, plus other modern art, including works of art by Pablo Picasso, Antonio Tapiès, Joan Miró, and Jesús Soto.

Taro de Tahiche, Manrique's former home

The broad terraces and garden are an essential part of the house. Situated within the garden, near the café, is a giant mural made in 1992 by Manrique, using volcanic rock and ceramic tiles.

🏛 **Fundación César Manrique**
Taro de Tahiche. 📞 *928 843 138.*
⏱ *Nov–Jun: 10am–6pm Mon–Sat, 10am–3pm Sun; Jul– Oct: 10am–7pm daily.* ♿

CÉSAR MANRIQUE (1919–1992)

César Manrique – painter, sculptor, architect, town-planner and art restorer – was born in Arrecife. Having completed his army service in 1937–39, he devoted himself to art. His abstract paintings were exhibited across Europe as well as in Japan and the United States, and he won international acclaim. In 1968, he returned to Lanzarote and brought his talent to bear on the task of protecting the natural environment against the uncontrolled development of the island for tourism. Manrique's efforts paid off and rules were introduced for developers dictating the height, style and colour of buildings. In addition, Manrique's own designs incorporating volcanic forms helped to create many architectural masterpieces on all the Canary Islands. Manrique died in a car accident in 1992 but he left his mark on Lanzarote, both in terms of his bold designs and in the restrained way traditional island life has adapted to tourism.

César Manrique, against the backdrop of immense lava fields

Giant metal cactus at the entrance to Guatiza's Jardín de Cactus

Guatiza ❹

🏠 820. 17 km (11 miles) northeast of Arrecife.

THE SMALL TOWN of Guatiza, situated north of Lanzarote and featuring the lovely 19th-century chapel of **Santa Margarita**, is surrounded by vast plantations of prickly pear. The plant is host to the cochineal insect – a source of vermilion or crimson dye.

Situated at the very centre of the cactus fields, on the outskirts of Guatiza, is the **Jardín de Cactus**, designed by César Manrique. At the entrance to the garden, established in 1987–92, stands an 8-m (26-ft) tall metal statue of a cactus. The large garden, which has a good restaurant, was built in an enormous pit, originally dug by the villagers who were excavating volcanic ash to fertilize their fields.

The Jardín de Cactus is arranged in the form of a giant amphitheatre, dominated by a white windmill. Growing on the terraces are about 10,000 specimens, representing over 1,000 varieties of cactus.

🌵 **Jardín de Cactus**
📞 *928 529 397.*
🕙 *10am–5:45pm daily.* 💷

Jameos del Agua ❺

Carretera de Orzola. 🚌 📞 *928 848 020.* 🕙 *9:30am–7pm daily, Wed, Thu & Sat until 2am.* 💷

IN THE LATE 1960s, César Manrique turned these natural caves, formed within a lava flow, into a complex of entertainment venues.

Situated in the northeastern part of the island, just a short walk from the sea, the caverns are well worth visiting. A staircase leads down to an underground restaurant and, further on, to a giant cave, 62 m (203 ft) long, 19 m (62 ft) wide and 21 m (70 ft) high.

The cave features a salt lake, connected to the ocean (look out for the unique blind species of crab). The bed is below sea level and the water level rises and falls with the tide.

Above the caves is Jameo Grande. This picturesque, irregularly-shaped swimming pool is surrounded by artistically arranged tropical flora. Jameo Grande opens to an underground auditorium, seating 600. This unique setting is famous for its outstanding acoustics. Apart from the natural features in the caves, another point of interest is the exhibition on volcanoes.

Three times a week Jameos del Agua changes its image and becomes a nightclub.

A palm beside the pool in one of Jameos del Agua's sunken craters

Cueva de los Verdes ❻

26 km (16 miles) north of Arrecife.
📞 *928 173 220.* 🕙 *10am–5pm daily.* 💷 📷

CUEVA DE LOS VERDES is a 7-km (4-mile) long underground volcanic tunnel, and was created by the eruption of the nearby Monte Corona, about 5,000 years ago. One of the world's longest volcanic tunnels, it is formed from a tube of solidified lava. The cave's name has nothing to do with its green colour. It derives from the name of a shepherd family, the Verdes (Greens), who inhabited it in the 18th

Exploring the Cueva de los Verdes

and 19th centuries. From the 17th century onwards, the cave was used by the local population as a shelter from pirates and slave traders.

In 1964, artificial lighting was installed and 2 km (1 mile) of the cave was opened to visitors. The tour takes about 50 minutes. One of the caves included in the tour features a small lake. Although only 20 cm (8 inches) deep, the stone vaults reflected in the water make it appear far deeper. Another cave has been converted to a concert hall.

Lichen growing on the volcanic debris in Malpaís de la Corona

Malpaís de la Corona **➐**

🚶 100. 🚌 🚤

THESE VOLCANIC badlands bear testimony to the extreme volcanic activities that shook the northernmost point of the island some 5,000 years ago. This wild terrain, strewn with volcanic rock and slowly being colonized by sparse vegetation, occupies 30 sq km (12 sq miles) between the village of Orzola and the headland of Punta de Mujeres, near Arietta.

On the western end of Malpaís, visible from far and wide, stands the mighty Monte Corona volcano. This measures 1,100 m (3,600 ft) in diameter at its base, and 450 m (1,500 ft) at its top section. Standing 609 m (2,000 ft) high, the eruptions of this volcano produced the wide belt of strange lava formations (the Malpaís de la Corona), which include the Cueva de los Verdes and Jameos del Agua.

Orzola **➑**

🚶 100. 🚌 🚤

THIS FISHING VILLAGE, lying at the northern tip of Lanzarote, is a haven of peace. It is known mainly for its excellent seafood restaurants, which stretch along the coastal seafront.

Orzola is also famous for the picturesque **Playa de la Cantería**, situated to the west. This beach is not suitable for bathing, however, as strong sea currents create unfavourable conditions.

A frequent motorboat service provides links with the neighbouring island of **Graciosa**. From here, you can travel by fishing boat as far as the islands of **Montaña Clara** and **Alegranza**.

You won't be allowed to explore, however, as these two small and uninhabited islands form part of the national park, which was founded in 1986, and are off-limits to visitors.

Isla Graciosa, seen from Mirador de Guinate

Isla Graciosa **➒**

🚶 500. 🚤

THE SMALLEST inhabited island of the archipelago has an area of just 27 sq km (10 sq miles). Separated from Lanzarote by the straits of El Río, it was dubbed the "gracious island" by Jean de Béthencourt and fully meets the expectations of visitors looking for a quiet rest.

An ideal place for scuba divers, anglers, hikers or anyone wishing to escape the brasher elements of tourism, Isla Graciosa plays to its strengths and offers a slow pace and a minimum of amenities. The island is fringed by long beaches of golden sand dunes.

The most beautiful of these is **Playa de las Conchas**, stretching over many kilometres of the northern shore. It is regarded as one of the most picturesque of all the beaches of the archipelago and provides a good view of the uninhabited smaller islands: **Montaña Clara**, **Roque del Este** and **Alegranza**.

There are no hotels on Graciosa, but the village of **Caleta del Sebo**, linked by small motorboats to Orzola, has a few pensions and restaurants.

Orzola, on the northern end of Malpaís de la Corona

Mirador del Río ⑩

C *928 173 536, 928 644 318.*
○ *10am–5:45pm daily.* 🖼

THE MOST FAMOUS viewpoint on Lanzarote is situated at the northernmost point of the island, 479 m (1,630 ft) above sea level. This spot, hidden among rocks, provides a breathtaking view over the high cliffs of the northern shore. Clearly visible is the island of **Graciosa** and, beyond it, **Montaña Clara** and **Alegranza**.

In 1898, when Spain was at war with the United States over Cuba, a gun emplacement was built here, guarding the straits of El Río, which separate Lanzarote from Graciosa.

In 1973, the former gun emplacement was transformed by César Manrique to provide a belvedere and visitors have been coming here ever since. Built into the rock, with an enormous window stretching the length of the room, is a minimalist bar and restaurant. Its stone walls are painted white. The only significant decorations inside are the huge mobiles by César Manrique. Their function is not merely decorative; they are also meant to dampen noise, because of the poor acoustics of the place.

Sign at the Mirador del Río

Tourists enjoying the wonderful view from the Mirador del Río

Haría's town square with its restored, whitewashed houses

Guinate ⑪

🏃 *50.* 🚌

SITUATED AT THE foot of the Monte Corona volcano, Guinate is a small village that is popular with bird lovers.

The **Parque Tropical**, spread out on terraces, features water cascades, ponds and fine gardens. Here you can see some 1,300 exotic birds, representing about 300 species, as well as many small apes. The famous shows featuring trained birds are a big hit with children (look out for the scooter-riding parrots!).

🦅 Parque Tropical
C *928 835 500.* **○** *10am–5pm daily.* 🖼

ENVIRONS: Just outside the village, the **Mirador la Graciosa** provides fine views over Graciosa, Alegranza and Montaña Clara.

Haría ⑫

🏃 *3,000.* 🚌 **ℹ** *Plaza de la Constitución, 928 835 251.* 🎉 *San Juan (23 Jun), San Pedro (29 Jun).*

CUBIC, WHITEWASHED houses, reminiscent of North African architecture, along with numerous palms, give this picturesque village an almost Middle-Eastern flavour. The scenic valley in which Haría is situated, known as the "valley of a thousand palms", was once home to far more of these trees. Many of them were burned during a pirate attack in 1856.

The shady, tree-lined **Plaza León y Castillo** is surrounded by restored historic houses. At one end of the square stands the church of **Nuestra Señora de la Encarnación.**

ENVIRONS: Not far south of Haría is the **Mirador de Haría**. A winding road leads to the mountain pass, providing a fine view over the village, the surrounding volcanoes, the high cliffs, and Arietta.

Teguise ⑬

🏃 *9,000.* 🚌 **ℹ** *C/ General Franco, 1, 928 845 072.* 🎪 *Sun.* 🎉 *Nuestra Señora del Carmen (16 Jul), Virgen de las Nieves (5 Aug).*

TEGUISE IS ONE of the oldest towns on Lanzarote. It was founded in 1418 by Maciot – nephew and successor of Jean de Béthencourt – who, it is said, lived here with Princess Teguise, the daughter of the Guanche king, Guadarfía.

Spacious squares and well-kept cobbled streets lined with beautifully restored houses are testimony to Teguise's former glory. A good time to visit is on Sundays, when there is a flourishing handicrafts market and folk dancing.

For centuries the town was one of the largest and richest on the island. Until 1852, it was its capital city. The fame and the wealth of Teguise, bearing the proud name of La Villa Real de Teguise (the Royal City of Teguise), attracted pirates who raided it repeatedly. The Callejón de la Sangre ("street of blood") owes its name to the worst of these raids and commemorates the victims of the massacre that took place in 1596.

The eclectic church of **Nuestra Señora de Guadalupe** stands in the town square. Since its construction in the mid-15th century, it has been rebuilt many times. The interior furnishing is Neo-Gothic and features a statue of the Virgin Mary of Guadalupe. On the opposite side of the square stands the **Palacio Spínola**. This beautiful residence, with its small patio and a well, was built in 1730–80. The reconstruction work, supervised by César Manrique, has restored the palace interiors to their former glory. Now the Palacio Spínola fulfils a double function as a museum and as the official residence of the Canary Islands' government.

Also of interest are two conventual churches. The 16th-century **Convento de**

Castillo de Santa Bárbara, high above Teguise

Lion from Teguise Palace

Miraflores was used as a burial site for the most prominent citizens of Lanzarote, and is now a venue for cultural events. Inside the 17th-century **Convento de Santo Domingo** is the original main altar. Now the abbey houses a modern art gallery – the Centro Arte. Towering over the town is the **Castillo de Santa Bárbara**. The castle was built in the early 16th century on top of the 452-m (1,480-ft) high Guanapay peak, and provides a view over almost the entire island. Within the castle is the **Museo del Emigrante Canario**, which tells the story of emigrants to South and Central America.

Palacio Spínola
Plaza de San Miguel.
928 845 181. 9am–3pm Mon–Fri, 9:30am–2pm Sat–Sun.

Museo del Emigrante Canario
Volcán de Guanapay.
928 845 001. 10am–4pm Tue–Fri, 10am–2pm Sat–Sun.

La Caleta de Famara ⑭

650. 35 km (22 miles) north of Arrecife.

A SMALL FISHING village, with only a handful of restaurants, attracts visitors to **Playa de Famara**, one of the most beautiful beaches on Lanzarote. **Urbanización Famara**, situated to the north, is a cluster of purpose-built holiday chalets.

The beautiful 3-km (2-mile) long sandy beach stretches along the base of tall cliffs formed during the most recent volcanic eruption in 1824. Behind the beach, which provides a wonderful view over **Isla Graciosa**, runs a long band of dunes. The heavy swell produces some splendid waves and makes this a popular surfing beach, though the strong currents can be dangerous.

The village also attracts quite a few painters. In view of its rich flora and fine scenery this whole area, including the cliffs and the Famara massif, has been declared a conservation area.

Playa de Famara, one of Lanzarote's most beautiful beaches

Windmill and camels at the Museo Agrícola El Patio, Tiagua

Tiagua ⓯

🏚 *300.* 🚌

THIS MODEST TOWN offers visitors an insight into local history and tradition.

The **Museo Agrícola El Patio** provides a glimpse of past agricultural practices. The complex was opened in 1994 on the site of a farm dating back to 1845 when a group of impoverished farmers began to cultivate the fertile land. A century later, it was the biggest and best-run estate on the island.

As well as a number of well-preserved windmills, the indoor exhibitions feature displays of folk costumes, agricultural tools, a loom, some fine examples of plaitwork, and a collection of original photographs.

🏛 **Museo Agrícola El Patio**
🄲 *928 529 134.* ◯ *10am–5pm Mon–Fri, 10am–2pm Sat.* 📷

San Bartolomé ⓰

🏚 *4,700.* 🚌
📅 *San Bartolomé (15 Aug).*

KNOWN TO THE Guanches as Ajei, San Bartolomé has some fine examples of traditional Canary architecture, including the 18th-century **Casa Pedromo**, with its beautiful courtyard

and tiny chapel of Nuestra Señora del Pino. Today it houses the **Museo Etnográfico Tanit**. Various exhibits, such as musical instruments, agricultural tools, furniture and wine production equipment, illustrate the island's economic history. In the town centre is a large, stylish square, containing the parish church of **San Bartolomé** (1789).

🏛 **Museo Etnográfico Tanit**
C/ Constitucíon, 1.
🄲 *928 520 655.*
◯ *9:30am–1:30pm Tue–Sun.* 📷

Manrique's homage to peasant life

ENVIRONS: A short way north, towards Mozaga, stands the **Monumento al Campesino** (Peasant's Monument). This 15-m (50-ft) tall construction was designed by César Manrique, and built in 1968 by Jesús Soto.

Made of old water containers once used on fishing boats, the monument is devoted, in Manrique's own words, "to the nameless farmers, whose hard work helped to create the island's unique landscape".

The nearby **Casa-Museo del Campesino** houses a cluster of workshops devoted to various crafts, illustrating former rural life on Lanzarote. Its restaurant is a good place for lunch.

🏛 **Casa-Museo del Campesino**
◯ *10am–6pm daily.*

Parque Nacional de Timanfaya ⓱

See pp92–3.

Yaiza ⓲

🏚 *2,000.* 🚌 🛈 *Departamento de Turismo, 928 830 333.* 📅 *San Marcial (Jun), Nuestra Señora de los Remedios (1st week in Sep).*

NESTLING AT THE FOOT of the Montañas del Fuego, Yaiza is regarded, along with Haría, as one of the most picturesque small towns on the island. In the 19th century, rich merchants settled here and to this day some houses with palm-shaded façades bear evidence of this former wealth. The parish church of **Nuestra Señora de los Remedios** dates from the 18th century.

One of the former residences in Yaiza, now a hotel

Los Hervideros, south of El Golfo

This triple-naved church was built on the site of a former chapel dating back to 1699 and has a number of fine 18th-century paintings.

The Baroque vault decorations, incorporating folk elements, give the church its unique atmosphere. Numerous shops along the main street sell embroidery, pottery and other items.

ENVIRONS: Just 2 km (1 mile) east of Yaiza, **Uga** is the departure point for camel trips across the volcanic landscape.

El Golfo ⑲

🏠 *110.* 7 km (4 miles) northwest of Yaiza.

THE SLEEPY VILLAGE of El Golfo is home to a small crater lagoon, **Lago Verde**, which was created by the an underwater volcano. Its emerald-green colour is due to the sea algae that thrive in it. El Golfo's restaurants make it popular with tourists while the presence of olivine (an olive-green semi-precious stone) attracts geologists and jewellery makers to the area.

Taking the path from the village, you get the best view of the lake, which is surrounded by dramatic, volcanic rocks resembling a petrified wave, and separated from the ocean by a narrow strip of black volcanic sand.

ENVIRONS: South of El Golfo are **Los Hervideros** ("the kettles"). As the name suggests, the waves "boil" inside the vast caves of the 15-m (50-ft) high cliffs.

Salinas de Janubio ⑳

9 km (6 miles) north of Playa Blanca.

THE GREENISH WATERS of a natural lagoon are employed to produce salt. Long used to preserve fish, the salt is still extracted by the traditional method of evaporation.

The sea-salt plant is believed to be the largest operating on the archipelago and currently produces about 2,000 tons of salt per annum. Years ago, the water was pumped into the lagoon by windpower; today the pumps are electrically driven.

Most of the local salt is still bought by fishermen, with a small portion sold as table salt. Each year, during the Corpus Christi festival, the local inhabitants use tons of dyed salt to create magnificent decorations for the streets and squares of the island's capital.

Sunset over the checkerboard salt pans of Salinas de Janubio

Playa Blanca ㉑

🏠 *500.* 🚌 🛥 🛈 *Muelle de Playa Blanca, 928 517 794.* 🛒 *Wed.* 🎉 *Nuestra Señora del Carmen (Jul).*

A FORMER FISHING village, Playa Blanca has become one of the largest resorts on the island in recent years, with regular ferry links to nearby Fuerteventura. Yet despite its numerous restaurants, bars and shops, the village remains relatively quiet and is a popular destination for family holidays.

It has several beaches. One of the best is the small beach situated near the centre, which has clear water and wonderful views over the neighbouring islands of Fuerteventura and Los Lobos. The **Playas de Papagayo** beaches, situated 4 km (2 miles) south of Playa Blanca, are also popular with visitors.

Castillo de las Coloradas, one of Playa Blanca's former defences

ENVIRONS: The **Castillo de las Coloradas**, in Punta del Águila, is a watchtower dating from 1741–8. Between here and Punta de Papagayo is a string of scenic coves with sandy beaches: **Playa de las Mujeres**, **El Pozo** and **Papagayo**. Their fine sand and warm, clear waters attract an ever-increasing number of visitors.

This area is a part of the **Los Ajaches** nature reserve, created in 1994, which includes a bird protection zone. There is an entrance charge and the only access from Playa Blanca is by a minor road. Nearby, on the very edge of a cliff, are the remains of the island's first Norman settlement, **San Marcial del Rubicón**, founded in 1402 by Jean de Béthencourt.

Parque Nacional de Timanfaya ⑰

ETWEEN 1730 AND 1736 the Montañas del Fuego – or
Fire Mountains – belched forth smoke and molten
lava, burying entire villages, and turning the island's
fertile lowlands into a sea of solidified lava, grey
volcanic rock and copper-coloured sand. Today, the
lava remains are Lanzarote's greatest attraction. Situated
to the southwest, they have become the heart of the
national park, established in 1974, and include the 517-
m (1,700-ft) Pico Portido. For the time being, the area is
quite safe, though the lava still bubbles away under the
surface and a whiff of sulphur hangs in the air.

Park Logo
*This mischievous little devil,
designed by César Manrique,
marks the boundaries of the
national park.*

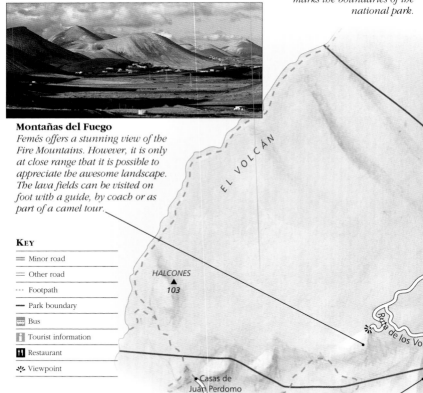

Montañas del Fuego
*Femés offers a stunning view of the
Fire Mountains. However, it is only
at close range that it is possible to
appreciate the awesome landscape.
The lava fields can be visited on
foot with a guide, by coach or as
part of a camel tour.*

EL VOLCÁN

HALCONES
▲
103

Ruta de los Vo

Casas de
Juan Perdomo

KEY

═══	Minor road
═══	Other road
···	Footpath
▬▬	Park boundary
🚌	Bus
🛈	Tourist information
🍴	Restaurant
�ખ	Viewpoint

**Echadero
de los Camellos**
*This dromedary station
includes a small
exhibition illustrating
the use of camels by
humans. Camelback
tours last half an hour
and take in the outer
reaches of the park.*

Fire in a Crater
Dry pieces of lichen, thrown into a shallow rock hollow, begin to burn quickly, demonstrating the continuing volcanic activity of this area.

Geyser
Water poured into underground pipes turns to steam within seconds. Islote de Hilario has the highest underground temperature in the park, reaching 600° C (1,112° F) at a depth of 12 m (40 ft).

CALDERA BLANCA
▲ 149

TINAJO

CALDERA ROYA
▲ 427

LZ-67

CALDERA DE LOS CUERVOS
▲ 502

PICO PARTIDO
▲ 517

YAIZA

0 km   1
0 miles   1

★ Volcanic Grill
Taking advantage of the 300° C (572° F) temperatures, the volcanic grill is used to cook meat and fish at the El Diabolo restaurant, designed by César Manrique (1970).

STAR SIGHTS

★ **Ruta de los Volcanes**

★ **Volcanic Grill**

★ Ruta de los Volcanes
This is the most interesting part of the national park open to visitors. However, there is a wide variety of different landscapes and volcanic formations elsewhere in the park.

Femés ㉒

🏠 230. 🎎 San Marcial (7 Jul).

OVERLOOKED BY THE 608-m (2,000-ft) high volcanic peak of Atalaya de Femés, this village once boasted one of the island's oldest religious buildings – the **Ermita San Marcial del Rubicón** cathedral, devoted to the patron saint of the island and destroyed in the 16th century by pirates. The present church, built on the site in 1733, is devoted to the same saint. Its white-painted walls are decorated with models of sailing ships, testimony to the seafaring heritage of the Canary Islands. Unfortunately, the church is open only during services.

In the centre of Femés, by the side of the road, is a fine viewpoint, which provides a scenic panorama of Montaña Roja and the ocean. The opposite side of town overlooks the panorama of Montañas del Fuego.

Ermita San Marcial del Rubicón, in Femés

La Gería ㉓

Northeast of Uga.

STRETCHING ON BOTH sides of the road from Masdache to Uga, the valley of La Gería is the main vine-growing area on Lanzarote. Set within this black cinder landscape that once featured only the occasional palm tree, the vineyards look as if they have been transplanted wholesale from another planet. They occupy 52 sq km (20 sq miles) and have been declared a protected area. The valley, right up to the volcanic slopes, is dotted with small hollows, sheltered from the drying wind by low, semicircular walls. Each hollow *(gería)* is covered with volcanic cinder that absorbs dew at night and maintains the required humidity. Each contains a single vine. There are over 10,000 such hollows here.

The grapes are used to produce the very sweet and

Lanzarote's Beaches

LANZAROTE'S 250-km (150-mile) long shoreline offers only 30 km (20 miles) of sandy beaches, some of which are popular with nudists *(see p181)*. In contrast to the long beaches of Fuerteventura, these are usually fairly small and consist of golden or white sand, with over 30 per cent of them artificial. Particularly beautiful beaches are found north of Arrecife.

Puerto del Carmen ③ has several easily accessible but built-up beaches. The main ones are Playa Blanca and Playa de los Pocillos, both over a kilometre (half a mile) long with golden sand.

Playas de Papagayo ①
A dirt track leads to several lovely sandy beaches, situated in a picturesque cove at the foot of a high cliff, on the southern shore of the island. The journey is rewarded by the sheer beauty of the area.

0 km   2

0 miles   2

Uga

LZ-2

Femés

LZ-2

Playa Blanca

aromatic Malvasía – an excellent quality wine for which Lanzarote is famous. Malvasía, as well as other brands of local wine, can be purchased cheaply in one of the many local *bodegas* (wine-shops). All visitors coming to *bodegas* may sample the wine before buying.

The vineyards tend to be small. El Grifo, situated at the northern end of La Gería, is a good example. Its outbuildings house a wine museum – **Museo del Vino de Lanzarote** – arranged in an old *bodega* dating from 1775. Apart from the old equipment used in the production and storage of wine, the museum has a library with more than 1,000 books, plus several 17th- and 18th-century manuscripts devoted to winemaking.

🏛 **Museo del Vino de Lanzarote**
📞 *928 524 951.*
🕐 *10:30am–6pm daily.*
🌐 *www.elgrifo.com*

Puerto del Carmen ㉔

🏨 *2,700.* 🚌 🚢 ℹ️ *Avda. de las Playas, 928 515 337.* 🎉 *Nuestra Señora del Carmen (Aug).*

IN RECENT YEARS this fishing village has become one of the island's top resorts. Visitors come for the beaches along the Avenida de las Playas, which are regarded as some of the island's most beautiful.

In Puerto del Carmen, which is densely filled with hotels, pensions and white villas, there is no shortage of shops, nightclubs, banks and restaurants. Numerous agencies encourage visitors to sample the local attractions, such as windsurfing, diving, fishing and trips by catamaran to Fuerteventura and Lobos.

ENVIRONS: Just 9 km (6 miles) to the north, **Puerto Calero** has the island's loveliest marina. It also offers boat rides to the Papagayo beaches and submarine trips for glimpses of the rich life beneath the Atlantic waves.

The harbour district, the oldest part of Puerto del Carmen

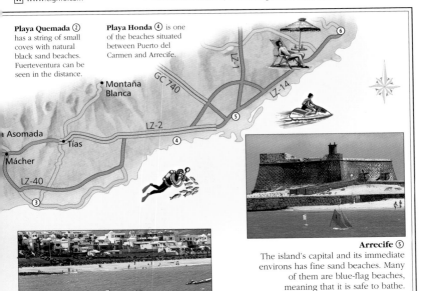

Playa Quemada ② has a string of small coves with natural black sand beaches. Fuerteventura can be seen in the distance.

Playa Honda ④ is one of the beaches situated between Puerto del Carmen and Arrecife.

Arrecife ⑤
The island's capital and its immediate environs has fine sand beaches. Many of them are blue-flag beaches, meaning that it is safe to bathe.

Costa Teguise ⑥
The sandy beach of Las Cucharas is not only ideal for sunbathing, but also provides opportunities to take windsurfing lessons and go on diving expeditions to a nearby shipwreck.

TENERIFE

I N THE LANGUAGE OF *the Guanches the name Tenerife meant "white mountain". This referred to the looming Pico del Teide – Spain's tallest peak. The 3,718-m (12,195-ft) volcano is at the heart of the island and forms part of the national park, attracting many thousands of visitors every year. Depending on the season, its summit is enveloped in clouds, sulphur or a good dusting of snow.*

Covering an area of 2,354 sq km (908 sq miles), Tenerife is the largest of the archipelago's islands. Situated between La Gomera and Gran Canaria, 300 km (186 miles) from Africa, it has about 800,000 inhabitants. The northern areas are the most densely populated, in particular around Santa Cruz – the island and provincial capital.

Balcony adorning a house in La Orotava

Pico del Teide divides the island into two distinct climate zones. Sheltered by the crater, the northwestern area is humid, covered in lush tropical vegetation, and supports evergreen vineyards. The southern part is hot, rocky and arid. Because of this, Tenerife, like Gran Canaria, is often referred to as a "miniature continent".

By far the most important element of the island's economy is tourism.

Its beginnings go back to the late 19th century when the first tourists arrived in search of blue skies, sun and clean air. The first hotel – the Grand Hotel Taoro in Puerto de la Cruz – was built in 1892 and was then one of the largest hotels in Spain.

However, the real boom in tourism began in the late 1960s. At first, tourists came mainly to the fertile, northern region of the island. Soon, however, tourism reached the south and, before long, its rocky shores were covered with many truck-loads of sand imported from the Sahara. Investment was stepped up with the addition of smart hotels and a dash of greenery. The gamble paid off and today most of the visitors to Tenerife prefer the southern resorts, such as Playa de las Américas and Los Cristianos.

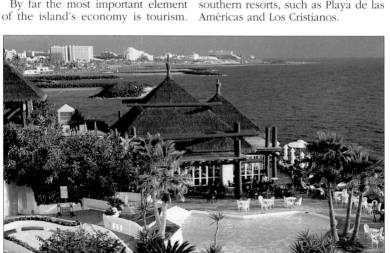

The seafront boulevard, Playa de las Américas

◁ **Pico del Teide, the symbol of Tenerife, visible from almost everywhere on the island**

Exploring Tenerife

ATTRACTED BY THE mild climate and an average coastal temperature of 20° C (68° F), Tenerife attracts thousands of tourists. Most visitors stay in large resorts where they have the opportunity to indulge in a variety of sports. The rocky, volcanic terrain of the national park, with its rivers of solidified lava, is fantastic for walking and there are still some relatively remote villages within the region of the Anaga Mountains. In February, the island explodes in a riot of colour for the carnival, which in terms of its exuberance ranks alongside that of Rio de Janeiro.

LOCATOR MAP

GARACHICO **11**

ICOD DE LOS VINOS **10**

9 LOS REALEJO

PUER DE LA CR

LORO PARQUE

MASCA **12**

SANTIAGO DEL TEIDE **13**

PARQUE NACIONAL DEL TEIDE
16

TF 82

TF 21

LOS GIGANTES AND PUERTO DE SANTIAGO **14**

TF 36

TF 47

GUÍA DE ISORA

TF 21

0 km   5

0 miles   5

17 VILAFLOR

GRANADILLA DE ABONA

TF 82

ADEJE   TF 51

ARONA

SAN MIGUE

SAN ISID

PLAYA DE LAS AMÉRICAS AND LOS CRISTIANOS **15**

TF 82

EL MI

LAS GALLETAS   COSTA DEL SILENCIO

Masca, one of the most beautiful villages on Tenerife

GETTING THERE

The island has two airports: Reina Sofía in the south and Los Rodeos in the north. Reina Sofía is the international airport, Los Rodeos is mainly for domestic inter-island flights (though it is due to take more charter traffic soon). Ferries from Tenerife sail to all the islands of the archipelago and to Cadiz. TITSA lines provide bus transport, although not everywhere on the island has bus links (make the most of organized coach tours or hire a car).

El Médano, a favourite destination for windsurfers

Golden sand beaches of Playa de las Américas

SIGHTS AT A GLANCE

Santa Cruz de Tenerife ❶

SANTA CRUZ DE TENERIFE took its name from the Holy Cross of the conquistadors, which Alonso Fernández de Lugo erected after landing on Añaza beach in 1494. During the 16th century, this former fishing village became an important port for land-locked La Laguna. Since 1723, the town has been the administrative centre of Tenerife, and was the capital of the entire archipelago from 1822–1927. Today, the economic life of Santa Cruz is dominated by its deep-water harbour, which can accommodate luxury liners, tankers arriving from Venezuela and the Middle East, and container ships loaded with bananas and tomatoes ready for export.

The imposing bell tower of Nuestra Señora de la Concepción

Exploring Santa Cruz de Tenerife

Though it does not have many historic sights, the capital of Tenerife has many attractions. The town's unique atmosphere is provided by the 19th-century, colonial-style architecture. Visitors come for the plentiful shopping opportunities, the museums and art galleries, the classical repertoire of the Teatro Guimerá, the annual classical music festival and, above all, the carnival.

🏛 Museo de la Naturaleza y el Hombre
C/Fuente Morales, s/n.
📞 922 535 816. ⏰ 9am–7pm Tue–Sun. ⬤ 1 Jan, 24–25 Dec. 📷
The natural history museum occupies a Classical building that was once a military hospital. The exhibition is a colourful multimedia show dedicated to the geology, archaeology, and flora and fauna of the Canary Islands.
In addition to the ever-popular mummies and skulls of the Guanches, it also displays a small collection of artifacts (including pottery, African carvings and pre-Columbian art) as well as fossils from around the world.

🔓 Iglesia de Nuestra Señora de la Concepción
C/Domínguez Alfonso.
Though this church was built in 1498, its present appearance is the result of reconstruction work carried out in the second half of the 18th century. Its richly furnished interior features paintings and sculptures, including the magnificent main altar by José Luján Peréz.
The church serves as a pantheon and houses mementoes of the island's history, including a silver cross (Santa Cruz) of the conquistadors and British flags captured during Nelson's attack on the city in 1797.

Madonna at Plaza de la Candelaria

🏨 Plaza de España
The circular Plaza de España is in the town centre near the harbour. The giant monument standing in the middle of the square – **Monumento de los Caídos** – featuring bronze figures, is the work of Enrique César Zadivar and commemorates the victims of the 1936–39 civil war.
The vast building on the south side of the square is the Cabildo Insular and was designed by José Enrique Marrero. An example of the Fascist architecture of the 1930s, it houses Tenerife's council building and Santa Cruz's main tourist office.

🏨 Plaza de la Candelaria
Plaza de Candelaria is a popular local meeting place and promenade. Laid out in 1701, it adjoins Plaza de España on the west. Its official name is Plaza de la Constitución. The monument standing at its centre – **El Triunfo de la Candelaria** – depicts the patron saint of the island. Carved in white Carrara marble and unveiled in 1787, it is the work of the Italian master, Antonio Canova. Another landmark on the square is the **Palacio de Carta** (1742). Formerly the Prefecture, it now contains a branch of the Banco Español de Crédito. It is worth seeking out for its fine example of a traditional Canary patio.

Plaza de España, a good orientation point when exploring the town

Calle Castillo, the main shopping street, also good for handicrafts

Calle Castillo

Many visitors come to Santa Cruz with the sole purpose of spending a few hours in the little shops in and around Calle Castillo – the main pedestrianized shopping precinct.

Except during the siesta, which takes place between 1–4:30pm, bargains are to be had in the local shops lining this attractive narrow street, whether they be electronic goods, watches or designer-label clothes. Several large handicraft centres sell embroidery, wickerwork and pottery.

Mercado de Nuestra Señora de África

Avenida de San Sebastián

9am–3pm Mon–Sat.

This large market-hall on two levels was built in 1943 in the style of North African architecture. Exotic fruit, vegetables, flowers, fresh fish, poultry, cheeses, herbs and spices are always available in this busy little spot.

Iglesia San Francisco

C/Villalba.

Opposite the Museo de Bellas Artes stands the monumental Franciscan abbey founded around 1680. It was restored and extended in the 18th century and acquired two naves and a coffered ceiling, as well as an additional chapel named Capilla de la Orden Tercera.

Inside the abbey church there is a fine 17th-century wooden altar and pulpit with beautifully painted decorations. The chapel, which was closed in the mid-19th century, was reopened in 1869, at which time it became the parish church.

Baroque portal of the Iglesia San Francisco

Museo de Bellas Artes

C/José Murphy, 12. 922 244 358.
10am–7:30pm Mon–Fri (phone to confirm).
Founded in 1898, the Museo de Bellas Artes' prize possessions are its exhibits from the Prado Museum, including works by old masters, such as Jan Brueghel and José de Ribera, as well as works by anonymous Spanish painters from the 17th and 18th centuries. In addition to collections of coins and armour, there is an exhibition of modern Canary art, with many paintings depicting local events and landscapes of the archipelago, such as *Santa Cruz Harbour* or *Landscape around Laguna*, by Valentín Sanza y Carta (1849–98).

SANTA CRUZ DE TENERIFE

0 m   100
0 yards   100

KEY

P Parking

Tourist information

Post office

PLAYA DE LAS TERESITAS

AIRPORT TENERIFE SUR

The palm-shaded Plaza del 25 de Julio

🌿 Parque Marítimo
Designed by the famous Canary architect and artist César Manrique *(see p85)*, the construction of the park began in 1995. The capital has thus acquired an innovative recreation area with two giant swimming pools, a children's paddling pool, and a beach. Work is currently under way to build an adjacent **"Palmetum"** – a park displaying all the world's species of palm trees.

⚓ Castillo de San Juan
Situated on the waterfront, the protective fort of Castillo de San Juan was built in 1643. One of its functions was to guard the safety of the port, once famous for the trade in African slaves that was carried out on the Los Llanos wharf.

The nearby small chapel of **Nuestra Señora de Regle** dates from the same period. Now both these buildings are overshadowed by the colossal edifice of the **Auditorio de Tenerife**, which is to become the island's leading performing arts venue.

⛲ Rambla del General Franco
This is one of the most elegant streets in Santa Cruz. With its smart houses, numerous restaurants and cafés, it sweeps in a semi-circle through most of the town. At its northern end, at the junction with Avenida de Francisco La Roche, stands an enormous monument to General Franco. Its wide central reservation separates two busy traffic lanes. Planted with tall palms and laurel trees, it is a veritable "art boulevard". Modern sculptures are set amid the trees, which are illuminated at night and bear plaques with the names of famous artists from around the world, including Michelangelo, Vermeer, Piranesi, Warhol and Pollock. Every Sunday, a lively antiques fair takes place here.

Lush, green avenue in Parque García Sanabria

⛲ Plaza del 25 de Julio
The 25th of July Plaza is a green oasis at the centre of the crowded, buzzing city. Its charm is enhanced by the central fountains and landscaped areas of trees and shrubs. The place, popular with the inhabitants of Santa Cruz, has a circle of original benches made of stone imported from Seville. Note the backrests decorated with ceramic tiles featuring old advertisements.

🌿 Parque García Sanabria
Established in the 1920s, this attractive and peaceful park was named after the mayor of Santa Cruz. The park is full of lush tropical plants and has a wonderful collection of trees. It has since been improved by the addition of a fountain and a number of modern sculptures. Besides being a good place to cool off, the park provides a brief lesson in Tenerife's history. The backrests of three benches depict the arrival of the conquistadors, the daily life of the Guanches and their defeat at the battle of Acentejo.

🏛 Museo Militar de Canarias
C/San Isidro, 2. 📞 922 274 224.
🕐 10am–2pm Tue–Sat. 📷
Founded in 1988, the museum occupies the former premises of the Curatel de Almeida, a fortress dating back to 1884. The exhibition features ancient weapons of the Canary Islands, 17th-century Spanish militaria, and weapons dating from the 19th century.

Banners, uniforms and the personal belongings of many famous soldiers form a major part of the exhibition. A separate section is devoted to the July 1797 battle against the British fleet under Nelson. The most famous exhibit – El Tigre – is a cannon that fired the grapeshot that tore into Nelson's arm during the attack on Santa Cruz.

Henry Moore sculpture in Rambla del General Franco

La Laguna ❷

🏠 130,000. 🚌 🛈 C/Carrera, 1,
922 601 106. 🎫 daily.
🎉 San Benito Abad (1st Sun in Jul),
Santísimo Cristo (7–15 Sep).

O FFICIALLY NAMED Ciudad de
San Cristóbal de la
Laguna, La Laguna is
Tenerife's second largest
town. Situated in the middle
of the fertile valley of
Aguerre, it owes its name to
the lagoon on whose shores
it stood, which was drained
in 1837.

Founded in 1496 by the
conquistador Alonso
Fernández de Lugo, the town
was the original residence of
the Adelantados – the island's
military governors. Until 1723,
La Laguna was capital of the
island but moving the capital
to Santa Cruz has done
nothing to hinder
the town's
development.

La Laguna is a
university town
and its academic
traditions go back to
the first half of the
18th century.
**San Fernando
University**, still in
existence, opened its doors
for the first time in 1817.
Since 1818, the town has
been a bishopric.

Despite its dynamic
development (with some of
the suburbs virtually merging
with Santa Cruz), the old
town's layout has maintained
its traditional form with
a network of narrow streets
and alleys following a
chequerboard pattern. The
district includes several
noteworthy houses that have
wooden balconies and lavish
portals crowned with crests.
They include **Casa del
Corregidor** and **Casa de la
Alhondiga** (both dating from
the 16th century), the 17th-
century **Casa Alvaro
Bragamonte** and the 18th-
century **Casa Mesa** and **Casa
de los Capitanes**.

The meticulously restored
Casa Lercaro, built in 1593
by Genoese merchants, now
houses the **Museo de
Historia de Tenerife**.
Opened in 1993, it presents

**St Christopher, La
Laguna's patron saint**

the history of the island from
the times of the Spanish
conquest through to the 20th
century. The collection
includes old documents, tools
and 16th-century paintings.
Among the highlights are
some of the oldest maps of
the archipelago.

Nearby is another
noteworthy building – the
Palacio Episcopal. The
bishop's palace features a
beautiful stone façade dating
from 1681. Of equal interest
are some 19th-century
buildings, such as the **Casino
de la Laguna** (1899)
whose creators drew on
French designs, and the
ayuntamiento – the town
hall of 1829 that houses the
banner under which de Lugo
fought during his conquest
of Tenerife (see p32).

The present town hall,
with its interior
frescoes illustrating
the island's history,
stands in **Plaza de
Adelantado**. The
adjacent church of
San Miguel (1507)
was founded by de
Lugo himself. Also
in the tree-shaded
square is the
**Convento de Santa
Catalina**, with its original
cloisters, and the **Palacio de
Nava** – a good example of
Spanish colonial architecture.
Behind the square is a large
market hall, selling fruit,
cheese and flowers.

Patio of the Palacio Episcopal

**Portal of Iglesia de Nuestra Señora
de la Concepción**

To the east of Plaza de
Adelantado stands the
Cathedral (1904–15). The
building features a twin-
towered façade dating from
1825. The main feature of the
interior is the magnificent
retable (or alterpiece) at the
back of the altar, dating from
the first half of the 18th
century. Behind the main
altar stands the simple tomb
of Alonso de Lugo.

In Plaza de la Concepción
stands the **Iglesia de Nuestra
Señora de la Concepción**
(1502) – an example of the
architectural style dating from
the time of the conquest.
This triple-naved Gothic-
Renaissance church features
a magnificent reconstructed
wooden vault. Each
year, in August,
thousands of pilgrims
flock to the **Santuario
del Cristo** – a small
church at the northern
end of La Laguna's old
quarter – to pay homage
to a statue of Christ
carved in the late 15th
century. This fine Gothic
sculpture by an
unknown artist was
brought to Tenerife
in 1520, by Alonso
de Lugo.

🏛 **Museo de Historia
de Tenerife**
C/San Augustín, 22. 📞 922
825 943. ◯ 9am–7pm
Tue–Sun. ● 1 & 6 Jan, 24–25
& 31 Dec. 📷

Anaga Mountains ❸

A PICTURESQUE RANGE OF volcanic peaks, the Anaga Mountains are lush and green thanks to a cool, wet climate. Narrow tracks lead through craggy, inaccessible valleys, and wind among steep rock faces and dense forests. For walkers, the effort required to deal with arduous paths is amply rewarded by the breathtaking views of the rocky coast below, and by the chance to see a wide variety of birds and plants.

Taganana ⑨
This enchanting village lies at the foot of the mountains, amid palm trees. The access road runs in the shadow of the Roque de las Animas – the Ghost Rock.

Cliffs ⑩
These tall, rugged cliffs, which run west of Taganana, thrust their way into an often rough ocean, creating picturesque nooks and inlets. They are difficult to reach, and are best admired from the deck of a cruising boat.

Road to La Laguna ⑪
Known as the gate to the Anaga Mountains, the road to La Laguna runs from Mirador Pico del Inglés, through the Las Mercedes plateau.

FLORA OF THE ANAGA MOUNTAINS

The lush, evergreen vegetation of this remote region, including forests of laurel and juniper trees, and heather, ferns and herbs gives the air its spicy scent. This area is deservedly popular with nature lovers. Dense bushes shelter the twisting roads from the wind, but are difficult to trek through when straying from a trail or path. Although the weather is not very warm, the humid air encourages the growth of vegetation.

Heather and ferns on the roadside near Chinobre

TF 12

LA LAGUNA

Valle Seco

0 km   1
0 miles   1

Santa Cruz de Tenerife ①
The capital of Tenerife, in the northeastern part of the island is the start of the two motorways – del Norte and del Sur.

Roque de las Bodegas ⑧
The bay and the rocky beach is a favourite place for surfers. Further to the east are Almaciga and Benijo, two fishing villages poised on top of the cliffs, which have a handful of restaurants.

VISITORS' CHECKLIST

Length of route: about 65 km (40 miles).
Stopping places: all stops along the route have a bar or restaurant.
Further information: Canarias Trekking, Santa Cruz, Calle Quevedo 1, 922 201 051. There are no fuel stations between La Laguna and San Andrés.

Faro de Anaga ⑦
From Chamorga – one of the loveliest villages on Tenerife – a steep path, 2 km (1 mile) long, runs eastwards to the Anaga lighthouse, which stands on a high peak.

Chinobre ⑥
The road leading from the El Bailadero Pass to Chinobre is where, according to folk legend, witches used to hold their Sabbaths. Thirteen kilometers (8 miles) to the west, at the foot of the Taborno summit, is the Mirador Pico del Inglés.

Igueste de San Andrés ④
The inhabitants of this quiet village at the mouth of a ravine grow mangoes, avocados and bananas. The plantations stretch all the way to the ocean.

Barranco de las Hubertas ⑤
The road from San Andrés to El Bailadero runs along the bottom of a ravine. On both sides are isolated farms standing in the cool shade of palm trees and mountain valley terraces, planted with crops.

San Andrés ②
This former fishing village is now a resort. It has narrow, shady streets and is justly famous for its handful of little seafood restaurants.

Playa de las Teresitas ③
The fine sand for this 2-km (1-mile) long artificial beach was imported from the Sahara. Lined with palm trees, which lend the place an exotic character, the beach is a favourite spot with people from Santa Cruz.

KEY

▬ Suggested route
═ Other road
••• Footpath
🌣 Viewpoint

Around the rocky swimming pools in Bajamar

Bajamar ❹

🏃 2,800. 🚌

T HE INHABITANTS of Bajamar once made their living from fishing and cultivating sugar cane. In recent years it has become popular as a resort and is a well-known tourist centre for Tenerife's northern coast. The high coastal cliffs and the soaring peaks of **Monte de las Mercedes** provide a scenic backdrop for the numerous hotels and bungalows. The main road is lined with restaurants and cafés. Visitors who like bathing will enjoy the large complex of sea-water swimming pools.

ENVIRONS: Some 4 km (2 miles) to the northeast is **Punta del Hidalgo** – a headland offering a fine view of the rocky coast and banana plantations. Strong winds create excellent conditions for windsurfing though the currents make it dangerous for novices. Punta del Hidalgo is a starting point for a marked hiking trail to the cave dwellings at Chinamada.

Tacoronte ❺

🏃 19,000. 🚌 🚊 Sat, Sun. 🗓 Cristo de los Dolores (1st Sun after 15 Sep).

A COASTAL VILLAGE, set 450 m (1,476 ft) above sea level, Tacoronte and its environs are famous for their excellent wines. When in the area, you should visit one of the many wineries to sample some of the fine local vintages.

Tacoronte has two churches: the **Iglesia del Cristo de los Dolores** features a revered 17th-century statue of Christ, which during the harvest festival is carried through the streets of the town. Also noteworthy are the Baroque woodcarvings decorating the interior. The **Iglesia de Santa Catalina** (1664) has a fine wooden vault and rich interior furnishings.

ENVIRONS: Famed for its wine, **El Sauzal** is a short way to the south. Its main attraction is La Casa del Vino La Baranda – a complex in a renovated country house, which comprises a wine museum, wine-tasting hall, bar and store, as well as an excellent restaurant.

La Orotava ❻

See pp108–11.

Puerto de la Cruz ❼

See pp112–13.

Loro Parque ❽

See pp114–15.

Los Realejos ❾

🏃 33,000. 🚌 🗓 San Sebastián (22 Jan).

A SPRAWLING TOWN overlooked by the peak of the Tigaiga Mountain, and criss-crossed with a network of steep and winding streets, Los Realejos consists of two parts: Realejo Bajo (the lower town) and Realejo Alto (the upper town).

The town played an important part in Tenerife's history. It was here that the last free chieftains of the Guanches surrendered to the Spanish invaders in 1496.

In the upper part of Los Realejos stands the **Iglesia de Santiago Apóstol** (1498). The oldest church on the island, it has a beautiful mudéjar (Spanish-Moorish) wooden vault. At the entrance to the town, from the direction of Puerto de la Cruz, stands a **romantic castle**, built in 1862. This square structure, with four almost round towers at its corners, is set in a beautifully tended garden. Unlike other fortresses on the Canary

Tacoronte, situated on the coast and surrounded by vineyards

Los Realejos castle, among its garden and tall palms

Islands, built during the 16th and 17th centuries on the ocean coast for defence, the Los Realejos castle was never used for military purposes.

Icod de los Vinos 🔟

🏠 8,000. 🎫 922 869 600. 🚍
🎭 San Antonio Abad (22 Jan), San Marcos (Mar), Fiestas del Cristo del Drago (1st Sun after 17 Sep).

As its name suggests, this small town is in the heart of a fertile wine-growing region.

However, tourists visit Icod mainly in order to see the legendary symbol of the islands – the **Drago Milenario**. Reputed to be over 1,000 years old, this dragon tree is probably half that age. The biggest specimen in the archipelago, it is best seen from the Plaza de la Iglesia.

The triple-naved church of **San Marcos** was built in the 15th and 16th centuries. Its interior features a beautiful coffered ceiling and a silver high alter. Other interesting items include the painting of Santa Ana, attributed to Bartolomé Murillo, and a fine marble font (1696).

One of the chapels houses the **Museo de Arte Sacro**. The jewel of its collection is an enormous filigree silver cross. Made in Cuba in 1663–8, by Jeronimo de Espellosa y Vallabridge, it is 2.45 m (8 ft) high. Weighing 48.3 kg (106 lb), this gleaming filigree silver cross is thought to be the largest ever made.

At **Mariposario del Drago**, close to the dragon tree, you can learn about the life cycle of butterflies. This covered attraction has many tropical butterflies, which flutter freely among jungle vegetation and water gardens.

Huge dragon tree, in Icod de Vinos

🏛 **Museo de Arte Sacro**
Iglesia San Marco.
📞 922 810 695.
🕐 9:30am–6pm. ⬤ Sun.

🏛 **Mariposario del Drago**
Avenida de Canarias, s/n.
📞 922 815 167.
🕐 9am–6pm daily. 🎫

Garachico 1️⃣1️⃣

🏠 5,900. 🚍
🎭 San Sebastián (20 Jan), Romería de San Roque (16 Aug).

Established in the 16th century by Genoese merchants, Garachico, on the north coast of Tenerife is a jewel of a town, with several historic buildings and traditional-style houses providing a rare sense of architectural unity.

Garachico was once the most important port on the island (later developing into a centre of sugar production) until the eruption of the Volcán Negro in 1706 put an end to its prosperity. Lava buried whole districts and most of the harbour, with only a handful of houses escaping destruction, together with the **Castillo de San Miguel** (1575), which guards Garachico Bay. The only portion of the former **Santa Ana** church to escape is the 16th-century façade. The restored interior has a Baroque font and a crucifix attributed to Martín de Andujar.

Other relics of the town's former glory include the **Palacio de Los Condes de la Gomera** (Palace of the Counts of Gomera), standing in Plaza de la Libertad, and several former convents, including the 17th-century **Santo Domingo**, now a modern art museum, and **San Francisco Nuestra Señora de los Angeles**. A section of this 18th-century convent is occupied by a modest museum – **Casa de la Cultura**. Also in the Plaza de la Libertad is a **monument** to **Simón Bolívar**, liberator of South America. Leading from the square, **Estaba de Porte** is lined with houses that have fine wooden balconies.

Every winter, Garachico is battered by Atlantic gales. The huge waves are truly spectacular, especially when the water level drops to reveal the vast **Roque de Garachico**.

🏛 **Museo de Arte Contemporáneo**
Plaza de Santo Domingo.
📞 922 830 000. 🕐 10am–1pm, 3–6pm Mon–Sat, 10am–1pm Sun. 🎫

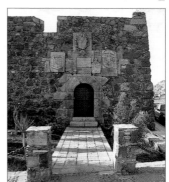

Entrance to Castillo de San Miguel, Garachico

La Orotava

Decorative gargoyle

PRIOR TO THE CONQUEST of the island, the town of La Orotava, situated at the heart of a valley, belonged to Taoro – the richest of the Guanche kingdoms on Tenerife. Soon after the Spanish conquest, settlers from Andalusia populated the valley and the first churches and residences appeared in the 16th century. The beauty of their wooden decorations is reminiscent of the Arabian palaces of Southern Spain. After gaining its independence from La Laguna in 1648, La Orotava began to develop rapidly and, today, it is one of the loveliest towns in the entire archipelago.

Exploring La Orotava

La Orotava is one of the best-preserved old towns on Tenerife. Its steep, narrow, cobbled streets captivate most visitors as do the enchanting 17th- and 18th-century townhouses. Their wooden, exquisitely carved balconies, fashioned from dark wood, represent the quintessence of Canary architecture.

Most of the interesting buildings are found in the compact old town. Excellent signposting makes it easy to find all of the sights.

🏠 Iglesia de la Concepción

Plaza Casañas. 922 330 187.
daily.
The Iglesia de la Concepción, or Church of the Immaculate Conception, presents a unique atmosphere.

The magnificent interior, with its wooden sculptures created by several local artists, including Fernando Estévez and José Luján Pérez, is only enhanced by the recordings of Mozart's music, which are played here almost all day. The original church, built in the 16th century, was destroyed by earthquakes in 1704 and 1705. The present triple-naved church is the result of restoration work carried out between 1768 and 1788 by two architects – Diego Nicolás and Ventury Rodríguez – who together produced this fine example of Canary Baroque architecture, which takes much of its inspiration from the sacral buildings of Latin America. In 1948, the church was listed as a national monument.

🏛 Calle Carrera Escultor Estévez

The town's defining feature is the chain of streets, including Doctor Domingo González Garcia, San Francisco and Calle Carrera Escultor Estévez, which run in a semicircle through the old part of La Orotava. Lined with charming houses built mostly

Carrera Escultor Estévez, the main street in La Orotava

in the second half of the 19th century, the streets wind up the hill toward Plaza del General Franco. The tourist office at No. 2 Calle Carrera Escultor Estévez can supply free town maps indicating the must-see sights along this street. One interesting stopping-off point is El Pueblo Guanche – an ethnographic museum occupying a renovated townhouse. The museum has a shop selling handicrafts and food products and also a restaurant.

🏛 Plaza del General Franco

During Corpus Christi, this pleasant square, which is situated at the very heart of the old town and towered over by its Neo-Classical town hall, becomes the focus of religious celebrations. At this time, the paving stones of the tree-lined square are covered with unusual, colourful "carpets", created from volcanic ash, soil and sand. Visitors can take home images of these fleeting works of art because they are recorded on colourful post-cards that can be found on sale throughout the town all year round.

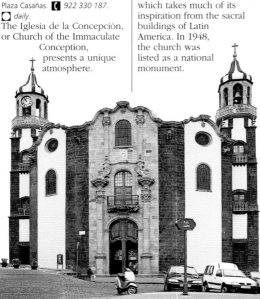

The imposing façade of the Iglesia de la Concepción

The tree-lined Plaza de la Constitución

Palacio Municipal

The town's administration centre is the *ayuntamiento* – the late Neo-Classical town hall, built in 1871–91, which has a modest façade virtually free of decoration. Its vault is painted with the heraldic arms of other towns on Tenerife, and with wall carvings depicting allegorical figures, which represent agriculture, history, morality and the law. Its patio once featured the oldest and largest dragon tree in the Canary Islands, which was destroyed during a storm in 1868.

Hijuela del Botánico

C/Hermano Apolinar.
daily from dawn till dusk.
La Orotava's botanical garden was established in 1923 using shoots and cuttings taken from the Jardín Botánico in Puerto de la Cruz, which is famous throughout the Canary Islands. This process gave the garden its name, Hijuela del Botánico, meaning "daughter of the botanical garden". Today, the relatively small garden is blooming and features over 3,000 species of tropical and subtropical plants.

Plaza de la Constitución

This is a good place to sit down and admire La Orotava from the comfort of one of the bars and cafés, which come to life in the evenings. The Plaza, a relic of the old town's merchant past, has a tree-lined terrace, offering fine views over the buildings below. The multicoloured roof tiles and slender church towers combine to produce a memorable panorama of the town and valley that is reminiscent of Florence.

Iglesia de San Agustín

The north side of the Plaza de la Constitución is occupied by the church and abbey of St Augustine. Dating from the 17th century, this building features a beautiful façade with a Renaissance-Baroque portal. The church has many fine historic remains and a panelled ceiling, while the former abbey is now a school of music.

Decorations on the
Iglesia de San Agustín

LA OROTAVA

0 m   100
0 yards   100

KEY

Tourist information

Post office

🏛 Calle Tomás Zerolo

Almost every street or alley in La Orotava offers some historic interest. Calle Tomás Zerolo, which passes through the lower part of the old town, is no exception. It features the **Convento de Santo Domingo**, which has a small museum of Latin American handicrafts, and, opposite it, the **Casa Torrehermosa** – a colonial-style house built in the 17th century for the Hermosa family. Today, this residence houses the Impresa Insular de Artesanía – a small workshop and museum devoted to local handicrafts.

Wooden galleries around the patio of the Casa de los Balcones

🏛 Casa de los Balcones

C/San Francisco, 3–4. 📞 922 330 629.
⏰ 8:30am–6:30pm Mon–Fri,
8:30am–5pm Sat.

The "House of Balconies", also known as the Casa de Fonseca, is a major landmark of La Orotava. Its light-coloured façade is adorned with a heavy, carved door, smart windows and long teak balconies. The palm-shaded patio, brimming over with greenery, is surrounded by the first- and second-floor galleries, which rest on slender wooden columns.

The house, built in 1632–70, has its own small museum of Canary art and handicrafts. Here, visitors can view and buy local products, including embroidery, lace, pottery, regional costumes and other souvenirs (don't miss the miniature balconies of La Orotava!).

🏛 Casa del Turista

Calle San Francisco, 4.
📞 922 330 629. ⏰ 9am–7pm
Mon–Fri, 8:30am–5pm Sat.

Standing on the opposite side of the road to the Casa de los Balcones is the Casa del Turista, also known as the Casa de Molina. This is a magnificent Canary townhouse once belonging to a wealthy family. It was known collectively (with the 17th-century Casa Mesa and the Casa de los Lercaro) as the Doce Casas or "twelve houses". The house is built in a style similar to that of Casa de los Balcones, but is older, dating from 1509. It also offers the chance to view and purchase local handicrafts. Its prize exhibit is a religious scene made from coloured volcanic sand. This type of decoration, for which the town is famous, is made during Corpus Christi. The terraces at the back of the house provide a fine view over the Orotava valley.

Stone portal of Casa del Turista

🏛 Iglesia San Francisco

C/San Francisco.

The church of San Francisco, with its Baroque portal and rather plain interior, stands in the palm-shaded Plaza de San Francisco and serves as the hospital chapel.

The church stands next to the **Hospital de la Santísima Trinidad** (Hospital of the Holy Trinity), which has occupied the 18th-century Convento de San Lorenzo since 1884. The interior is closed to visitors. Note the revolving drum on the door where foundling babies were placed to be cared for by the nuns.

🏛 Gofio Mills

C/Doctor Domingo
González García.
In the south, Calle San Francisco becomes Calle Doctor

Domingo González García. The street features a number of 17th- and 18th-century mills that once produced *gofio* (a roasted mixture of wheat, maize or barley). One of these mills is still working. Here, visitors can see the entire process of flour production, as well as buy the end product. One room has a display showing the production process prior to the introduction of electrical machinery.

🏛 Iglesia San Juan Bautista

C/San Juan Bautista

The single-nave church of St John the Baptist was built in the 18th century. Its modest façade, with a monumental belfry, does nothing to hint at the magnificence of its interior. Thanks to the beautiful *artesonado* – the wooden coffered ceiling – and the opulent interior decorations featuring sculptures by Luján Peréz and Fernando Estévez, the church is regarded as one of the most precious historic sites in La Orotava. The fine altars deserve special attention.

In front of the church is a bust of the Venezuelan President, Rómulo Betancourt (1909–81).

The simple façade of Iglesia San Juan Bautista

🏛 Museo de Cerámica – Casa de Tafuriaste

C/León, 3. ☎ 922 321 447.
🕙 10am–6pm daily. ♿

The island's passion for ceramics reached its peak even before the advent of the European conquerors, and remains alive to this day, particularly among the local population of La Orotava. The primitive designs, which are based on old Guanche forms, are popular with many tourists, as are items representing a more modern style of pottery.

Orotava's Museo de Cerámica was founded to cater for this interest. The museum is housed in the Casa de Tafuriaste – a much-restored Canary townhouse from the 17th century, which is about 2 km (1 mile) west from La Orotava's old town on the La Luz-Las Candias road.

On the museum's first floor, there is a fine display of antique ceramics. The collection includes nearly 1,000 vessels from the Canary Islands and Spain. Down on the ground floor there is a pottery workshop, where visitors can see demonstrations of how modern jugs and bowls are made.

The gift shop sells a wide variety of these items to take home as souvenirs.

Modern pottery from Casa de Tafuriaste

🏛 Liceo de Taoro

C/San Augustín. ♿
Above the Plaza de la Constitución stands the charming, eclectic building of the former grammar school, with a well-maintained 100-year-old garden. These days, it houses a club with elegant reception rooms, a bar (which is open to non-members), games room and a library.

🌿 Jardín Victoria

Plaza de la Constitución.
🕗 8am–9pm daily. ♿
Bordering the Liceo de Taoro is the 19th-century Jardín Victoria – full of beautiful flowers and palm trees, arranged on terraces along a shallow ravine with a stream running at the bottom. The main architectural feature of this garden is the mausoleum of **Diego Ponte del Castillo**, made of Carrara marble.

🏛 Ex-convento Santo Domingo

C/Tomás Zerolo, 34.
On the outskirts of La Orotava's old town stands a 17th–18th-century Dominican convent, which has a triple-naved church featuring a magnificent polychromatic wooden coffered ceiling. The remaining rooms of the

Jardín Victoria, situated in a ravine

former convent are arranged around a patio with lovely balconies resting on wooden columns. These rooms are occupied by the compact **Museo de Artesanía Iberoamericana**, which opened in 1991. This ethnographic museum has an interesting exhibition of handicrafts from Spain and Latin America. The collection includes traditional musical instruments (look out for the Canary *timple* – a kind of ukelele), pottery, textiles, wickerwork and some fine locally produced furniture.

🏛 Museo de Artesanía Iberoamericana

☎ 922 323 376. 🕘 9am–6pm Mon-Fri, 9am–2pm Sat. ♿

ENVIRONS: The **Mirador de Humboldt** is 5 km (3 miles) northeast. This splendid viewpoint overlooks the entire Orotava valley and is named after the geographer, traveller and naturalist, Alexander von Humboldt, who visited Tenerife in 1799.

Some 30 km (19 miles) south, along a scenic road that crosses the Orotava valley, stands the **Izaña Astrophysical Observatory**. The observatory is near the entrance to the Parque Nacional del Teide, and occupies a picturesque spot 2,200 m (7,210 ft) above sea level, close to the top of the Izaña mountain.

CORPUS CHRISTI

Apart from Epiphany, Corpus Christi is one of the most celebrated religious festivals in the Canary Islands. The most extravagant festivities on Tenerife are held in La Orotava and La Laguna, which try to outdo each other in the splendour of the occasion. The streets of the town are lined with magnificent floral decorations, and the Plaza del General Franco is adorned with pictures and "carpets" made of volcanic sands, which can take months to prepare.

Preparing a floral picture from volcanic sand

Puerto de la Cruz **❼**

RISING UP FROM the sea front, Puerto de la Cruz was the principal port of the island after the destruction of Garachico. By the late 19th century, it had already become a resort and a popular destination for upmarket British visitors and remains so to this day. The hotels tower above banana plantations, shopping arcades, casinos, restaurants, cafés and nightclubs, as well as numerous historic sites. An artificial lagoon and warm, clear water attracts over 100,000 visitors each year to the area.

Portal of the Iglesia de Nuestra Señora de la Peña de Francia

🔒 Iglesia de Nuestra Señora de la Peña de Francia

The triple-naved cathedral was built in 1684–97. Its tall tower was added in the late 19th century.

In the dark interior of the church the eye is drawn to Baroque sculptures – the work of the local artist Fernando Estévez, and José Luján Pérez, a well-known island artist. No less precious are the paintings by Luís de la Cruz. The cathedral's organ was brought from London in 1814.

A bust of Augustín de Bétancourt (1758–1824), founder of the Engineering College in Madrid, stands in front of the church.

🏛 Calle Quintana

The street leads to Punta del Viento, a terrace poised on the edge of the ocean and affording a fine view over the rocky coast and **Lago Martiánez**. Branching off eastwards is **Calle de San Telmo**, a seaside promenade with stone seats and numerous bars. The **Monopol Hotel** – one of the oldest hotels in Puerto de la Cruz – stands in Calle Quintana.

🏛 Plaza de Europa

Hugging the shoreline, this square was laid out in 1992, but is based on 18th- and 19th-century European-style town planning. Its features include the **town hall** (1973) and the **Casa de Miranda** (1730), a fine old town house, which now accommodates a restaurant specializing in local fare. The tourist information bureau is also in this square.

🏛 Casa de la Real Aduana

Calle de las Lonjas. **☎** *922 378 103.* **◯** *Mon–Sat.*
This was built in 1620 for Juan Antonio Lutzardo de Francha and is the oldest house in town. Following the destruction of Garachico it became the seat of the governor and from 1706 to 1833 served as the customs house. The building was restored in the 1970s and now houses a shop selling old furniture and handicrafts.

Town crest at Plaza de Europa

🏛 Puerto Pesquero

The history of this picturesque fishing harbour, situated on a small, stony beach, goes back to the 18th century, when the town was the main exporter of the island's agricultural produce. Today you can buy freshly caught fish direct from the fishermen.

🔒 Iglesia de San Francisco

C/San Juan.
The Church of St Francis is built around the Ermita de San Juan, which was constructed in 1599. One of the oldest buildings in Puerto de la Cruz, it is decorated with sculptures and paintings, from the 16th century up to modern times.

Today, this modest building serves as an ecumenical church, and holds services for all Christian denominations in the town.

🏛 Plaza del Charco de los Camerones

Many of the town's most historic buildings are found in Plaza del Charco, a square shaded by palm and laurel trees, which were brought in 1852 from Cuba.

The centre is occupied by a stage used for musical concerts. Many tourists enjoy watching chess games played with giant pieces on a chessboard that has been constructed of paving stones.

🏛 Museo Arqueológico

C/Lomo, 4. **☎** *922 371 465.* **◯** *10am–1pm & 5–9pm Tue–Sat, 10am–1pm Sun.* 🈲
This small museum, opened in 1991, is devoted to the history and cultural heritage of the Canary Islands. Its exhibits include a collection

View of the entrance to Puerto Pesquero fishing harbour

Lush banana plantations south of Parque Taoro

of Gaunche products and the mummified remains of the island's original inhabitants.

♣ Castillo de San Felipe

This small 17th-century fort once guarded the harbour entrance against attacks from pirates and the ships of Spain's two maritime rivals: France and England. Now the fort, situated in the western part of town, often serves as a venue for temporary exhibitions. To the west of the fort is the **Playa Jardín** – the town's longest beach.

♣ Parque Taoro

This majestic park is an enchanting spot and a good place to escape the bustle of town. The park, which is home to the ultra-smart **Casino Taoro**, has cascades, waterfalls, streams crossed with bridges, small ponds and viewing terraces. At the centre of the park lies the **Jardín Risco Bello Acuático** – a tropical water garden.

🏊 Lago Martiánez

Playa Martiánez. ☎ 922 385 955.
🕐 10am–6pm daily. ● May. 📷
This artificial lagoon, designed by César Manrique, was built in 1969. Conjuring up a subtropical paradise, it has lush plants and white sand. It consists of a complex of seawater swimming pools and gurgling fountains, which contrast with the surrounding lava field.

♣ Jardín Botánico

C/Retama, 2. ☎ 922 383 572.
🕐 9am–7pm daily. 📷
The local botanical garden is one of the oldest in the world. It was established in 1788 at the request of Carlos III of Spain, by Alonso de Nova Gimón.

Today, the lush garden is crammed with over 1,000 species of plants and trees from the Canary Islands, as well as flora from all over the world.

Playa Jardín, a popular beach with tourists

PUERTO DE LA CRUZ

Calle Quintana ②
Casa de la Real Aduana ④
Iglesia de San Francisco ⑥
Iglesia de Nuestra Señora de la Peña de Francia ①
Plaza de Europa ③
Plaza del Charco de los Camerones ⑦
Puerto Pesquero ⑤

0 m   50
0 yards   50

KEY

🅿 Parking
❙ Tourist information
⊠ Post office

Loro Parque ⓳

FROM THE DAY it opened in 1972, this tropical plant complex has been hugely popular and has been visited by over 11 million tourists. The huge area contains many animals and birds, magnificent orchids and dragon trees. It offers numerous tourist attractions, including shows of performing seals, parrots and dolphins. It even has a bat cave! The entrance to the park leads through an authenic Thai village. Built in 1993, it consists of six buildings which were constructed in Thailand and shipped in sections to Tenerife, where they were reassembled by Thai craftsmen.

★ Dolphinarium
This is Loro Parque's biggest draw and can accommodate 1,800 spectators at a time to watch the show in what is claimed to be Europe's largest dolphinarium.

Jaguars
Two jaguars live in a reconstructed volcanic landscape. You can see them through a series of large windows.

Alligators

Parrot hatchery

"Natural Vision" cinema complex

Parrot Show
Trained-parrot shows, including roller-skating antics, are held in the building at the centre of the park.

KEY

- 🅿 Parking
- ☕ Café
- 🍴 Restaurant
- 🚻 Toilets

★ Penguin House
With frost-covered rocks and a water temperature of 8° C (46° F), the Penguin House recreates a natural habitat, enabling the inhabitants to forget that they are living on Tenerife.

VISITORS' CHECKLIST

Puerto de la Cruz, C/San Felipe.
📞 922 373 841.
⏰ 8:30am–5pm daily. 🅿 ♿
🌐 www.loroparque.com
Free transport by tram from Playa Martiánez (every 20 min).

Tower of Fish
A school of fish swim inside an illuminated glass cylinder, more than 8 m (26 ft) tall, which stands next to the Penguin House.

Entrance

0 m   50
0 yards   50

Amphitheatre and trained seal shows

Gorillas
A sizeable number of gorillas live out their days in relative freedom in the park, in an area of 3,500 sq m (4,200 sq yards).

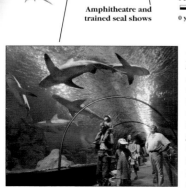

★ Shark Aquarium
Several species of shark can be viewed in the aquarium. A specially designed glass-tunnel walkway allows visitors to watch sharks swimming directly overhead.

STAR ATTRACTIONS

★ **Dolphinarium**

★ **Penguin House**

★ **Shark Aquarium**

Masca ⑫

🚶 150. 🚌

Masca, with its scenic position at an altitude of 600 m (2,000 ft), is a popular destination for day trips from many of the big resorts. Just above the small village is a terrace, which offers an impressive outlook, especially at sunset, towards Mount Teide on one side, and the Atlantic on the other.

Masca was once a refuge for pirates and accessible only by mule. Even today, it can only be reached via a steep, winding road. Though narrow, the road is a feat of modern engineering and uses small lay-bys along the roadside to allow vehicles to pass each other. The incredible views as the road winds through the mountains are reason enough to visit.

The village is charming and consists of a handful of old, red-tiled, stone houses clinging to the sides of the gorge, and surrounded by lush palm trees. Roadside vendors offer prickly pears and oranges to passers-by.

Crops are grown in small fields on terraces, which descend towards the Barranco de Masca ravine. The villagers also keep bees that gather nectar from the surrounding flowering meadows. The village is an excellent starting point for hikers. One of the best routes leads along the Masca ravine, to the seashore. A fit mountain walker should be able to get there and

The green square of Plaza de la Iglesia in Los Silos

back again in under four hours. Take care, however, as the return hike is steep and fairly arduous.

Environs: Past the village, the road leads north through the Macizo de Teno massif, towards the coastal flatland. Some 10 km (6 miles) along the route is the scenic village of **El Palmar**. The nearby **Montaña de Talavera** has had chunks cut out of it to provide soil for the banana plantations.

Another 4 km (2 miles) further on is **Buenavista**, the island's westernmost village, which has a small fishing harbour and a pebble beach.

A short way eastwards in the midst of banana plantations, **Los Silos** is a quiet little town with a compact 19th-century layout. In the town centre is a typical tree-shaded square, with a coffee pavilion. The shady square is idyllic and has traditional Canary houses with wooden balconies.

Santiago del Teide ⑬

🚶 7,000. 🚌 ℹ️ Paseo Marítimo, Playa de la Arena, 922 860 348.

Should you visit Santiago del Teide in February, when the countless almond trees are in bloom with pink and white blossom, you will see it is particularly lovely. The small town is surrounded by vineyards and cornfields, and nestles among the foothills of the Teno massif. La Gomera can be seen in the distance.

The pride of the town is the Baroque parish church of **San Fernando**, which was built in the mid-16th century and stands at the end of the main street. Its asymmetric façade is adorned with a wooden, grill-shaded balcony. A tall belfry has been added at the northern end of the church. The small, Moorish-looking domes give the building its distinctive look.

Look out for the strange figure in front of one of the side altars: it represents Christ on horseback, wearing a black Spanish hat and carrying a sword.

Environs: Branching off from the southern approach road to the village is a path to **Camino de la Virgen de Lourdes**. The path, dedicated to the Virgin Mary of Lourdes and with a shrine and an ornamental bridge, leads along the slope of the mountain to a grotto decorated with flowers.

The façade of San Fernando with its wooden balcony, Santiago del Teide

Los Gigantes and Puerto de Santiago ⓮

THE GIANT CLIFFS, known as the **Acantilados de los Gigantes** ("Cliffs of the Giants"), form the ridge of the Teno massif. Some 10 km (6 miles) long, this steep cliff-face plunges 500 m (1,600 ft) into the ocean. The dark rocks are best seen by boat. Trips often leave from Puerto Deportivo and usually travel further north to include a wonderful view over the **Barranco de Masca**.

Situated beneath the cliffs, the small town of **Los Gigantes** is a typical Canary holiday resort, the biggest on the northwest coast of Tenerife, with apartment complexes sprawling over the slopes. Its yachting marina has diving clubs and offers angling trips.

The town itself, with its concentrated development, gives the impression of being overcrowded. Only narrow alleys separate small hotels and apartment blocks.

A seaside boulevard connects Los Gigantes with nearby **Puerto de Santiago**, which has long been a resort, although on a smaller scale. The main attraction here is the dark volcanic-sand beaches, including the most popular of them, **Playa de la Arena**, situated to the south. Most of the fishermen here have traded in their rods and nets and take tourists out for boat trips instead.

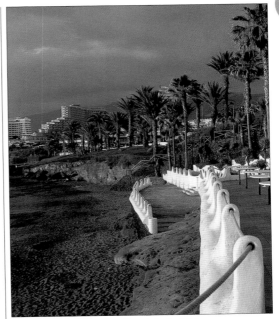

Boulevards along the beach in Playa de las Américas

Playa de las Américas and Los Cristianos ⓯

🏘 20,000. 🚌 🛳 🚹 C/General Franco, 922 757 137. 🎉 Fiesta del Carmen (beg. of Sep).

YOU WOULD NOT think so to look at it now but Los Cristianos was once a sleepy fishing village. Today, it is a year-round provider of fun and sun with artificial beaches, sprawling hotel-apartments, and countless bars, discos and souvenir shops. Many people embrace the noise and kitsch good humour of the place and Los Cristianos is one of the most popular resorts in the archipelago. It extends into the virtually identical Playa de las Américas, which merges in its turn with **Costa Adeje** a little further up the coastline.

A promenade, running alongside the crowded beaches and the harbour wall, has shops, restaurants and bars. In Las Américas the promenade turns into a palm-shaded boulevard several miles long, which runs above numerous sheltered beaches. The most exclusive among them are **Torviscas** and **Bahía del Duque**. Ferries and hydrofoils make regular trips from Los Cristianos' port to La Gomera and El Hierro.

ENVIRONS: A short way northeast, **Parque Ecológico Las Águilas** has displays of condors in flight, evening variety shows and a floodlit pool full of crocodiles. Some 7 km (4 miles) north, and a two-hour walk from the town of Adeje, is the **Barranco del Infierno**, a wild gorge with an impressive waterfall.

Harbour in Puerto de Santiago, against the steep cliffs of Los Gigantes

Parque Nacional del Teide ⑯

Some 3 million years ago a huge volcano exploded, leaving behind the 16-km (10-mile) Las Cañadas crater with the much smaller volcano, Teide, on its northern edge. In 1954 the area was turned into one of the largest national parks in Spain. Marked paths guide visitors round the best of this awesome wilderness of ash beds, lava streams and mineral tinted rocks. The refurbished parador, next to the road leading along the plateau, is the only hotel in the park. The same road leads to the lower cable-car station and the El Portillo visitor centre.

Pico Viejo
The crater of this volcanic cone, which last erupted in the 18th century, measures 800 m (2,624 ft) in diameter.

Los Roques de García
Close to the parador is a much photographed set of strangely shaped rocks, rising some 150 m (500 ft) above the crater floor.

Boca de Tauce
This lookout provides a stunning view of the gulleys and slopes of Mount Teide.

SANTIAGO DEL TEIDE

PICO VIEJO ▲ 3134

TF 36

Llano de Ucanca
This treeless plain contains the rocks of Los Azulejos. Their blue-green glitter is due to the copper deposits within them.

MONTAÑA GANGARRO ▲ 2191

TF 21

GRANADILLA DE ABONA

Pico del Teide

The most recent eruption of Mount Teide occurred in 1798. At 3,718 m (12,195 ft), it is the highest mountain in Spain. Today, you can only visit its peak if you have a permit (ask at the visitor centre for details). The viewing platform in La Fortaleza, reached by a footpath leading from the top cable-car station, affords (on a clear day) an incredible view of the entire archipelago, stretching hundred of miles.

Early map showing Teide as the world's highest mountain

Key

▬ Major road
▬ Minor road
═ Other road
··· Footpath
▬ Park boundary
`·-. Seasonal river
🅿 Parking
ℹ Tourist information
☀ Viewpoint
🍴 Restaurant

Izaña Astrophysical Observatory
At the entrance to the park, the observatory gives astronomers the chance to make the most of the island's clear skies.

VISITORS' CHECKLIST

🚌 342 from El Portillo.
ℹ️ Oficina del Parque Nacional, C/Emilio Calzadilla, 5–4a, Santa Cruz de Tenerife, 922 290 129.
🕐 9am–2pm Mon–Fri.
♿ cable-car only.

Refugio de Altavista
This modest shelter is located along the trail leading to Pico del Teide, at an altitude of 3,270 m (10,726 ft).

LA OROTAVA
El Portillo
LA LAGUNA
TF 24
TF 21
MONTAÑA BLANCA 2760
MONTAÑA RAJADA 2509

Cable-car
Built in 1971, the cable-car takes only eight minutes to whisk tourists to within 200 m (656 ft) of Teide's summit.

Las Cañadas
The seven cañadas (sandy plateaux) are the result of the collapse of ancient craters. Only a few species of plant can grow in this dusty, arid wasteland.

0 km 2
0 miles 2

Echium wildpretii
This striking plant, a kind of viper's bugloss, has bright red stalks. It can grow up to 2m (6 ft) high and is one of the symbols of Tenerife.

Roque Cinchado
One of the Roques de García, the Cinchado is this strange shape because it is wearing away faster at the bottom than the top.

Vilaflor ⓱

🚶 *1,600.* 🚍

WITH AN ELEVATION of 1,400 m (4,600 ft), Vilaflor is the highest village in the Canaries. In the 19th century the village became famous for its lacework. Close

The giant "Pino Gordo" just outside Vilaflor

to the village, which is surrounded by pine forests, is "Pino Gordo", a pine tree over 40 m (130 ft) tall. In the plaza at the top of the village is the **Iglesia de San Pedro** (1550), which has a statue of the church's patron saint.

ENVIRONS: Hikers can set out from Vilaflor for the so-called **Paisaje Lunar** ("Lunar Landscape"), a curious rock formation made of weathered cones of sandstone.

El Médano ⓲

🚶 *1,500.* ℹ️ *Plaza del Médano, 922 176 002.* 🚍 🛥 *San Antonio de Padua (14 Jun).*

EL MÉDANO, a former fishing village, is now famous for its bay, fringed by long, sandy beaches. These stretch south to the **Punta Roja**, towered over by the **Montaña Roja** volcano (now a nature reserve). The strong winds (known as *alisios*)

make the place enormously popular with windsurfers (international competitions are held here every year). The winds are also utilized in the **Parque Eólico de Granadilla** – a wind farm, supplying electricity to over 3,000 homes.

ENVIRONS: Some 5 km (3 miles) to the northwest, at the end of the runways of Reina Sofia Airport, is the **Cueva del Hermano Pedro** – a cave converted into a sanctuary, dedicated to Father Peter, the first Canary saint (1626–67).

Candelaria ⓳

🚶 *12,000.* 🚍 🛥 ℹ️ *C/Antón Guanche, 1, 922 500 415.* 🛒 *Sat, Sun.* 🛥 *Nuestra Señora de la Candelaria (2 Feb, 14–15 Aug).*

CANDELARIA IS FAMOUS for its religious sanctuary, the most important in the archipelago. Twice each year *(see above)*, crowds of pilgrims come to the **Basílica**

Tenerife's Beaches

WITH THE POSSIBLE exception of Las Teresitas, near Santa Cruz, the beaches of Tenerife are not nearly as scenic as those of Fuerteventura, though they are nevertheless popular with tourists. Numerous diving packages are on offer to visitors, from courses aimed at beginners to expeditions into the depths of the ocean. Reliable winds make the place popular with windsurfers and conditions are also good for many other watersports, from paragliding to waterskiing.

Playa San Blas ④ is situated near Los Abrigos. From here a modern road leads to Golf del Sur, the biggest golf course on Tenerife and one of the finest on the Canary Islands.

Los Abrigos ⑤ is a fishing village next to a quiet, rocky beach, and is known for its many excellent fish restaurants.

Playa de las Américas ①
To satisfy the taste of visitors, the local volcanic beaches with black and grey sand are covered each year with light sand imported from the Sahara.

Los Cristianos ② is one of the Canary Islands' most popular resorts with newly laid-out sand beaches close to its centre.

Costa del Silencio ③, as its name suggests, is quieter than many resorts, though it is right next to the international airport.

Imposing façade of the basilica, Candelaria

de Nuestra Señora de Candelaria to pray to the Black Madonna – the patron saint of the Canary Islands.

According to legend, in 1390 two fishermen from a Guanche tribe found a miraculous statue that had been washed up on the beach (it was probably a figurehead from a shipwreck). The tribe placed it in one of the coastal caves as an object of veneration and there it remained until 1826, when it was swept away during a violent storm.

The basilica itself was built in 1958 on the site of an earlier 16th-century church. The present statue of the Madonna is the work of Fernando Estévez (1827). It has been placed inside a niche above the main altar. The wall around the niche has paintings by Jose Aguiar and Manuel Martín Gonzáles. The church's main entrance features a vast painting of the Black Madonna by Dimas Coello (1986).

The basilica adjoins the 17th-century church of **Santa Ana**. Both churches stand along the northwest frontage of **Plaza de la Patrona de Canaria**, a huge square that includes nine bronze statues depicting the legendary Guanche rulers, known as the *Menceyes*.

Statue of a Guanche chieftain, Candelaria

Güímar ⑳

🏠 15,500. 🚌 🎉 San Pedro (29 Jun).

THE LARGEST TOWN in southeast Tenerife, Güímar has an eclectic mix of 19th-century houses. On a small square in the town centre stands the 18th-century church of **San Pedro Apóstol**.

The town is famous for the terraced **pyramids** made from uncut stone that were unearthed in the suburb of Chacona in the 1990s. The anthropologist Thor Heyerdahl and the ship owner Fred Olsen persuaded the authorities to seal off the area and founded the **Parque Etnográfico** museum.

🏛 **Parque Etnográfico Pirámides de Güímar**
C/Chacon, s/n.
📞 922 514 510.
🕙 9:30am– 6pm daily.
⬤ 1 Jan & 25 Dec. 🎫
🌐 www.fredolsen.es

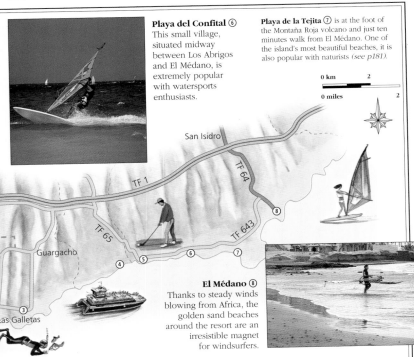

Playa del Confital ⑥
This small village, situated midway between Los Abrigos and El Médano, is extremely popular with watersports enthusiasts.

Playa de la Tejita ⑦ is at the foot of the Montaña Roja volcano and just ten minutes walk from El Médano. One of the island's most beautiful beaches, it is also popular with naturists (see p181).

0 km 2
0 miles 2

San Isidro

TF 1
TF 64
TF 643
TF 65

Guargacho

Las Galletas

El Médano ⑧
Thanks to steady winds blowing from Africa, the golden sand beaches around the resort are an irresistible magnet for windsurfers.

La Gomera

*L*a gomera, *the Isla Redonda or Round Island, is the "alternative" Canary Island. A mere 378 sq km (146 sq miles), it has little tourism infrastructure and only small pebble-and-sand beaches. Many visitors treat it as a day trip. Some, however, come for this very absence of commercialism, drawn by the mountainous countryside and an ancient laurel forest that is perfect for hiking.*

Despite the poor soil and the hilly conditions, the inhabitants of La Gomera, who lived on the island during the Guanche era as well as those who arrived after the Spanish conquest, made a living as farmers. Fields were set on terraces cut into the slopes of ravines. Crops included potatoes, tomatoes, bananas and grapes. To this day many of the local people are engaged in farming and the island has maintained its agricultural character.

Cacti decorating an island windowsill

The isolation of the island, its inaccessibility and the difficulties in cultivating the fertile land all contributed to its poverty and often caused many of the Gomerans to leave for South America (though quite a few are returning now). Signs of emigration are still visible in the form of numerous deserted villages.

In the 1960s, La Gomera was discovered by people seeking an alternative lifestyle. The island became a symbol of unspoiled nature. This was the beginning of the development of tourism. Today, the island authorities try to maintain a balance between the traditional economy and the proceeds of tourism, and strive to protect the historic landscape from the trappings of civilization that threaten it.

One of the outstanding features of La Gomera that attracts many visitors each year is the Garajonay national park. This is one of the world's oldest natural forests and provides an excellent area for walking. Equally interesting are the local customs. Some of them, including a unique whistle language, have survived since the times of the Guanches.

Harbour entrance in San Sebastián de La Gomera

◁ **Green terraces of cultivated fields, on the slopes of the Valle Gran Rey**

Exploring La Gomera

MOST VISITORS COME to La Gomera on day trips, arriving from nearby Tenerife. This small island, though somewhat short of historical sites, such as those on Gran Canaria or Tenerife, is extremely attractive in terms of its landscape. Deep ravines, rocky summits, mist-shrouded laurel forests and valley slopes descending in terraces all compensate for the lack of long, sandy beaches. Rich in unspoilt areas and seemingly untainted by tourism, the island is an excellent place for hiking. With no industry, motorways and few large hotels, La Gomera is a haven of peace and suits those wishing to escape the bustle of the larger resorts.

LOCATOR MAP

SIGHTS AT A GLANCE

Agulo **3**
Alajeró **8**
El Cercado **6**
Hermigua **2**
Parque Nacional de Garajonay pp130–31 **7**
Playa de Santiago **9**
San Sebastián de La Gomera **1**
Valle Gran Rey **5**
Vallehermoso **4**

VALLEHERMOSO **4**

ALOJERA

PARQUE NACIONAL DE GARAJONAY

ARURE

TE-713

EL CERCADO **6**

CHIPUDE

VALLE GRAN REY
5

ALAJERÓ

The parador courtyard in San Sebastián de La Gomera

SEE ALSO

• *Where to Stay* pp161–2.

• *Where to Eat* pp174–5.

GETTING THERE

The distance between La Gomera and Tenerife is 32 km (20 miles). The journey by ferry from Los Cristianos takes 1 hr 40 min, by hydrofoil it is 45 min. There are also ferry links with La Palma and El Hierro. The island has direct air links with Tenerife and Gran Canaria. All main routes on the island are served by buses, although these are not very frequent. It is therefore preferable to hire a car. A few unmade roads on the island are only suitable for a four-wheel-drive vehicle.

Black sand beach near the harbour in San Sebastián de La Gomera, one of the few beaches on the island

KEY

▬	Minor road
▬	Scenic route
✈	Airport
⛴	Ferry harbour
✹	Viewpoint

View towards Ermita San Isidoro, from around Alajeró

0 km — 3
0 miles — 3

Façade of Iglesia de la Virgen de la Asunción in San Sebastián

San Sebastián de La Gomera ❶

🏚 1,600. 🚌 ⛴ ℹ️ C/Real, 1, 922 141 512. 🎉 Fiesta de San Sebastián (20 Jan), Bajada de la Virgen de Guadalupe (5 Oct, every 5 years).

WITH THE DAILY arrival of tourists on the Tenerife ferry, the island's sleepy capital and main harbour comes alive. The road from the harbour into town passes through the laurel-shaded **Plaza de las Américas**, which is lined with street cafés.

To the west of the square stands the **Torre del Conde**. This Gothic tower was built in 1447 by the first Spanish governor of La Gomera, Hernán Peraza the Elder. Restored in 1997, it is the only remaining fragment of the town's fortifications. Torre del Conde is a reminder of a tragic uprising in the town. In 1448, Beatriz de Bobadilla, wife of Hernán Peraza the Younger, barricaded herself within its walls after her husband was killed by a Guanche in revenge for his illicit affair with a native princess. When help arrived from Gran Canaria, Beatriz avenged herself by putting almost every male Guanche on Gomera to death.

The island's main church is the **Iglesia de la Virgen de la Asunción** in Calle Real. The foundations were laid in the mid-15th century and Christopher Columbus is said to have knelt down to pray in the church's dim interior before continuing on his first

voyage. **Casa de Colón**, at 56 Calle Real, is where Columbus is said to have stayed before setting off for the New World, while the **Pozo de Colón**, a well standing in the courtyard of a former customs building, has the inscription "With this water America was baptized".

The Gothic defensive tower of Torre del Conde

Another sight to look out for is the small **Ermita de San Sebastián**. Built around 1450, this is the oldest church on the island, and is dedicated to La Gomera's patron saint.

Heading towards **Mirador de la Hila**, which offers views over the whole of San Sebastián, the road leads to the **Parador de San Sebastián**. This comfortable hotel was built in 1976 and is a modern replica of a Canary colonial mansion.

ENVIRONS: Some 4 km (2 miles) north, the gravel road divides: one route descends towards the quiet beach at **Playa de Abalo**; the other leads to **Ermita de Nuestra Señora de Guadalupe** – every five years a statue of the Virgin Mary is carried to San Sebastián from here (the next "Bajada" is in 2003).

Hermigua ❷

🏚 500. 🚌 ℹ️ near Iglesia de la Encarnación, 922 144 025.

A WINDING ROAD leads from San Sebastián to Hermigua. Along the route, the scenery is attractive and varied with weathered rocks, forests of willow and laurel, juniper groves, deep ravines and lush green valleys.

Hermigua, known as Mulagua during the times of Guanches, was once an important town but is today little more than a village. The fertile soil in the lower

---

CHRISTOPHER COLUMBUS (1451–1506)

The name "Isla Colombina" evokes La Gomera's links with Christopher Columbus. Columbus stopped here three times, in 1492, 1493 and 1498. The island provided his fleet with food and fresh water and was a good launch pad for his historic expeditions. The many stories surrounding his visits include an alleged romance with Beatriz de Bobadilla. Columbus will always remain an unofficial patron of the island and the Fiesta Colombina, held on 6 September each year, commemorates his first voyage.

Statue of Columbus in Playa de las Américas

regions of Barranco de Monteforte still allows cultivation of grapes, bananas and dates.

Today the only evidence of past glories is a handful of old buildings along the small scenic streets and the **Convento de Santo Domingo de Guzmán** in the Valle Alto district. Dating from the 16th century, the church's interior features a fine 19th-century image of the Madonna by Fernando Estévez.

Hermigua is famous for its handmade rugs and other woven products. These can be seen and purchased in **Los Telares**, the local handicraft centre. Nearby is **Playa de Hermigua** – covered with shingle, it is not the most beautiful of beaches and is subject to rough weather.

ENVIRONS: An hour's hike along the footpath, to the northeast, brings you to **Playa de la Caleta**, one of the best black sand beaches on the island.

Banana plantation on the coast near Agulo

The pretty Iglesia de la Encarnación in Hermigua

Agulo ❸

🏛 1,200. 🚌

THE 17TH-CENTURY TOWN of Agulo lies in the north-eastern part of the island, high above the sea at the foot of a natural rock amphitheatre and surrounded by banana plantations. Together with the nearby hamlet of Lepe, inhabited by hardly more than handful of crofters, this is a picturesque little place and a popular destination for sightseers around La Gomera.

One unique feature of Agulo's architecture is the church of **San Marcos** (1939). Moorish in design, its four white domes are visible from far away. The town's best-known native son is the painter José Aguiar (1895–1976) who was born in Cuba of Gomeran parents, and spent his childhood in Agulo.

ENVIRONS: A steep, twisting road leads upwards from Agulo to **Mirador de Abrante**. This stone terrace offers a splendid view over the rocky coast and the ocean and is a fine spot to appreciate Mount Teide on Tenerife. A little further along the road, at the end of a ravine, is the village of La Palmita, renowned for its traditional lifestyle.

Vallehermoso ❹

🏛 1,800. 🚌 🛈 Avda. de Guillermo Ascanio, 18, 922 800 181.

VALLEHERMOSO TRANSLATES as "beautiful valley" and the surrounding agricultural landscape is evidence of the island's fertile soil. Some 17 km (11 miles) along a winding road from Agulo, this compact town, with its bustling centre (including shops, a post office, a bank and a petrol station) is a good starting point for sightseeing and walking tours around this green and pleasant region.

At the centre of the town is the Iglesia San Juan Bautista, which was designed by the Tenerife architect, Antonio

Pintor. One of the town's other attractions is a small park enlivened by bizarre groups of roughly hewn sculptural figures.

ENVIRONS: A short way to the north is **Playa de Vallehermoso**, which is good for windsurfing. Those who prefer to swim in calmer waters can make use of the swimming pool built next to the pebble beach.

Some 4 km (2 miles) to the north is **Los Órganos** – an impressive section of steep cliff that can be seen only from the sea, on cruising trips from Valle Gran Rey, Playa de Santiago or San Sebastián. This basalt wall, 80 m (262 ft) high and 200 m (656 ft) wide, resembles the pipes of an organ and is one of the most unusual (and least accessible) attractions on La Gomera.

Just 2 km (1 mile) to the east, along the road to Agulo, is the **Roque Cano**. This 650-m (2,132-ft) high fang-shaped rock was created by erosion of a volcanic peak.

Las Rosas, situated just 11 km (7 miles) from Vallehermoso, is a popular stopping place for coach tours. It has a restaurant where tourists are treated to demonstrations of El Silbo – the island's famous whistle language *(see p128)*.

Mother and Father **in Vallehermoso's park**

Black sand beach at Valle Gran Rey

Valle Gran Rey **5**

🏠 3,600. 🚌 ⛴ 🛈 La Playa, Calle de la Noria, 922 805 458.

THE CENTRE OF tourism on the island, Valle Gran Rey ("valley of the great king") was known even before the Spanish conquest of Gomera, when it was named Orone after a Guanche leader. Today's Valle Gran Rey is really a complex of several seaside villages – **La Calera**, **La Playa**, **La Puntilla** and **Vueltas** – which are the measure of the tourism boom that has even reached La Gomera. The developing estates try hard to meet the demands of modern European guests, particularly Germans, who look for comfort but are also keen to sample a different lifestyle. The place attracts many visitors who come not only for the idyllic scenery, but also for the excellent new pensions and restaurants. The magnificent Atlantic waves will satisfy even the most demanding surfing fanatics.

La Calera, with its picturesque setting in the midst of banana plantations, has been nicknamed the Montmartre of La Gomera, thanks to its small boutiques and cosy restaurants. It is regarded as one of the archipelago's prettiest towns and the house prices here are some of the highest on the island. Like La Playa, it also has a small beach.

The harbour at **Vueltas** offers hydrofoil links to Los Cristianos on Tenerife, as well as short cruises along the coast of La Gomera and to

Los Órganos. It is also used by fishing boats and numerous yachts. Several restaurants tempt visitors with tasty dishes of freshly caught fish. The most scenic road on the island is surrounded by massive basalt rocks and runs through the valley, renowned for its fertility. Local crops include dates, bananas, papayas, avocados, mangoes and tomatoes. Small fields,

New houses at the mouth of the Valle Gran Rey

cutting into the valley slopes in the form of terraces, are similar to Balinese rice fields.

For hikers there are several walking trails, representing various degrees of difficulty. Above the town, at the entrance to the valley, is a **viewpoint** made according to a design by César Manrique, and featuring one of the island's best restaurants.

ENVIRONS: Perched above the valley, 11 km (7 miles) to the north, is the village of **Arure**, which prior to the island's conquest used to be its main centre. Today the place has a desolate look about it and is known mainly for its excellent *miel de palma* – "palm honey". The palms from which the honey is made have flanges fitted around their trunks to protect them against hungry ants.

The nearby **Mirador del Santo** offers a splendid view over the ravines and on to La Palma and El Hierro.

El Cercado **6**

🚌 Chipude.

THIS SMALL VILLAGE is best-known for its handicrafts, especially the primitively shaped earthenware products that are made of dark Gomera clay, without the use of a potter's wheel.

Local traditions are also being upheld by a small number of bars offering traditional cuisine.

EL SILBO GOMERA

Long before the invention of the telephone, Gomera's inhabitants needed a way of communicating across the island's inhospitable terrain. A unique whistle language, known as El Silbo, was the solution. Modulating the whistle by changing finger positions produced many different sounds to produce a limited vocabulary, which could be transmitted up to 4 km (2 miles). Nowadays the whistle is just used to impress tourists but the local Guanches once relied on it when threatened or during hunting expeditions.

Cupping the hands to carry the sound further

Terraced fields of El Cercado

ENVIRONS: Some 3 km (2 miles) to the south, at the foot of **La Fortaleza** – a large basalt rock that is almost as flat as a table top – lies **Chipude**. At 1,050 m (3,444 ft) above sea level, this is the highest village on La Gomera. It is known for its 16th-century church, the Iglesia de la Virgen de la Candelaria. Like El Cercado, Chipude is renowned as a pottery village. A steep country road that later becomes a walking trail leads from El Cercado to **La Laguna Grande** – an information point at the entrance to the Parque Nacional de Garajonay.

Some 15 km (9 miles) to the south is **La Dama**. Surrounded by banana plantations, this small village is poised high above the ocean.

Parque Nacional de Garajonay ❼

See pp130–31.

Alajeró ❽

🏠 *1,150.* 🚌 📷 *Fiesta del Paso (Sep).*

Aⁿ TYPICAL GOMERA village, Alajeró sprawls along a mountain road in the southern part of the island. Most of the village's inhabitants make a living by growing bananas. The 16th-century **Iglesia del Salvador** is one of the few remains of the village's historic past.

From Alajeró a path leads westward, along a very deep ravine, to **La Manteca**. Though many of the people who were born in the area have left in search of a better life, this ghost village, set in a very picturesque spot, is one of the few villages to be totally abandoned.

ENVIRONS: In Agalán, 2 km (1 mile) north of Alajeró down a cobbled road, is the island's only surviving dragon tree. The **Drago de Agalán** is about 150 years old.

Playa de Santiago ❾

🏠 *1,600.* 🚌 ℹ️ *Casa de Cultura, Avenida Marítima, 922 895 650.*

Pᴸᴬʸᴬ ᴅᴇ sᴀɴᴛɪᴀɢᴏ plays a vital role in La Gomera's transport system. It lies at the junction of two ravines – **Barranco de los Cocos** and **Barranco de Santiago** – and has a fishing harbour and a newly constructed airport, situated on a bare stretch of land to the west. In addition, the town lies along the road that runs in a loop around the southern part of the island.

Traditional pottery made in El Cercado

As recently as 50 years ago Playa de Santiago was probably the busiest centre on the island with a thriving food industry, a small shipyard and a harbour with facilities for the export of the local cash crops, including bananas and tomatoes. Then, in the 1970s, an economic crisis hit and the town went into a steep decline.

Affordable holidays provided the town's route back to prosperity and these days Playa de Santiago is orientated mainly towards tourism. It is the second largest resort on the island, besides Valle Gran Rey, and is slowly but surely returning to its past glory.

Visitors are attracted mainly by the weather, since the place is believed to be the sunniest spot on La Gomera. Further temptations include the local beaches and the modern hotel and beach club facilities.

If proof were needed of Playa de Santiago's tourist-friendly credentials then look no further than the **Jardín Tecina**. The complex has numerous bars, restaurants, tennis courts and a new golf course. Perched on top of cliffs, the complex consists of unobtrusive white bungalows, built in the local style. A lift, running in a shaft carved into the rock face, whisks guests to the beach and the Club Laurel beach club, which has a huge salt-water pool and a good restaurant. To the east of the hotel are other beaches, including **Tapahuga**, **Chinguarime** and **Playa del Medio**.

Shingle beach in Playa de Santiago

Parque Nacional de Garajonay ❼

COVERING AN AREA of 400 sq km (154 sq miles), Gomera's national park is the largest intact area of ancient woodland in the archipelago. The unique weather conditions, caused by the constant flow of mist produced when the cool Atlantic trade winds encounter warm breezes, ensure constant dew and humidity conducive to the growth of some 450 species of plants and trees. The vegetation often reaches unprecedented sizes, providing an illustration of what a Mediterranean forest looked like before the last Ice Age. So precious is this region that it is the only national park in Spain to be declared a World Heritage Site by UNESCO.

Walking Trails
The high viewpoints situated along the park trails provide fantastic views over to Tenerife.

La Laguna Grande
Often shrouded in mist, La Laguna Grande is a good stopping-off point for walks around the park. It also features an excellent restaurant, a children's playground and a picnic area.

El Cercado
The village, enjoying a scenic position and easily reached by bus, provides a starting point for walks around the park.

Chipude
This village, on the outskirts of the park, has a small hotel and restaurant.

Epina

Banda de las Rosas

TF 713

VALLE GRAN RAY

▲ QUEMADO 1136

Las Hayas

El Cercado

Chipude

Igua

PL
DE SANTIA

0 km   1

0 miles   1

VEGETATION

The term *laurisilva*, meaning "laurel grove", is used to describe the ancient laurel forest at the heart of the park. The evergreen laurel trees grow to 20 m (65 ft). These trees provide large areas of the park with a thick ceiling of green, which keeps in much of the mist and provides enough shade to keep walkers cool on the many hiking trails that wind through the forest. As well as laurel trees, the park has dense tree heather and juniper groves.

Lichen hanging from the branches of tree heather

KEY

═	Major road
═	Other road
•••	Footpath
━	Park boundary
⋯	Seasonal river
☀	Viewpoint

Mirador de Vallehermoso
From this fine viewpoint, just inside the park boundary and surrounded by dense heather, you can get a magnificent overview of the park and the north side of the island.

Ravines
The park is criss-crossed by many densely wooded ravines, which provide shelter for numerous species of rare birds, including the long-toed Canary pigeon.

Garajonay
At 1,487 m (4,877 ft), El Alto de Garajonay is La Gomera's highest mountain. A marked trail leads to the summit.

Visitors' Centre
The excellent visitor centre, near Las Rosas, has craft workshops, an exhibition on Gomera handicrafts, a well-labelled garden, and a pleasant Canary restaurant.

Los Roques
The volcanic formations, including Zarcita (1,236 m/4,054 ft), Carmen (1,140 m/3,739 ft) and Agando (1,250 m/4,100 ft), are situated just outside the park's boundaries, and are best seen from Mirador El Bailadero.

EL HIERRO

EL HIERRO IS *the smallest and westernmost island of the archipelago. Known locally as "La Isla Chiquita" – the Small Island – it occupies a mere 278 sq km (107 sq miles). Rural and, for the most part, untouched by tourism thanks to its lack of sandy beaches, the entire island has only 8,000 or so inhabitants, a quarter of whom live in the island's capital – Valverde.*

The shape of El Hierro is the result of a strong earthquake that struck the island some 50,000 years ago. At that time one third of the island broke away from its northern side and sank beneath the ocean waves, creating the El Golfo bay. The most recent volcanic eruption on this mountainous island, numbering 500 volcanic peaks, occurred more than 200 years ago.

Prior to the Spanish invasion of 1403, the island's population consisted of Bimbache tribes. Following the island's conquest most of these tribes fell victim to slave traders and their land was appropriated by Norman and Castilian settlers. A feudal system, introduced at that time, survived until the mid-19th century.

Aeonium, growing on the rocks

Today, the population lives mainly off agriculture, growing grapes and bananas, as well as almonds, peaches, potatoes and tomatoes. As elsewhere, fishing is another key element of the local economy, particularly on the southern coast.

Tourism plays little part in the economy of the island. The accommodation on offer extends to some 800 beds (taken mainly by Canary islanders in July and August). The pine forest camping site of Hoya del Morcillo is also very popular.

There is no industry on El Hierro, but handicrafts thrive, particularly pottery, weaving and woodcarving. Many tourists shop for local products, particularly at village markets where buyers and sellers are entertained by folk musicians and dancers.

Natural pools in Charco Manso lava near Valverde

◁ **Red and yellow carpets of flowering plants covering the rocks**

Exploring El Hierro

EL HIERRO'S CHIEF draw is its romantic wildness. Before Columbus's voyages, this was the westernmost point of the known world. Even today the island is largely untouched by tourism and retains its "end of the world" feel. The magnificent mountain scenery compensates for the lack of sandy beaches. Wild terrain, shrouded in mist and often overgrown with dense pine forest, attracts nature lovers. Some less accessible places can only be reached on foot. Equally attractive is the maritime nature reserve, to the south, a paradise for divers. The local cuisine revolves around fresh fish and the island is known for its delicious wines.

LOCATOR MAP

POZO DE SABINOSA

EL SABINAR 5

SABINOSA 4

SANTUARIO DE NUESTRA SEÑORA DE LOS REYES

6

HI

EL JULÁN

0 km   2

0 miles   2

Giant junipers, twisted into fanciful shapes by the wind, in El Sabinar

SEE ALSO

• *Where to Stay* pp162–3.

• *Where to Eat* p175.

SIGHTS AT A GLANCE

El Sabinar 5
Frontera 2
Isora 8
La Restinga 7
Las Puntas 3
Puerto de la Estaca 10
Sabinosa 4
San Andrés 9
Santuario de Nuestra Señora
  de los Reyes 6
Valverde 1

Tiny Puerto de la Estaca, on the east coast – the island's only ferry harbour

EL GOLFO
BAY

TAMADUSTE

MOCANAL

VALVERDE ❶

GUARAZOCA

HI 1

LAS PUNTAS ❸

TIÑOR

❿ ⚓
*PUERTO
DE LA ESTACA*

❾
*SAN
ANDRÉS*

TIGADAY ❷ *FRONTERA*

❽ *ISORA*

HI 1

HI 30

EL PINAR

TAIBIQUE

GETTING THERE
El Hierro has air links with Tenerife,
Gran Canaria and La Palma. A regular
ferry service connects Puerto de la
Estaca with Tenerife and La Gomera. In
view of the scarcity of bus services and
their limited range, it is necessary to hire
a car when planning sightseeing. Ideally,
rental cars should be booked before you
arrive; most companies will meet you at
the airport. The roads have recently
been improved, but some more remote
places require an all-terrain vehicle.

❼
LA RESTINGA

KEY

🟫	Major road
▬	Other road
▬	Scenic route
✈	Airport
⚓	Ferry harbour
✲	Viewpoint

Iglesia de la Concepción in Valverde

Pools in Pozo de las Calcosas near Valverde

Valverde ❶

🏘 2,000. 🚌 ℹ️ C/Dr. Quineiro, 11, 922 550 302. 📅 Fiesta de San Isidro (15 May), Bajada de la Virgen de los Reyes (every 4 years in Jul).

THE FULL NAME of the island's capital is La Villa de Santa María de Valverde. Unlike the other island capitals, Valverde has no harbour. The small town is poised on the slope of an evergreen valley (hence the name), and is extremely quiet and often rather foggy.

The only noteworthy local historic sight is **Iglesia Santa María de la Concepción**. Built in 1767 on the site of a former 16th-century chapel, this vast church was erected in thanksgiving for the repulse of a pirate attack. The belfry includes a large clock brought from Paris in 1886. The main feature of the interior is the Baroque altar. The town hall, standing opposite the church, took 30 years to build (1910–40), and is in the local style.

ENVIRONS: Tamaduste, 10 km (6 miles) to the northeast, is the islanders' favourite resort, and has a quiet cove with a pleasant beach.

Charco Manso, 8 km (5 miles) to the north, is a complex of natural pools set in volcanic rock. These are reached by a narrow road with hairpin bends. The sea here can be dangerous and swimming is not advisable.

Pozo de las Calcosas, 8 km (5 miles) to the northwest, is a good place to swim and features pools similar to those of Charco Manso, and a number of black stone huts on the ocean shore, all reached by steep steps.

An unforgettable view over **El Golfo** bay is to be had from **Mirador de La Peña**, 8 km (5 miles) to the west. The restaurant here was built in 1988 following a design by César Manrique.

Frontera ❷

🚌 📅 Fiesta de la Virgen de la Candelaria (Aug).

MANY OF THE inhabitants of the island's second largest town make their living by growing grapes. These are the source of Viña Frontera – wines famous throughout the archipelago.

The **Iglesia de la Candelaria**, standing on the outskirts of the town, was built in 1818 and occupies the entire square. The interior, covered with a wooden ceiling, features a striking, gilded altar. Standing above the church, on a hill of red volcanic ash, is a belfry that is visible from afar.

ENVIRONS: Tigaday, 1 km (half a mile) to the west, is a relatively large village and a great wine-producing centre. It is the starting point for the road to Las Puntas.

Las Puntas ❸

ℹ️ 922 559 081 📅 Fiesta de San Juan (24 Jun).

STANDING ON THE old wharf, where until 1930 ships arrived bringing supplies, is the Hotel Puntagrande, which had an entry in the *Guinness Book of Records* as the world's smallest hotel. It began life in 1884 as a harbour building until it was transformed into a hotel. It has four rooms, a bar and a restaurant. Although it is difficult to get a room here it is still worth coming in order to admire the beautiful sunset and enjoy a swim in one of the rocky coves.

Another noteworthy local feature is the **Roques de Salmor**. These scenic rock formations rise from the sea, and are one of the island's most important bird colonies.

ENVIRONS: A short way to the south, **Casas de Guinea** is an old Norman settlement dating from the early 15th century. Along with Las Montañetas, it claims to be the oldest village on El Hierro. Today it houses the Ecomuseo de Guinea – a complex of former shepherds' huts that have been restored and kitted out with furniture from different periods.

The world's smallest hotel in Las Puntas

A small site known as **Lagartario**, above the museum, is used to provide natural breeding conditions for a rare species of lizard from Salmor, found only in El Hierro. A project to restore this species of giant, 1.5-m (5-ft) lizard, extinct since the 1930s, commenced in 1975. Public viewing of the giant lizards is limited; apply to the town hall in Tigaday. Skeletons of the extinct giant lizards can today be seen in London and Vienna's main natural history museums.

🏛 **Ecomuseo de Guinea**
⏰ *10am–2pm and 4–6pm Tue–Sun*
⬤ *Mon.* 📷

Pozo de la Salud, poised on the shore of El Golfo bay

Sabinosa ➍

🚌 📷 *San Simón (end Oct).*

Swamped with flowers, Sabinosa is pleasantly remote, with picturesque narrow streets and paths. Poised high up on a steep slope, overlooking almost all of El Golfo bay, it is known for its "well of health" – **Pozo de la Salud** – which can be found by the sea below Sabinosa. The water, which must be drawn up by bucket from a well, is highly radioactive and is believed to be something of a cure-all for any number of ailments. A modern hotel, built here in 1996 to cater to the needs of health-seeking visitors, is the only one of its type in the Canary Islands.

BAJADA DE LA VIRGEN DE LOS REYES

In the early 18th century, during a period of drought, the Madonna was carried down from the Nuestra Señora de los Reyes by villagers to Valverde and, hey presto, it rained. Since then a feast has been held every four years (2005, 2009) on the first or second Saturday in June. The statue of the Holy Mother follows the same route along unmade country lanes – the Camino de la Virgen – and is carried on a litter to Valverde. The ceremony, which begins at 5am and goes on till late, is accompanied by a week of merriment, with many villagers dressed in red and white costumes.

The "Descent of the Virgin"

ENVIRONS: Playa de Arenas, 6 km (4 miles) to the west, is a sandy beach, popular with tourists and locals alike.

Some 10 km (6 miles) to the west is **Playa de Verodal**. This small, scenic, windswept beach, with its rust-coloured volcanic sands, lies at the foot of a high cliff. Accessible via a bumpy, coarse-gravel road, it is generally considered to be the most beautiful stretch of beach on the island.

East of Sabinosa, the road runs to **Los Llanillos**, a tiny village with a small chapel built of blocks of volcanic rock. Standing by the roadside is a workshop producing all shapes and sizes of birdcages. A little further along, the road reaches **Charco Azul**, where rocky coves with turquoise water tempt visitors to swim.

El Sabinar ➎

The name of this upland, swept by Atlantic winds and crossed by a gorge, derives from the local word *sabina* (juniper). It features almost 300 white-trunked juniper trees that have bent and twisted into bizarre shapes.

El Sabinar is reached by a road that starts out as asphalt and later becomes a dirt track running among pastures and crossing cattle gates. It is a little under 4 km (2 miles) from the sanctuary of Nuestra Señora de los Reyes.

ENVIRONS: Mirador de Basco, 3 km (2 miles) to the north, offers a view (on sunny days) not only of El Golfo, but also of La Palma, La Gomera and Tenerife.

The island's symbol – a wind-twisted juniper tree in El Sabinar

Santuario de Nuestra Señora de los Reyes, surrounded by a low wall

Santuario de Nuestra Señora de los Reyes 6

S ET AMONG WOODED hills in the western part of the island, surrounded by a low wall, is the pilgrim sanctuary of the Holy Mother of the Kings (Magi) – the patron saint of El Hierro. Inside is a statue of the Madonna, kept on a silver litter. Every four years, in the course of a ceremonial procession known as the Bajada de la Virgen de los Reyes, the statue is carried to Valverde *(see p137).*

Legend has it that a French ship was becalmed near the shores of the island, and the crew were only able to survive thanks to the help of El Hierro's inhabitants. Having no money to pay for food and water, the captain presented the islanders with a statue of the Virgin Mary. On the same day, 6 January 1577, the day of the Epiphany, a strong wind sent the ship on her way.

ENVIRONS: The **Faro de Orchilla** lighthouse is 7 km (4 miles) to the southwest. The road leading to it is initially asphalt but later becomes an unmade track. In AD 150, the Greek geographer Ptolemy declared this western end of the island to be the end of the world. In 1634, the zero meridian was drawn through this point and remained recognized as such until 1884, when it was moved to Greenwich. Even so, El Hierro still refers to itself as "Isla del Meridiano" and visitors can buy a decorated certificate confirming that they have crossed the zero meridian.

La Restinga 7

🏠 🎭 *Fiesta de San Juan (24 Jun), Fiesta de la Virgen del Carmen (16 Jul).*

L A RESTINGA IS a small fishing harbour and yacht basin, situated on the sunniest, southern end of the island. It is also one of the most popular resorts on El Hierro. There's a large hotel and a small apartment complex and the coastal road – Avenida Marítima – features a wide variety of shops, bars and restaurants. This is a good place to sit out and watch the world drift by.

In the centre is a small, black sand beach that is sheltered by the large harbour. Though generally rather quiet, La Restinga has plenty of facilities for water sports including diving. The local waters around here have protected status and feature rich marine fauna and flora combined with underwater gullies and interesting rock formations to explore. Diving centres are open all year round and offer trips and night-time expeditions.

ENVIRONS: A short way to the northwest is **Bahía de Naos** –

which is known principally as the place where Jean de Béthencourt landed in 1403.

Some 10 km (6 miles) to the northwest is **Cala del Tacorón** – a number of small coves carved into the volcanic shore of Mar de las Calmas. Here, swimmers find the clear waters and steps down to the sea particularly inviting.

Cueva Don Justo, 2 km (1 mile) to the north, within the Montaña de Prim massif, is a great attraction to potholers, with its 6-km (4-mile) labyrinth of underground volcanic tunnels.

Spectacular view from Mirador de las Playas

Isora 8

🎭 *Fiesta de San José (19 Mar).*

S ITUATED IN THE eastern part of the island, Isora is a picturesque assembly of several hamlets, and is famous for cheese production. It is well worth trying to arrive here at dawn to admire the magnificent sunrise.

Volcanic peaks around La Restinga

Another attraction is the famous *lucha canaria* games, when feats of Canary-style wrestling take place at the local stadium.

ENVIRONS: About 1 km (half a mile) to the south, at the edge of the mountain range of El Risco de los Herrenos, is the **Mirador de Isora**, offering enchanting panoramic views over the ocean. A narrow footpath, some 4 km (2 miles) long, leads down to the coast.

About 3 km (2 miles) to the south is **Mirador de las Playas** – a high viewpoint, set among Canary pines. The broad terrace provides magnificent panoramic views over Las Playas bay, from Roque de la Bonanza up to the parador.

El Pinar, 6 km (4 miles) to the south, is the collective name often used to describe two villages – **Las Casas** and **Taibique** – which has a main street featuring bars, restaurants, shops, a hotel and bank. The local Artesania Cerámica sells ceramics and handmade jewellery. There is also a small church – **Iglesia de San Antonio**. As well as displaying local relics, the **Museo de Panchillo** also sells figs and honey.

🏛 **Museo de Panchillo**
C/El Lagar, 53. 🕐 *no fixed opening hours.*

San Andrés ❾

📷 *Fiesta de la Apañada (1st Sun in Jun).*

A HEADY 1,100 m (3,600 ft) above sea level, San Andrés is often shrouded in thick fog. This small agricultural town tends to be hot in summer, but winters are cold, with strong winds.

Its inhabitants live mainly off the land, cultivating crops and grazing sheep and goats. Despite the fertile soil, the unfavourable weather

Mist-shrouded fields around San Andrés

conditions cause many of them to leave this rough and inhospitable terrain.

ENVIRONS: To the north, an asphalt road a little under 4 km (2 miles) long, which later becomes a footpath, leads to **Árbol Santo** – the holy Bimbache tree, known to locals as the *Garoé*. According to legend, water once flowed from the tree to give the island its entire supply (in fact the pine tree's needles had the ability to accumulate large quantities of water). The ancient tree was destroyed in 1949 by a hurricane; in its place grows a lime tree, planted here in 1957.

Some 2 km (1 mile) to the southwest is **Mirador de Jinama**. It is reached by road through fields divided by dry stone walls. In clear weather, the viewpoint provides a fine panorama over El Golfo bay.

Goat's cheese produced in San Andrés

Puerto de la Estaca ❿

📷 *San Telmo (14 Sep).*

U NTIL 1972, when the airport opened, this small harbour, cut off from the land by high volcanic cliffs, was the island's only link with the world. The name of the harbour, built in 1906, is derived from the word *estaca*, which is a type of wooden pile, to which fishermen tied their boats.

ENVIRONS: The **Roque de la Bonanza**, a bare basalt rock rising vertically from the sea a few steps from the shore, is 9 km (6 miles) to the south. It can be reached via a beautiful coastline road that is in the shadow of a steep volcanic slope. Take care: at one point, the road passes through a single-lane tunnel with intermittently functioning traffic lights.

Some 2 km (1 mile) further south, set amid picturesque scenery, stands the **Parador del Hierro** – the most comfortable hotel on the island. The hotel has an isolated waterfront location, with views of the cliff walls round the bay, and was built in the Castilian style between 1973 and 1976. Its opening was delayed by five years, due to the slow building of the road that terminates here.

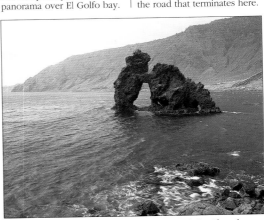
Roque de la Bonanza or "Rock of the Silent Ocean" in Las Playas bay

LA PALMA

THE PALMEROS REFER to *La Palma as La Isla Bonita – "the Beautiful Island", or La Isla Verde – "the Green Island". Both nicknames are justified since the island is both extremely pretty and strikingly lush. The rich vegetation of ferns and laurel forests, together with the fine domestic gardens, regarded as the best-kept in the archipelago, make this one of the greenest spots in the region.*

The island's greenery is in large part thanks to the highest rainfall in the Canary Islands. In spring and autumn the sun stays behind the clouds for an average of 63 days and the plants enjoy excellent growing conditions.

The fifth largest island of the archipelago, La Palma is shaped like the head of a stone axe. It is claimed to be among the world's most mountainous islands, in terms of its height to area ratio (the island is 706 sq km/273 sq miles). The highest peak – Roque de los Muchachos – measures 2,426 m (7,957 ft). Like the rest of the archipelago, La Palma is a volcanic island and its volcanoes cannot be regarded as truly extinct. The last eruption occurred in 1971 in the south of the island, where the black lava fields and reddish brown volcanic rocks contrast with the lush greenery of the remaining part of the island. Opinion is divided as to when the next eruption is likely to take place.

Statue of a "dancing dwarf"

The island's population engages mainly in agriculture. An abundance of water ensures good crops of grapes, avocados, bananas and tobacco. The latter is used to make cigars that are considered by experts to be as good as the cigars produced in Cuba. La Palma is also known for its production of honey while, like many of the islands, fishing plays an important part in the local economy. Mass tourism remains less of a feature here, due in part to the shortage of pleasant beaches along the island's craggy coastline, though there are good tourist centres on the west and east coasts.

Glittering volcanic rocks, providing a fairytale-like spectacle of colour around Pico de la Cruz

◁ **Green areas of Caldera de Taburiente national park**

Exploring La Palma

L A PALMA IS excellent for walking trips and can cater for all tastes from a gentle stroll to a strenuous hike. Its varied landscapes, from the volcanic ash region of El Pinar to the lush, almost tropical forests of Los Tilos, fully compensate for the lack of great historic sights. Free of the bustle of the larger resort islands, there's ample opportunity for rest and relaxation, while the coastal waters of La Palma, rich in aquatic life, will attract divers. An excursion along the volcano trail, in the south of the island, is one of the highlights of a visit here, as is sampling the local wines and cuisine.

Colourful wooden balconies on the sea promenade at Santa Cruz de La Palma

SIGHTS AT A GLANCE

0 km   3

0 miles   3

SEE ALSO

• *Where to Stay* p163.

• *Where to Eat* p175.

GETTING THERE

La Palma has air links with Tenerife, Gran Canaria and El Hierro, as well as with some cities of mainland Spain. There are charter flights to and from several Western European airports. Planes touch down at the airport on the east coast, which connects to Santa Cruz de La Palma via an 8-km (5-mile) motorway. Ferries from Tenerife and La Gomera sail to Santa Cruz de La Palma harbour. Most of the island's towns and villages have bus transport. However, in order to explore the more remote parts of La Palma, you will have to hire a car.

BARLOVENTO 5

LOS SAUCES 4 SAN ANDRÉS

3 LOS TILOS

1032

RQUE CIONAL DE LA DERA TABURIENTE

LP 1

PUNTALLANA

LAS NIEVES 2

1 SANTA CRUZ DE LA PALMA

BREÑA ALTA

BREÑA BAJA

13 MAZO

RUTA LOS VOLCANES 12

LP 1

TIGALATE

MONTE DE LUNA

11 FUENCALIENTE DE LA PALMA

Astronomical observatory on top of the Roque de los Muchachos

KEY

▬	Major road
═	Other road
▬	Scenic route
✈	Airport
⚓	Ferry harbour
☀	Viewpoint

Bathing area in Charco Azul, near San Andrés

Santa Cruz de La Palma ●

SANTA CRUZ DE LA PALMA, situated on a bay known to the Guanches as Timibucar, has from its early days played a vital role in the economic and political life of Spain. During the 16th century it was the third most important port in the entire Spanish empire, after Seville and Antwerp. It was also considered the best shipbuilding centre in the Canary Islands. The town's wealth attracted pirates, who plundered it on several occasions, including a particularly brutal raid in 1553 by Jean-Paul de Billancourt, otherwise known as "Pegleg". However, Santa Cruz de La Palma always managed to recover and today it is the capital of the island and an important communications centre.

Calle O'Daly, the main street of Santa Cruz's old town

Exploring Santa Cruz de La Palma

Poised on the slopes of a volcanic crater, this is one of the Canary Islands' loveliest towns. Its compact layout features many modern houses and a picturesque old town. The centre developed within a short space of time and consequently has a harmonious appearance.

But Santa Cruz de La Palma is more than a collection of colonial architectural relics. Numerous bars and restaurants along Avenida Marítima are popular with locals and tourists alike, and add to the town's atmosphere.

Statues of musicians in Calle O'Daly

🏛 Calle O'Daly

The main street, now turned into a pedestrian precinct, bears testimony to the town's former wealth and prestige. It was named after an Irish banana merchant who settled here. The street is lined on both sides with historic houses and residences. The most outstanding of these are the **Palacio de Salazar** (No. 22), which dates from the early 17th century and features distinctive wooden balconies, and the 19th-century **Casa Pinto** (No. 2).

🏛 Ermita de San Sebastián

Plaza de San Sebastián.
This small chapel, which is usually closed, is one of several in Santa Cruz; the others include the 16th-century **Ermita de Nuestra Señora de la Luz**, which stands in the picturesque San Sebastián Square. Inside is a statue of Saint Catherine, which was brought here from Antwerp.

🏛 Plaza de España

At the very heart of Santa Cruz lies the Plaza de España. This triangular space, with its 16th-century fountain, is surrounded by historic buildings. The statue in the middle is of Manuel Díaz Hernández (1774–1863), a priest of San Salvador church who preached political liberalism in his sermons.

🏛 Iglesia de El Salvador

Plaza de España. ⏰ 8:30am–1pm & 4–8:30pm daily.
Built at the end of the 15th century, the church acquired its present shape in the second half of the 16th century. This is the most monumental example of the Canary Islands' Renaissance architecture. Its façade has a portal in the form of a triumphal arch (1503) – an allegory of Christ and his Church. The interior features a *mudéjar* (Spanish-Moorish) coffered ceiling and sculptures by Fernando Estévez.

🏛 Casas Consistoriales

Plaza de España.
Casas Consistoriales, formerly the bishop's palace and now the town hall, was built in 1559–63. Its Renaissance façade, resting on columned arcades, is decorated with the bust of Philip II, carved in low relief, and the crests of La Palma and the Habsburgs. The inside walls are decorated with paintings by Mariano de Cassio, depicting island life.

🏛 Avenida Marítima

Avenida Marítima is regarded as one of the Canary Islands'

Iglesia de El Salvador in Plaza de España

most beautiful and best-preserved shorelines. At its southern end stands a dragon tree *(see p14)*, with curiously twisted branches. At the northern end of the shore stands the **Casas de los Balcones** – a row of picturesque old houses, which have been wonderfully restored, with colourful elevations, featuring beautiful wooden balconies.

Main altar in Iglesia de San Francisco

🔒 Iglesia de San Francisco
Plaza de San Francisco. ⬤ 9am–2pm & 4–6:30pm Mon–Fri. 📷

In 1508, Franciscan monks accompanying Alonso Fernándo de Lugo in his conquest of the island began to build their abbey in Santa Cruz. The church, built in the 16th–17th centuries, is one of the earliest examples of Renaissance architecture on La Palma. Outstanding features of the interior include the main altar and the coffered ceiling, as well as the richly painted décor. Today, the abbey houses the **Museo Insular** exhibiting local relics, along with Guanche skulls, stuffed animals and Spanish-school paintings.

🏛 Museo Naval
⬤ 9:30am–2:30pm Mon–Fri; summer: also 4–7pm. 📷

Near Plaza de la Alameda stands a 1940 replica of the *Santa María* – the tiny ship in which Christopher Columbus set off in 1492 to discover the New World.

The inhabitants of Santa Cruz have named the ship *El Barco de la Virgen* – the Ship of the Holy Virgin. Inside is a modest maritime museum. The core of its collection consists of fascinating old charts, navigational instruments and a variety of ships' flags.

VISITORS' CHECKLIST
👥 20,000. 🚌 ⛴ ✈ 11 km (7 miles) south. 🛈 Calle O'Daly, 8. (Casa Salazar), 922 412 106. 📅 Sat, Sun. 🎭 Carnival (Jan/Feb), Fiesta de la Cruz (3 May), Bajada de la Virgen (Jun/Jul, every 5 years).

♣ Castillo de Santa Catalina
Avenida Marítima.
This 16th-century castle is also known as Castillo Real. Similar to the **Castillo de la Virgen** – a smaller fortress standing on the opposite side of Barranco de las Nieves – it was built as a defence against pirate attacks. In 1585, the gunfire from both castles prevented Sir Francis Drake from taking over the island.

***El Barco de la Virgen**, a replica of Christopher Columbus's ship*

SANTA CRUZ DE LA PALMA
Avenida Marítima ⑥
Calle O'Daly ①
Casas Consistoriales ⑤
Ermita de San Sebastián ②
Iglesia de El Salvador ④
Plaza de España ③

KEY
🅿 Parking
🛈 Tourist information

0 m 100
0 yards 100

Rich interior of Santuario de Las Nieves

Las Nieves ❷

📮 🖼 *Bajada de la Virgen de las Nieves (Jun/Jul, every 5 years).*

T HIS VILLAGE, lying among green hills above Santa Cruz de La Palma, is the main pilgrimage centre and the most important religious shrine on the island.

Standing in a picturesque spot is the **Santuario de la Virgen de las Nieves**. Its small church was built in 1657 on the site of the original chapel. It forms a historic complex together with the neighbouring buildings: the 17th-century **Pilgrim's House**, the early 18th-century **Parish House**, and several houses that once belonged to members of the local aristocracy.

The church is a typical example of colonial Canary architecture, with wooden balcony façades, whitewashed walls and a lovely *mudéjar* (Spanish-Moorish) ceiling made of Canary pine. The lights of flickering candles, lit by the faithful, and the rich interior décor give the place its unique atmosphere. The central position on the gilded Baroque main altar is occupied by a 14th-century 82-cm (32-inch) high terracotta statue of the Madonna of the Snow, the island's patron saint, which was made in Flanders and stands on a base of Mexican silver. Her image refers not so much to the snowy peaks of the archipelago as to

her miraculous appearance during a freak August snowstorm in Rome. The side walls of the church are decorated with a row of *ex voto* canvases. These votive pictures are in thanks for numerous miracles performed by the island's patron saint, including saving a ship caught in a storm, calming the stormy seas and answering the prayers of couples hoping to have children.

Los Tilos ❸

3 km (2 miles) west of San Andrés. ℹ️ *Centro de Investigaciones e Interpretación de la Reserva de Biosfera "Los Tilos".* ⏰ *9am–4pm Mon–Fri.*

T HE ROCKY, almost vertical sides of the deep Barranco del Agua ravine are overgrown with a misty, evergreen rainforest, which includes moss-covered laurel trees – the island's largest concentration of the ancient *laurisilva* – as well as lime, myrtle and ferns.

In 1983, Los Tilos was declared a biosphere reserve by UNESCO. A 3-km (2-mile) winding asphalt road, running along the bottom of the ravine, leads to the tourist centre, with its information point and a small café.

The reserve area, measuring some 5 sq km (2 sq miles), has several marked walking trails. One of them leads to the **Mirador de las Barrandas**

viewpoint. A longer and much more difficult (6-km/4-mile) trail with steep ascents leads in a southwesterly direction to **Caldera de Marcos y Cordero**, where a determined tourist can admire the picturesque waterfalls.

San Andrés ❹

🏠 *1,100.* 🚌 🖼 *Fiesta de San Andrés (30 Nov).*

T HIS PRETTY SEASIDE village, with cobbled streets and squares planted with flowers and palms, is filled with typical local houses. At its centre stands the **Iglesia de San Andrés Apóstol**. Built as a fortified church in the 16th century and extended in the 17th century, this is one of the oldest churches in the Canary Islands. The interior features a Baroque main altar and retable and a *mudéjar*-style coffered ceiling. Look out, too, for the paintings of assorted human limbs on the wall, hung here in thanks for the supposed healing powers of the church's patron saint.

San Andrés remains under joint administration with the larger town of **Los Sauces**, hence the combined name of San Andrés y Los Sauces. The environs of both towns are famous for the cultivation of bananas and sugar cane.

The only noteworthy building in Los Sauces is the **Iglesia Nuestra Señora de Montserrat**, the largest church on the island, which dates back to 1515. Its present Neo-Romanesque appearance

The modest Iglesia de San Andrés Apóstol

is the result of refurbishment in 1960. Inside is a picture of the Madonna, attributed to the Dutch artist, Pieter Poubrus.

ENVIRONS: A short way to the south is **Charco Azul** – a tiny village set among banana tree plantations. High cliffs provide effective shelter for a natural tidal pool of a startling blue shade.

About 7 km (4 miles) to the south is **Puntallana**. One of its historic sights is the Iglesia San Juan Bautista. However, Puntallana owes most of its popularity to Playa de Nogales – a long, black sand beach backed by steep cliffs.

Picturesque gullies criss-crossing the area around Barlovento

Barlovento ❺

🏃 2,500. 🚌 🎎 Fiesta de la Virgen del Rosario (2 Aug, every 2 years).

BESIDES THE **Iglesia de Nuestra Señora**, with its altar of 1767 and some 16th–18th-century Spanish sculptures, Barlovento's main claim to fame is its fiesta held every two years in August, when the villagers recreate bloody scenes from the Battle of Lepanto (1571).

ENVIRONS: For a dip, try the **Piscinas de Fajana**, 6 km (4 miles) to the northeast where the Atlantic keeps a rock pool topped up with cool water. The nearby lighthouse at **Punta Cumplida** has been operating non-stop since 1860.

Mysterious rock carvings in La Zarza

La Zarza ❻

10 km (6 miles) west of Barlovento.

THE ARCHAEOLOGICAL SITE of La Zarza provides visible evidence of the Benahoares – the former inhabitants of La Palma – who left strange signs carved into the rock in several sites throughout the north of the island, including Roque Faro, Don Pedro and Juan Adalid. These carvings consist mostly of spirals, circles and linear figures, and have survived in their natural environment, though their meaning remains unknown.

The information centre has a small museum illustrating the everyday life of the Benahoares. The exhibition includes a 20-minute video and shows how the ancient inhabitants of the island lived, and reveals their diet, medical practices and burial rites. The illuminated screens display images of erupting volcanoes, island scenery, its flora, fauna, and a map pointing out where the rock carvings were found.

When the carvings were discovered here in 1941 they became an archaeological sensation. Apart from the puzzling pictures, the ancient inhabitants of the island also left two Aztec-style carved images: one of a man, and an abstract figure of a woman with the head of an insect.

🏛 **Parque Cultural La Zarza**
La Mata, s/n . ☎ 922 695 005.
🕐 winter: 11am–5pm; summer: 11am–7pm. 🎫

Tazacorte ❼

🏃 6,600. 🚌 🎎 Fiesta de San Miguel (29 Sep).

IN 1492, Alonso Fernandez de Lugo commenced the conquest of the island from Tazacorte. Today, the skyline of this small town, surrounded by banana plantations, is dominated by the **Iglesia de San Miguel Arcángel**. The church, built in the 16th century, was extended in 1992 and given a magnificent, abstract stained-glass window. Next to the church is a pergola lined with ceramic tiles and overgrown with bougainvillea – the traditional meeting place of the locals.

ENVIRONS: Just 12 km (7 miles) to the north is **Mirador del Time**, which provides a fine view over Los Llanos, Tazacorte, the surrounding mountains and the ocean.

Banana plantations growing almost in the centre of Tazacorte

Wide boulevard leading to Plaza España in Los Llanos de Aridane

Los Llanos de Aridane ❽

🏠 *10,000.* 🚌 🎭 *Fiesta de los Remedios (2 Jul, every 2 years).*

THE SECOND LARGEST town of La Palma is a modern affair, with the exception of the **Plaza de España**. This charming square, with laurel trees casting a pleasant shade over café tables, is a venue for concerts.

One side of the square is occupied by the **town hall**. Opposite it stands the **Iglesia de Nuestra Señora de los Remedios**. This white 16th-century church is built in the Canary colonial style. Its Baroque main altar features a 16th-century Dutch statue of its patron saint.

ENVIRONS: About 3 km (2 miles) to the east is **El Paso**, a small town famous for its handmade cigars. Its main feature is the old quarter, with traditional Canary-style buildings surrounding the **Ermita de la Virgen de la Concepción de la Bonanza**. Next to the chapel stands a modern church with Neo-Gothic furnishings, dedicated to the same saint.

A short way south of El Paso is the **Parque Paraíso de las Aves** – a combination of botanical garden and miniature zoo, housing exotic birds from many corners of the world.

Parque Nacional de la Caldera de Taburiente ❾

See pp150–51.

Puerto Naos ❿

🏠 *500.* 🚌 ℹ️ *Palmaclub, Paseo Marítimo, s/n, 922 408 121.*

A SMALL, QUIET resort, Puerto Naos features an ever-increasing number of low-built apartment complexes. Its main tourist attraction is the guaranteed good weather, with some 3,300 annual hours of sunshine.

Running along the black sand palm-lined beach, the longest on La Palma, is a small promenade with cafés, restaurants and small shops. It also features the four-star Hotel Sol Palma, opened in 1990. This modern, tiered hotel is the biggest on the island and can accommodate nearly 1,000 guests.

ENVIRONS: Charco Verde, about 2 km (1 mile) to the south, is a scenic sandy beach. The beach is sheltered from the Atlantic waves, and ideal for families.

Fuencaliente de La Palma ⓫

🏠 *1,800.* 🚌 🎭 *La Vendimia (14–30 Aug), San Martín (11 Dec).*

THE NAME OF this place derives from the words *fuente caliente*, meaning "hot spring". However, the spring has long since been swallowed by a series of volcanic eruptions.

Set amid vineyards, the small town is best-known for its sweet, heavy wine and is the home of the oldest and largest winery on the island, established in 1948. Evidence of the town's historic past can be seen in the parish church of **San Antonio Abad** (1730).

ENVIRONS: A little over 10 km (6 miles) to the south is **Punta Fuencaliente**, the southernmost point of La Palma. It features a lighthouse and a desalination plant.

Mazo ⓭

🏠 *5,300.* 🚌 🚢 *Sat, Sun.* 🎭 *Corpus Christi (May–Jun).*

MAZO IS FAMOUS for its handmade cigars (*puros*). Tourists also shop here for handicrafts including woven baskets and lacework. The **Escuela Insular de Artesanía** has these for sale and also holds demonstrations of how they are made. Other sights include the **Cerámico Molino**, known for its production of replica black Guanche vessels, and the **Museo de Corpus**, in a villa called Casa Roja, which exhibits street decorations for the feast of Corpus Christi.

The **Iglesia de San Blás** (1512), which looks out towards Tenerife, was extended in the 19th century and features a beautiful Baroque altar and richly carved decorations.

A Madonna from Mazo's San Blás

ENVIRONS: Just 4 km (2 miles) to the south is the **Cueva de Belmaco**, a cave with original Guanche inscriptions.

San Antonio volcano near Fuencaliente de La Palma

Ruta de los Volcanes ⑫

A SOMEWHAT ARDUOUS TRAIL leads along the Cumbre Vieja mountain ridge, from Refugio el Pilar (alt. 1,450 m/4,756 ft) towards Fuencaliente. The hike, which should take a fit walker some 6-7 hours, is an unforgettable experience. Winding round steep volcanic rims, the path leads past striking geological formations and provides magnificent views of the eastern and western coasts of the island.

Refugio del Pilar ①
This ridge, with a walkers' shelter, is a popular picnic spot. It can be reached by car and is a good starting point for hikes.

Fuencaliente ⑥
From here the trail continues further south, towards the nearby volcanoes of San Antonio (last eruption in 1949) and Teneguía (last eruption in 1971).

Montaña de los Charcos ②
A powerful eruption of this volcano took place in 1712 when a vast flow of lava swamped much of the southwestern part of the island.

Volcán Martín ⑤
The eruption of the volcano in 1646 destroyed the former springs (believed to be a cure for leprosy) that gave the nearby town its name.

LOS LLANOS DE ARIDANE

SANTA CRUZ DE LA PALMA

El Charco

LP 1

LP 1

Las Indias

Cráter del Duraznero ④
This crater, rising 1,902 m (6,238 ft) above sea level, was left after the eruption of San Antonio in 1949. To the left of it stands the peak of Nambroque.

Cráter del Hoyo Negro ③
The trail runs along the edge of the San Juan volcano, which most recently erupted in 1949. The crater, with its rubble of solidified lava, is a reminder of how relatively recent the eruption was.

0 km   1

0 miles   1

TIPS FOR WALKERS

Length: 19 km (12 miles).
Stopping-off points:
Fuencaliente is a good place to halt for a meal.
Note: Don't stray from the marked trail, and make sure you carry a supply of drinking water.

KEY

▬ Main trail

▬ Scenic route

═ Other road

••• Footpath

✻ Viewpoint

Parque Nacional de la Caldera de Taburiente 9

LA CALDERA DE TABURIENTE, a massive crater formed in the course of several powerful volcanic eruptions, is a natural fortress and served as a refuge for the last Benahoares when the Spanish invaded in the 15th century. Some of its walls reach up to 2,000 m (6,560 ft). Awarded national park status in 1954, the crater has many walking trails (some walks require a very good head for heights!). No roads run right through the park, and walkers should make sure they take with them enough water and a snack.

Roque de los Muchachos
Six telescopes have been placed along the steep, mountain road around Roque de los Muchachos, which passes through scrubland.

Caldera de Taburiente
The lush vegetation, much of it unique to the region, and the bare, rugged summits of the park, often shrouded in mist, appeal to lovers of nature.

ASTRONOMICAL OBSERVATORY

Thanks to their clear skies, the Canary Islands are regarded as one of the best places for conducting observations of the cosmos. The International Astrophysical Observatory near Roque de los Muchachos was opened in 1985, in the presence of King Juan Carlos and many European heads of state. Six telescopes, including the largest Anglo-Dutch one, named after William Herschel and measuring 420 cm (165 inches) in diameter, are used for night observations. There is therefore a ban between 8pm and 9am on the use of lights while driving in the park (once a year the entire island switches off its lights to make certain experiments possible).

The Herschel telescope inside the observatory

KEY

═══ Major road

── Other road

••• Footpath

━ Park boundary

┄ Seasonal river

P Parking

i Tourist information

�લ Viewpoint

0 km   1

0 miles   1

Mirador de los Andenes
These bare rocks, eroded by wind and moisture over thousands of years, have been shaped into curious natural works of art.

VISITORS' CHECKLIST

Tourist centre: east of El Paso.
922 497 277.
FAX 922 497 081.
9am–6:30pm daily.

Pico de la Cruz
This is one of park's highest peaks. A challenging 4–5 hour walking trail, connecting Pico de las Nieves with Roque de los Muchachos, leads over the peak through some breathtaking scenery.

SANTA CRUZ DE LA PALMA

Trail to Roque de los Muchachos
The trail, running along the highest peaks of Caldera de Taburiente, provides a view over the stunningly steep walls of the crater, shrouded with dense fog.

La Cumbrecita
A good asphalt road leads to La Cumbrecita, which has an information point. This is a good point of departure for exploring the park.

Lomo de las Chozas
A short and easy trail leads through Canary pines from La Cumbrecita westwards, to Lomo de las Chozas, where the views are at their best at sunset and sunrise.

EL PASO

TRAVELLERS' NEEDS

WHERE TO STAY

THE CANARY ISLANDS are seventh on the list of the world's most frequently visited places, with a sophisticated and highly organized tourist industry. Popularity has its downside, however, and the accommodation prices are high. This applies in particular to the larger islands, such as Tenerife and Gran Canaria, where it can be difficult

Tenerife's parador

to find cheap places to stay. The smaller, less-frequented islands, such as El Hierro and La Gomera, offer lower prices, but do not have many hotels. In recent years, *casas rurales* have become more widespread. Generally in country properties of charm and character, they provide much more varied and individual alternatives to conventional hotels.

Guest lounge in Las Cañadas del Teide parador on Tenerife

HOTELS

HOTELS ARE THE most expensive form of accommodation on the Canary Islands. Many of them belong to international hotel chains, such as NH Hotels, Riu, TRYP or the Spanish chains (Sol Meliá, H10 Hoteles and Paradores Nacionales) and are block-booked by foreign package tour operators for most of the year.

The hotels in large town centres cater mainly for business visitors. Popular coastal resorts have huge hotel complexes, aimed squarely at the tourist market. These have been built relatively near the beaches and are generally surrounded by lush tropical gardens. Hotels are designed so that most rooms have sea views.

Complexes vie with each other to offer their guests maximum fun, day and night. Many have tennis courts, large swimming pools, mini-golf, gymnasia or exercise rooms.

It is certainly advisable to check in advance to find out whether these facilities are included in the price or are charged for separately.

PARADORS

THE SIX STATE-RUN parador hotels (one on each island except Lanzarote) are attractively located in coastal or national park settings.

They provide a first-class service and usually have excellent restaurants. Despite their high prices, they offer good value and are well worth considering.

APARTMENTS

APARTMENTS ARE THE most popular form of accommodation on the islands and there are many more of these than there are hotels. They can either be situated within hotel buildings or as separate blocks or complexes.

Quality varies, but most include a lounge, fully equipped kitchen, bathroom and one or two bedrooms. Most sleep between two and six people, but it is sometimes possible to combine two apartments into one. Apartments are especially suitable for families with young children.

Apartments are generally better value for couples or families than staying in a hotel, though many require you to stay at least three to five nights and sometimes a week is the minimum.

Some apartments form part of a complex and provide similar facilities to those offered by hotels. Most of these have a swimming pool and a small playing field or tennis courts. Some have much more.

Bungalows in Las Puntas on El Hierro

CASAS RURALES

RURAL HOTELS *(casas rurales)* are generally converted farms or village houses and are aimed at those seeking quiet, out-of-the-way places. Most of them are located far from the traditional resorts and can be found in small towns and villages. Some have no public transport so it is wise to check whether you will need to hire a car.

However, they are not necessarily a cheap option. Neither can they offer the same variety of facilities as the large hotel complexes, but this is the very reason that many visitors seek them out. *Casas rurales* offer a degree of authenticity and individuality not found elsewhere and the rooms and communal spaces are often characterful and furnished with local handicraft items. This is definitely the best choice for those who appreciate a personal touch.

All tourist information offices have full lists of organizations offering this type of service. Information can also be found on the Internet or in the *Guía de Alojamiento en Casas Rurales de España* publication.

CAMPING SITES

CAMPING SITES ARE rather primitive and most islands have only one or two sites at most. Before travelling it is wise to find out about the situation on a particular island. Just turning up and pitching your tent on the beach is generally forbidden.

BOOKING

MOST OF THE islands' hotel rooms and apartments are booked by travel agents and tour operators in advance. They then sell on the holidays, including flights and half-board. Such holidays do not suit everyone but are the cheapest way to visit the Canary Islands.

One of the few camp sites to be found on Lanzarote

It is obviously possible to make a booking without using a travel agent. It is best to do so well in advance, although it is sometimes possible to find something at short notice.

Hotels and pensions can be booked over the telephone, or via the Internet. Some places, particularly the smaller hotels and *casas rurales*, may require a deposit. When booking, bear in mind peak tourist times, and festivals and carnivals, especially when going to Gran Canaria or Tenerife.

Entrance to Jardín Tropical hotel in Playa de las Américas

PRICES

HOTEL PRICES DEPEND on the season and the island. The dates when prices change are determined by individual hoteliers, so it is worth finding out in advance what prices apply at particular times. Tariffs will obviously be higher during popular

Club La Santa apartments on Lanzarote

holidays and carnivals. It should be understood that hotels quote their prices in various ways. Some are per night in a twin room; others are per person per night.

The price is subject to 5 per cent IGIC tax, which is generally included in the quote. Prices quoted by apartments, pensions and *casas rurales* do not usually include breakfast. Until recently, hotels always included breakfast in the price of the room, but this habit seems to be gradually disappearing.

Most hotels accept credit cards. Pensions and *casas rurales* usually prefer to be paid in cash.

Choosing a Hotel

HOTELS OF VARIOUS price categories have been chosen for their standard, their good value and their attractive location. They are listed separately for each island, in the order in which they appear in the guide. For each island, they are listed in alphabetical order according to location. For more information on hotels see page 154.

	NUMBER OF ROOMS	CREDIT CARDS	CHILDREN'S PROGRAMME	ROOMS WITH A VIEW	SWIMMING POOL
GRAN CANARIA					
AGÜIMES: *Casa de los Camellos* €€ C/Progreso, 12. **☎** 928 785 003. **FAX** 928 785 053. **@** rcamellos@hecansa.com This hotel occupies a historic building with stylish décor. Features include a restaurant/bar and immaculately kept gardens. The hotel exudes a quiet and peaceful atmosphere. 📺 🍸 🍽	12	●			
CRUZ DE TEJEDA: *El Refugio* €€ **☎** 928 666 513. **FAX** 928 666 520. **@** elrefugio@canariasonline.com The quiet and cosy rooms of this hotel feature stylish furniture, most of which is handcrafted. The hotel restaurant serves a mixture of local and international cuisine. 📺 🗒 🍸 🍽	10				▓
FATAGA: *Molino de Agua de Fataga* €€ Ctra. Fataga – San Bartolomé, 1. km (half a mile). **☎** 928 172 089. **FAX** 928 172 244. Occupying a 200-year-old building, restored by its present owners, this hotel is only a few steps away from the 19th-century water mill that gives the establishment its name. 📺 🍸 🍽 🄿 🛏	20	●		●	
LAS PALMAS DE GRAN CANARIA: *Fataga & Centro de Negocios* €€ C/Néstor de la Torre, 21. **☎** 928 290 614. **FAX** 928 292 786. **@** fataga@hai.es This luxurious and modern hotel, situated in the Las Palmas shopping district, provides an attractive option for tourists and business travellers. 📺 🗒 🍸 🍽 🄿	94	●			
LAS PALMAS DE GRAN CANARIA: *Parque* €€ C/Muelle de las Palmas, 2. **☎** 928 368 000. **FAX** 928 368 856. **@** hparque@idecnet.com The hotel stands opposite the magnificent park of San Telmo, and the restaurant terrace offers unforgettable views over the park and the ocean. The facilities include a Turkish bath. 📺 🗒 🍸 🍽	102	●		●	
LAS PALMAS DE GRAN CANARIA: *Reina Isabel* €€€€€ C/Alfredo L. Jones, 40. **☎** 928 260 100. **FAX** 928 274 558. **@** h.reina.isabel@retemail.es This central, luxurious five-star hotel on Las Canteras beach has lovely sea views from many rooms, and from its restaurants. 📺 🗒 🍸 🍽 🄿	224	●		●	▓
LAS PALMAS DE GRAN CANARIA: *Santa Catalina* €€€€ C/León y Castillo, 227. **☎** 928 243 040. **FAX** 928 242 764. **W** www.hotelsantacatalina.com **@** hsantacatalina@entorno.es Occupying a Canary-style building, this hotel is listed as a historic and artistic heritage site. The hotel entertains many prominent guests and is situated in the town centre and surrounded by magnificent gardens. 📺 🗒 🍸 🕓 🍽 🎮 ♿ 🄿	208	●			▓
MASPALOMAS: *Gran Hotel Costa Meloneras* €€€ C/Mar Mediterraneo, 1. **☎** 928 128 100. **FAX** 928 128 122. **@** info@meloneras.com Opened at the end of 2000, this huge hotel complex offers its guests countless sporting attractions and a wonderful atmosphere thanks to its traditional local architecture. 📺 🗒 🍸 🍽 🎮	1136	●	▓		▓
MASPALOMAS: *Maspalomas Oasis (Riu)* €€€€€ Centro Hotelero de Maspalomas. **☎** 928 141 448. **FAX** 928 141 192. **@** roasismaspalomas@riu.es A smart, five-star hotel, offering splendid facilities for recreation even to the most fastidious guests. The rooms are arranged in three- to five-storey buildings, which stand in a large park, with direct access to the beach. 📺 🗒 🍸 🍽 🎮 📶	372	●		●	▓

		Price categories / info	NUMBER OF ROOMS	CREDIT CARDS	CHILDREN'S PROGRAMME	ROOMS WITH A VIEW	SWIMMING POOL

Price categories for a standard double room per night including breakfast, service and tax.

€ below 50 euros
€€ 50–100 euros
€€€ 100–150 euros
€€€€ 150–200 euros
€€€€€ over 200 euros.

CREDIT CARDS
Accepted credit cards include American Express, MasterCard, Visa, Diners Club.

CHILDREN'S PROGRAMMES
Hotel provides programmes for children and/or child-minding facilities.

ROOMS WITH A VIEW
Hotel rooms have splendid views, including the ocean.

SWIMMING POOL
The hotel has a pool for the exclusive use of its guests.

Listing	Rooms	Credit Cards	Children's Programme	Rooms with a View	Swimming Pool
MOGÁN: *Steigenberger La Canaria* €€€€€ Barranco de la Verga. 📞 928 150 400. FAX 928 151 003. @ reservas@lacanaria.com The hotel's wonderful style manages to combine simplicity with elegance. Situated right on the coast, each balcony is decorated with a different type of flower. TV ▤ Ⓨ 🍴 ♜ ⊙ ▦ & P	249	●	■	●	■
PLAYA DEL INGLÉS: *Catarina* €€ Avda. de Tirajana, 1. 📞 928 762 812. FAX 928 760 615. @ catarina@creativhotels.com The hotel has large rooms, with double or twin beds (a third can be provided on request). It features swimming pools and offers various health treatments. TV ▤ Ⓨ 🍴 ▦	402	●	■		■
PLAYA DEL INGLÉS: *Neptuno* €€ Avda. Alféreces Provisionales, 29. 📞 928 777 492. FAX 928 766 965. @ info@hotelneptuno.com The hotel combines modern style with a family atmosphere. It is adjacent to a small shopping centre and not far from the beach. TV ▤ Ⓨ 🍴 ▦	171	●	■		■
PLAYA DEL INGLÉS: *Palace Maspalomas (Riu)* €€€€ Avda. Tirajana, s/n. 📞 928 769 500. FAX 928 769 800. @ rpalacemaspalomas@riu.es The magnificent architecture, resembling an amphitheatre, and an excellent restaurant are among the many attractions of this hotel, which offers exceptionally varied entertainments. TV ▤ Ⓨ 🍴 ♜ ⊙ ▦ & P	368	●	■		■
PLAYA DEL INGLÉS: *IFA Dunamar* €€€€€ C/Helsinki, 8. 📞 928 772 800. FAX 928 773 465. @ dunamar@ifacanarias.es The hotel stands on a slope, descending towards the ocean. The architects took advantage of its location to create numerous terraces and swimming pools at different levels. TV ▤ Ⓨ 🍴 & P	273	●		●	■
SAN AGUSTÍN: *Costa Canaria* €€€€ Las Retamas, 1. 📞 928 760 220. FAX 928 720 413. @ reservas@costa-canarias.com Quiet and restful, the hotel is by the beach and features colourful tropical gardens. It offers bungalows as well as rooms. TV ▤ Ⓨ ▦ &	235	●	■	●	■
SAN BARTOLOMÉ DE TIRAJANA: *Hotel Las Tirajanas* €€ C/Oficial Mayor José Rubio, s/n. 📞 928 123 000. FAX 928 123 023. @ info@hotel-lastirajanas.com The building's décor includes a number of Canary motifs by Francisco López. Three suites have the luxury of their own Jacuzzi. The restaurant offers good local cuisine. TV ▤ Ⓨ 🍴 P	68	●			■
TAFIRA ALTA: *Escuela Santa Brígida* €€ C/Real de Coello, 2. 📞 928 355 511. FAX 928 355 701. @ reservas.hesb@hecansa.org The hotel building, lovingly restored in 1922, can boast more than 100 years of history as well as an excellent catering school. It is surrounded by magnificent greenery and provides an ideal place for a rest. TV ▤ Ⓨ 🍴	41	●			■
TAURITO: *Taurito Princess* €€€ Urb. Costa Taurito – Playa Taurito. 📞 928 565 250. FAX 928 565 566. This hotel has its own private beach. It is situated 4 km (2 miles) from Puerto Mogán. All rooms have sea views. It offers many recreational facilities to its guests. TV ▤ Ⓨ & ♜	402	●	■	●	■
VEGA DE SAN MATEO: *La Cantonera* Avda. de Tinamar, 17. 📞 928 661 795. FAX 928 661 777. The building, typical of the Canary Islands' architecture, features wooden balconies decked out with a variety of local plants. It is equipped with all the facilities expected of a modern hotel. 🍴	15				

For key to symbols see back flap

Price categories for a standard double room per night including breakfast, service and tax.

€ below 50 euros
€€ 50–100 euros
€€€ 100–150 euros
€€€€ 150–200 euros
€€€€€ over 200 euros.

CREDIT CARDS
Accepted credit cards include American Express, MasterCard, Visa, Diners Club.

CHILDREN'S PROGRAMMES
Hotel provides programmes for children and/or child-minding facilities.

ROOMS WITH A VIEW
Hotel rooms have splendid views, including the ocean.

SWIMMING POOL
The hotel has a pool for the exclusive use of its guests.

FUERTEVENTURA

Hotel	Price	Number of Rooms	Credit Cards	Children's Programme	Rooms with a View	Swimming Pool
ANTIGUA: *Hotel Elba Palace Golf* — Urb. Fuerteventura Golf Club. 928 163 922. FAX 928 163 923. www.elbapalacegolf.com. The island's only five-star hotel was designed in typical Canary style, with wooden balconies and patios with palms, and is ideal for golf and water sports enthusiasts.	€€€€€	61	●	■	●	■
CALETA DE FUSTE: *Bungalows Fuerte Sol* — 928 163 017. FAX 928 163 060. Two or three-person bungalows, including kitchen, lounge, and a separate bedroom.	€	110	●	■		■
CALETA DE FUSTES: *Barceló Club El Castillo* — 928 163 101. FAX 928 163 042. www.barcelo.com. Situated in a small cove, this complex has attractive apartments, all with direct access to the beach. An ideal location for water sports and for families with small children.	€€	420	●	■	●	■
CORRALEJO: *Sol las Olas* — Avda. de Las Palmeras, s/n. 928 536 299. FAX 928 536 297. Pleasant and spacious apartments in two-storey buildings that can accommodate up to three persons. Each apartment includes kitchen, lounge and bedroom. All apartments have balconies.	€	250	●			■
CORRALEJO: *Corralejo Beach* — 928 866 315. FAX 928 866 317. informacion@corralejobeach.com. A quiet, low-built hotel situated near the beach. Spacious and modern apartments include terraces. The hotel offers a variety of entertainment to its guests.	€€	79	●		●	■
CORRALEJO: *Hesperia Bristol Playa* — Urb. Lago de Bristol, 1. 928 867 020. FAX 928 866 349. hotel@hesperia-bristolplaya.com. Modern apartments set among gardens provide a peaceful environment for a restful holiday.	€€	186	●			■
CORRALEJO: *Dunapark* — C/General Franco, s/n. 928 535 251. FAX 928 535 491. The hotel stands less than 50 m (55 yards) from the beach and is surrounded by a colourful garden. Hotel buildings do not exceed two storeys.	€€€	79	●			■
COSTA CALMA: *Club Barlovento* — 928 547 002. FAX 928 547 038. barlovento@intercom.es. The hotel stands near a yachting marina.	€€€€	256	●	■		■
COSTA CALMA: *Risco del Gato* — 928 547 175. FAX 928 547 030. This luxury hotel, poised on a scenic escarpment, comprises strikingly designed apartments, which are built into the cliff-face. It has an excellent restaurant, serving local and international cuisine.	€€€€	51	●			■
CORRELEJO: *Riu Palace Tres Islas* — Avda. Grandes Playas. 928 535 700. FAX 928 535 858. All the stylish double rooms have balconies overlooking dunes. Single rooms have no ocean view.	€€€	365	●		●	■
MORRO JABLE: *Garonda Jandía* — Avda. del Saladar, 28. 928 540 430. FAX 928 540 218. Elegant rooms, furnished to a high standard. Buffet offers varied and plentiful breakfasts.	€€€€€	238	●		●	■

MORRO JABLE: *Robinsón Club Jandía Playa* €€€€€ 362
Solana Matorral. 928 169 100. FAX 928 169 540. @ jandiaplaya@gmx.net
Situated right on the beach, the hotel is an ideal place for
indulging in various water sports.
TV ▤ Y ♊ 🍴 ⚅

LANZAROTE

ARRECIFE: *Lancelot* €€ 113
Avda. Mancomunidad, 9. 928 805 099. FAX 928 805 039.
The hotel has direct access to the beach, where there is a safe shore, with
no eddies or currents. TV Y ♊ 🍴 P

ARRECIFE: *Miramar* €€ 90
C/Coll, 2. 928 801 522. FAX 928 801 533.
A terrace situated on the hotel roof provides views over the ocean.
Clean and spacious rooms, modestly furnished. TV ♉ ⚅

COSTA TEGUISE: *Oasis de Lanzarote* €€€ 372
Avda. del Mar, s/n. 928 590 410. FAX 928 590 791.
@ oasis@occidental hoteles.com
A modern, luxurious hotel standing on the coast with direct
access to the beach. Spacious and comfortable rooms.
TV ▤ Y ♊ 🍴 P

COSTA TEGUISE: *Occidental Teguise Playa* €€€€ 314
Avda. Jablillo, s/n 928 590 654. FAX 928 590 979.
@ comerciallanzarote@oh-es.com
All rooms are of a good size and benefit from ocean views.
The hotel stands next to the beach.
TV ▤ Y ♊ 🍴 🍽 ⚅

COSTA TEGUISE: *Gran Meliá Salinas – The Garden Village* €€€€€ 310
Avda. Islas Canarias, s/n. 928 590 311. FAX 928 590 390.
@ gran.melia.salinas@solmelia.com
A striking building with terraces descending towards the ocean. Some of its
architectural elements were designed by César Manrique and the hotel has
been declared a National Cultural Heritage Site.
TV ▤ Y ♊ 🍴 P

PLAYA BLANCA: *Lanzarote Park* €€ 332
Avda. Canarias, 5. 928 517 048. FAX 928 517 348.
The hotel offers a quiet, family atmosphere. Rooms feature modest
furnishings and have fully equipped bathrooms. TV Y 🍴 P

PLAYA BLANCA: *Lanzarote Princess* €€ 410
Maciot, s/n. 928 517 108. FAX 928 517 011. @ lanpr@hio.es
A four-storey building with three lifts, situated within a
luxurious hotel complex, with direct access to the beach.
TV ▤ Y 24 🍴 ⚅ P

PLAYA BLANCA: *Hesperia Playa Dorada* €€€ 466
Urb. Costa Papagayo, s/n. 928 517 120. FAX 928 517 432.
Modern hotel, standing on the beach, with fine ocean views. All rooms
have balconies. An extra bed can be provided on request.
TV ▤ Y ♊ 🍽 ⚅ P

PUERTO DEL CARMEN: *Lanzarote Village* €€ 220
Avda. de Suiza, 2. 928 511 344. FAX 928 512 030.
New hotel, with simple but elegant décor. Situated near the beach.
TV ▤ Y ♊ ⚅ P

PUERTO DEL CARMEN: *La Geria* €€€ 240
Júpiter, 5. 928 510 441. FAX 928 511 919. @ lageria@hipotels.com
Spacious, double rooms, with third and fourth beds provided
on request. Diving lessons are offered on the hotel beach.
TV ▤ Y ♊ 🍴 🍽 ⚅ P

PUERTO DEL CARMEN: *Los Fariones* €€€ 249
Roque del Este, 1. 928 510 175. FAX 928 510 202. @ hotel@grupofariones.com
Los Fariones is a luxurious hotel, which stands on the coast in a
picturesque corner of town. Diving lessons and other water sports facilities
are available from the hotel.
TV Y ♊ 🍴 🍽

For key to symbols see back flap

Price categories for a standard double room per night including breakfast, service and tax. € below 50 euros €€ 50–100 euros €€€ 100–150 euros €€€€ 150–200 euros €€€€€ over 200 euros.	**CREDIT CARDS** Accepted credit cards include American Express, MasterCard, Visa, Diners Club. **CHILDREN'S PROGRAMMES** Hotel provides programmes for children and/or child-minding facilities. **ROOMS WITH A VIEW** Hotel rooms have splendid views, including the ocean. **SWIMMING POOL** The hotel has a pool for the exclusive use of its guests.		NUMBER OF ROOMS	CREDIT CARDS	CHILDREN'S PROGRAMME	ROOMS WITH A VIEW	SWIMMING POOL

	ROOMS	CARDS	CHILDREN'S	VIEW	POOL
YAIZA: *Finca de las Salinas* C/La Cuesta, 17. ☎ 928 830 325. FAX 928 830 329. @ fsalina@santandersupernet.com Historic, 18th-century building. Rooms are furnished modestly but tastefully, in rustic style. TV ≣ ⑨ ⑪ ⑨ €€€€€	19				▨

TENERIFE

	NUMBER OF ROOMS	CREDIT CARDS	CHILDREN'S PROGRAMME	ROOMS WITH A VIEW	SWIMMING POOL
COSTA ADEJE: *Bouganville Playa* €€€ Urb. S. Eugenio – C/Eugenio Domínguez, 23. ☎ 922 790 200. FAX 922 794 173. Modern hotel, on the coast. Guests can expect all the usual comforts. TV ≣ ⑨ ⑨ ⑪ ⑨ &	496	●		●	▨
COSTA ADEJE: *Gran Tinerfe* €€€ Avda. Rafael Puig Lluvina. ☎ 922 791 200. FAX 922 791 265. @ grtin@h10.e The hotel stands near the beach. Besides numerous entertainments, guests may enjoy the local casino. TV ≣ ⑨ ⑨ ⑨ & P	1,100	●		●	▨
COSTA ADEJE: *Guayarmina Princess* €€€€ Playa de Fañabe – C/Londres, 1. ☎ 922 712 584. FAX 922 712 000. Luxurious hotel, standing in a beautiful garden. Its main decorative features are white columns, set amid the greenery. TV ≣ ⑨ ⑪ ⑨ ⑤ &	513	●			▨
COSTA ADEJE: *Jardín Tropical* €€€€€ C/Gran Bretaña, s/n. ☎ 922 746 000. FAX 922 746 060. An extremely striking hotel of Moorish design, set in spectacular gardens. With several restaurants, the El Patio is particularly worthy of recommendation. TV ≣ ⑨ ⑪ ⑨ ⑨	400	●			▨
COSTA ADEJE: *Torviscas Playa* €€€ Urb. Torviscas – Avda. Ernesto Sarti, 5. ☎ 922 712 300. FAX 922 713 155. The hotel stands in one of the quietest corners of Costa Adeje. Modern building, with garden and swimming pools. TV ≣ ⑨ ⑨ & P	482	●	▨	●	▨
COSTA ADEJE: *Gran Hotel Bahía del Duque Resort* €€€€€ Playa de Fañabe – C/Alcalde Walter Paetzmann, s/n. ☎ 922 713 000, 922 746 900. FAX 922 746 925, 922 712 616. @ comercial@bahia-duque.com Strikingly beautiful hotel, set on a large site with separately designed buildings in a variety of Mediterranean styles. Rooms are furnished in Baroque style, with brown colour schemes. TV ≣ ⑨ ⑪ ⑨ ⑨ & P ⑭	482	●	▨	●	▨
LA LAGUNA: *Nivaria* €€ Plaza del Adelantado 11. ☎ 922 264 298. FAX 922 259 634. This elegant, classic hotel stands in the middle of town and offers both rooms and apartments. TV ⑨ ⑪ P	76	●			
LA OROTAVA: *Parador de las Cañadas del Teide* €€ Ctra. Orotava – Teide, 43 km (27 miles). ☎ 922 386 415. FAX 922 382 352. This fully refurbished hotel offers a quiet and restful atmosphere. Situated in the National Park amid crater landscapes, it commands astonishing views of the Teide peak and Los Roques. TV ⑨ ⑪ ⑨ P	37			▨	
LOS CRISTIANOS: *Arona Gran Hotel* €€€€€ Avda. Los Cristianos. ☎ 922 750 678. FAX 922 750 243. This hotel, situated on the beach with views over the old harbour in Los Cristianos, is one of the most popular hotels in south Tenerife. TV ≣ ⑨ ⑪ ⑨ ⑤	401	●		●	▨
LOS CRISTIANOS: *Princesa Dacil* €€ Camino Penetración, s/n. ☎ 922 753 030. FAX 922 790 658. High-rise hotel, close to the beach. Spacious rooms feature traditional décor. TV ⑨ ⑪ ⑨ & P	366	●			▨

PLAYA DE LAS AMÉRICAS: *Bitácora* €€ 314
Avda. A. Domínguez Alfonso, 1. 922 791 540. FAX 922 796 677.
Situated in the best part of Playa de las Américas, near the shopping centre,
bars and nightclubs. Rooms are very large and comfortable.
TV ≡ ♈ ♙ ⬛ &

PLAYA DE LAS AMÉRICAS: *Gala Tenerife* €€€ 308
Avda. Litoral, s/n. 922 794 513. FAX 922 796 465. @ hotelgala@interbook.net
Modern hotel, with family atmosphere, situated 100 m (110 yards) from
the seafront. TV ≡ ♈ ♙ ⬛ & P

PLAYA DE LAS AMÉRICAS: *Vulcano* €€€ 371
Avda. Domínguez Alfonso, 8. 922 787 740. FAX 922 792 853.
Hotel situated in a beautiful garden, 300 m (330 yards) from the ocean.
All rooms have furnished terraces. TV ♈ &

PUERTO DE LA CRUZ: *Atlantis* €€ 320
Avda. Venezuela, 15. 922 374 545. FAX 922 382 153. W www.hap.es
@ atlantis@hap.es
The hotel stands 50 m (55 yards) from the beach. The management offers
interesting entertainment programmes. TV ♈ ♙ ⬛ &

PUERTO DE LA CRUZ: *LTI – Chiripa Garden* €€€ 192
Urb. San Fernando – C/Bélgica, 54. 922 381 450. FAX 922 380 893.
@ ltihotel@lachiripa.es
The hotel stands amid tropical gardens. Most rooms have a kitchen annexe.
TV ≡ ♈ ♦ ♙ P

PUERTO DE LA CRUZ: *Tigaiga* €€€€ 83
C/Parque del Taoro, 28. 922 383 500. FAX 922 384 055. W www.tigaiga.com
Four-storey hotel, with family atmosphere. TV ≡ ♈ ♦ ♙ & P

PUERTO DE LA CRUZ: *Botánico* €€€€€ 252
C/Richard J. Yeoward, s/n. 922 381 400. FAX 922 381 504.
@ hotelbotanico@hotelbotanico.com
This sumptuously furnished hotel offers immaculately designed gardens
and magnificent interiors, and excellent leisure facilities. The hotel
restaurant has a dress code. TV ≡ ♈ ♦ ♙ & P

SANTA CRUZ DE TENERIFE: *El Dorado* € 50
C/Cruz Verde, 24. 922 243 184. FAX 922 243 259.
This small, simply furnished hotel is clean and tidy and offers,
above all, good value for money. ♈

SANTA CRUZ DE TENERIFE: *Escuela Hotel Santa Cruz* €€ 65
Avda. San Sebastián 152, Parque Viera y Clavijo. 922 010 500.
FAX 922 010 501. @ reservas.ehscehecansa.net
Situated on the outskirts of town, this catering school hotel is a must for all
gourmets. It organizes popular gastronomic "weeks" and also holds its own
cookery competitions. TV ♈ ♦

SANTA CRUZ DE TENERIFE: *Taburiente* €€ 116
C/Dr. José Naveiras, 24-A. 922 276 000. FAX 922 270 562.
@ hoteltaburiente@teleline.es
The hotel stands in the town centre, close to Parque García Sanabra.
TV ≡ ♈ ♦ 24 ♙ ♦ & P ♙

SANTA CRUZ DE TENERIFE: *Mencey* €€€€€ 286
Avda. José Naveiras, 38. 922 609 900. FAX 922 280 017.
@ reservations.hotelmencey@LuxuryCollection.com
Situated in the centre of Santa Cruz, this luxurious hotel occupies a historic
building, typical of Canary architecture.
TV ♈ 24 ♙ & P

LA GOMERA

HERMIGUA: *Ibo Alfaro* €€ 17
922 880 168. FAX 922 881 019. This small hotel, opened in 1996, is
surrounded by a pleasant garden and terraces.

PLAYA SANTIAGO: *Jardín Tecina* €€€€ 434
Lomada de Tecina. 922 145 850. FAX 922 145 851. W www.jardin-tecina.com
Standing in a magnificent garden, on a craggy shore of the ocean, this
hotel has access to the beach by lift. One of the best hotels on the island.
TV ≡ ♈ ♙ ♦ & P

For key to symbols see back flap

Price categories for a standard double room per night including breakfast, service and tax.

€ below 50 euros
€€ 50–100 euros
€€€ 100–150 euros
€€€€ 150–200 euros
€€€€€ over 200 euros.

CREDIT CARDS
Accepted credit cards include American Express, MasterCard, Visa, Diners Club.

CHILDREN'S PROGRAMMES
Hotel provides programmes for children and/or child-minding facilities.

ROOMS WITH A VIEW
Hotel rooms have splendid views, including the ocean.

SWIMMING POOL
The hotel has a pool for the exclusive use of its guests.

		NUMBER OF ROOMS	CREDIT CARDS	CHILDREN'S PROGRAMME	ROOMS WITH A VIEW	SWIMMING POOL
SAN SEBASTIÁN DE LA GOMERA: *Hesperides* C/Ruiz de Padrón. 922 871 305. Small, clean and inexpensive hotel. It is worth booking early.	€	9				
SAN SEBASTIÁN DE LA GOMERA: *Villa Gomera* C/Ruiz de Padrón, 68. 922 870 020. FAX 922 870 235. The hotel offers a good location and above average facilities. The price is a bargain considering the standard. TV	€	16				
SAN SEBASTIÁN DE LA GOMERA: *Parador de la Gomera* 922 871 100. FAX 922 871 116. @ gomera@parador.es Although modern, with a swimming pool, this hotel has been designed as a 16th-century colonial house. TV Y ‖ P	€€€	60	●			
VALLE GRAN REY: *Casa Bella Cabellos* La Calera. 922 805 182. *Casa rural* in a Canary-style house surrounded with palms.	€€	5			●	
VALLE GRAN REY: *Gran Rey* La Puntilla. 922 805 859. FAX 922 805 651. W www.hotel-granrey.com The hotel stands near the beach and 500 m (550 yards) from a yachting marina. Free use of hammocks and umbrellas. TV Y ‖	€€	99				▨
VALLEHERMOSO: *Hotel Rural Tamahuche* La Hoya, 20. 922 801 176. FAX 922 801 176. W www.ecoturismocanarias.com This traditional house has been sympathetically renovated and its location, near the Parque Nacional de Garajonay, makes it ideal for walkers and nature lovers. Most rooms have either a terrace or balcony with views over the old village of Vallehermoso. TV P	€€	10	●		●	▨
EL HIERRO						
LA RESTINGA: *Kai Marino* 922 557 034. FAX 922 557 034. Inexpensive hotel, in a scenic location. Depending on price, the rooms are with bath, shower or washbasin. P	€	7				
LAS PUNTAS: *Apartamentos Roques Salmor* Ctra. Punta Grande, s/n. 922 559 016. FAX 922 559 401. Modest bungalows, surrounded by greenery, overlooking the Roques de Salmor.	€€	10				
LAS PUNTAS: *Puntagrande* Las Puntas, 1. 922 559 081. FAX 922 559 081. The world's smallest hotel. Entered in the *Guinness Book of Records*, it has just four rooms. Early booking necessary. Y P	€€	4			●	
SABINOSA: *Balneario Pozo La Salud* Pozo La Salud. 922 559 561. FAX 922 559 801. @ meridiano@el-meridiano.com Sanatorium standing on an escarpment above the ocean. Nearby is the water outlet flowing from the health-giving Pozo de la Salud. On offer is a variety of health and beauty treatments. TV Y &	€€	18	●		●	▨
VALVERDE: *Boomerang* C/Dr. Gost, 1. 922 550 200. FAX 922 550 253. A modest hotel in the town centre. It also has some bungalows standing directly on the beach. TV Y ‖	€	17	●			
VALVERDE: *Casa Rural El Tesón I* Calle Esquina Campo, 14, San Andrés. 922 551 824. FAX 922 550 575. W www.ecoturismocanarias.com This small country cottage with its organic vegetable garden and fruit trees is ideal for walkers and nature lovers. Other cottages are available in the area.	€€	2	●		●	

VALVERDE: *Parador del Hierro* €€€ 47
Ctra. General Las Playas, 26. 922 558 036. FAX 922 558 086.
@ hierro@parador.es W www.parador.es
Situated in a quiet spot, right by the sea. The restaurant serves dishes prepared from typical island produce. TV Y 11 & P

LA PALMA

BARLOVENTO: *La Palma Romántica* €€€ 46
Topo de Las Llanadas. 922 186 221. FAX 922 186 400.
Luxurious hotel in the Barlovento mountains. Large, comfortable rooms, meticulously furnished. Excellent place for a quiet rest.
TV Y 11 P

BREÑA BAJA: *Apartamentos Costa Salinas* €€ 140
Urb. Las Salinas – Playa de los Cancajos. 922 434 348. FAX 922 434 510.
@ salinas@h10.es
Apartments situated a mere 300 m (330 yards) from the Los Cancajos beach and 5 km (3 miles) from Santa Cruz de La Palma. Typical, smart centre belonging to the H10 chain. TV Y 11

BREÑA BAJA: *Hacienda San Jorge* €€ 155
Playa de los Cancajos. 922 434 075. FAX 922 434 528.
@ comercial@hsanjorge.com
With lush gardens and stylish décor, this quiet hotel is 4 km (2 miles) from the island's capital. It has private access to the beach. TV Y 11 & P

BREÑA BAJA: *Hotel Las Olas* €€ 182
Playa de los Cancajos. 922 434 052. FAX 922 434 085. W www.a-caledonia.com
This modern hotel complex has well-equipped apartments spread across six buildings. Situated on the seafront, all its rooms have a terrace or balcony with good views. TV Y 11 & P

BREÑA BAJA: *Parador de Breña Baja* €€€ 78
El Cumacal s/n. 922 435 828. FAX 922 435 999. @ lapalma@parador.es
Situated in the mountains with beautiful views. TV P 11 &

BREÑA BAJA: *Taburiente Playa* €€€ 293
Urb. Las Salinas – Playa de los Cancajos. 922 181 277. FAX 922 181 285.
@ taburiente@h10.es
A hotel belonging to the popular H10 chain, situated on the front line of the beach. All rooms are spacious and have a sea view.
TV Y 11 & P

LOS LLANOS DE ARIDANE: *Valle Aridane* € 42
Glorieta Castillo Olivares, 3. 922 462 600. FAX 922 401 019.
W www.hotelaridane.com
A small hotel, overlooking the national park of La Caldera de Taburiente. A good base from which to explore the island. TV Y 11 P

LOS LLANOS DE ARIDANE: *Amberes* €€€ 17
Avda. General Franco, 13. 922 401 040. FAX 922 402 441.
The hotel occupies a recently restored 17th-century building. Its restaurant specializes in vegetarian dishes.
TV Y 11

PUERTO NAOS: *Sol Élite La Palma* €€€ 307
Punta del Pozo, 24. 922 408 000. FAX 922 408 014.
A modern hotel complex, situated next to a black-sand volcanic beach, featuring all the modern facilities. It has a number of apartments on offer to its guests. TV Y 11 & P

SANTA CRUZ DE LA PALMA: *Castillete* €€ 42
Avda. Marítima, 75. 922 420 840. FAX 922 420 067. @ h.castillete@airtel.net
An inexpensive option for tourists not expecting excessive luxury. Conveniently situated and clean. TV Y 11 & P

TAZACORTE: *Apartamentos Atlantis* €€ 23
Mariano Benlliure, 14. 922 406 146. @ atlantis@la-palma.de
A small hotel with pleasant apartments and large balconies. TV Y

VILLA DE MAZO: *Arminda* €€ 5
Lodero, 182. 922 428 432.
The hotel occupies an old farmhouse. Rooms are decorated in a rustic style. TV & P

For key to symbols see back flap

WHERE TO EAT

THE CANARY ISLANDS can offer a good selection of restaurants, able to satisfy the most discerning palates. Traditional Canary cuisine is in plentiful supply, as are dishes from other regions of Spain. In addition, speciality food, which includes German, French, Italian, Chinese, Arab and Indian cuisine, can easily be found to cater for the varied tastes of tourists.

Icod de los Vinos restaurant décor

Numerous restaurants offer hybrid menus and many chefs create sophisticated dishes by experimenting with a range of local ingredients and various culinary traditions. Some of these restaurants are highly regarded and very popular. The majority of Canary Island restaurants, however, are actually small bars near beaches and tourist centres, which cater for the fast-food market.

A modest restaurant in one of El Golfo's quiet streets

WHERE TO EAT

THE ISLANDS OFFER countless bars and restaurants, with diverse menus. The majority of restaurants open for lunch and dinner. Tourists and locals alike enjoy going to restaurants, which accounts for the variety on offer, including *marisquería* (seafood) and *cervecería* (pubs).

There is no dress code in restaurants, apart from a very few exclusive places that require evening dress. Apart from the fast-food bars close to the beaches, swimming costumes are not acceptable in bars and restaurants.

There are also fast-food chains, local and foreign, including McDonald's, Tele Pizza, Slow Boat (Chinese), Little Italy (pizza and pasta) and Bocatta as well as cafés serving English-style breakfasts, fish and chips and pizzas. For the genuine article, visitors will need to head inland, away from the popular resorts, where the majority of authentic Canary restaurants (*típico*) can be found.

WHAT TO EAT

THE ISLANDS' CUISINE is the basic Mediterranean diet. Ingredients include fish, meat, rice, sweetcorn, potatoes, vegetables and tropical fruit.

The most popular meats are goat and lamb, although beef is also becoming popular. Typical species of fish include *dorada* (sea bass) and *pez espada* (swordfish).

Lagomar restaurant in Lanzarote

Canary dishes are quite easy and quick to prepare. Most types of fish and meat are fried or roasted. They are usually served with the local *mojo* sauces, made of olive oil, seasoning and herbs.

Local bars serve basic *raciones* (portions), including *tortilla de patata* (omelette with potatoes), *jamón Serrano* (Spanish ham), *queso* (cheese) and many others.

Another option are the so-called *platos combinados* – inexpensive combinations of basic dishes, including chips, fried egg and cutlet. These are large helpings, and usually competitively priced.

Also available are "single pot" courses. These consist mainly of potatoes and pulses, along with any combination of meat, fish and vegetables.

One should also not forget *gofio*. This roasted sweetcorn flour can be added to everything: soups, stews, desserts and even ice cream!

WHEN TO EAT

AS WITH THE rest of Spain, mealtimes on the Canary Islands have fairly irregular hours. Lunchtime (*la comida*) is usually between 1pm and 3pm, but restaurants that cater principally for locals tend to have unusually late meal times. Regardless of the hour, however, having ordered a meal you are generally allowed to finish it in peace.

Restaurants by the harbour in Puerto de Mogán

Outside traditional mealtimes it is always possible to eat in bars, which offer a wide variety of food. Beachside restaurants are good for snacks any time of day.

Dinner *(cena)* starts late, at about 9pm. It is served in all restaurants until 11pm or midnight. After this, it is generally only possible to buy sandwiches, kebabs or hot dogs in small bars.

Dinner in Spain is usually a hot meal. Like lunch, it may include two courses. During dinnertime, the restaurants offer only meals *à la carte*. Spaniards like to meet from time to time for dinner, in bars that serve *tapas* or *raciones*. When in a group it is fun to order a selection of *tapas* and sample a little bit of each dish.

The Spanish breakfast *(desayuno)* tends to be a light affair and usually consists only of coffee with milk and a sweet bun. An alternative is toast with ham and cheese. Many bars offer a set breakfast, generally including coffee, natural orange juice and a snack. If you want a bowl of breakfast cereal or a fry-up you had better head for a hotel restaurant.

BOOKING

THE LARGE NUMBER of restaurants on the islands means that there are no problems with finding a table. Nevertheless, sometimes it is worth booking in advance in order to avoid disappointment, particularly when you fancy a specific restaurant.

VEGETARIANS

ALL RESTAURANTS OFFER some vegetarian dishes, but the concept of a strictly meatless or fishless diet is not always understood. It is wise to check before ordering whether vegetarian dishes contain meat stocks or ham.

Stylish interior of Finca de las Salinas hotel restaurant in Yaiza

PRICES

PRICES IN THE islands' restaurants can vary enormously. In smart, exclusive establishments a full meal, including wine, may cost up to 50 euros per head. In other, provincial restaurants, the same meal could cost around 15 euros.

During lunch hours many restaurants offer, besides *à la carte* dishes, an inexpensive and tasty *menu del día* (menu of the day). Such menus always include a selection of starters, main courses and desserts, as well as bread and often beverages (wine, beer or soft drinks). The average price of such a meal is from 4 to 10 euros.

Some more upmarket restaurants also offer "taster" menus. The dishes from these menus are much more expensive, since they include all of the specialities recommended by the chef.

PAYING

ALMOST ALL restaurants accept credit cards to pay *la cuenta* (the bill). Even bars are willing to accept this form of payment, if it is more than a certain amount. You must, however, be prepared to pay in cash in smaller restaurants, not oriented towards tourists. Also, bills of under 30 euros are usually settled in cash. It is best to ask before ordering, if in doubt. Traveller's cheques are sometimes accepted.

TIPPING

TIPS ARE NOT obligatory and may be left depending on the quality of service. If the service was bad, then don't tip! Generally, tips are below ten per cent. As a rule, you leave loose change or round up the bill. The IGIC tax is included in the price.

Restaurants lining the ocean boulevard in Playa de las Américas

What to Eat in the Canary Islands

Goat's cheese – a popular snack

THE ISLANDS' CUISINE, though influenced by mainland Spain and Latin America, has its own character and combines elements of Guanche cooking with ingredients from the New World, including bananas and sweetcorn.

Mojo verde

Papas arrugadas *are potatoes cooked in their skins, in brine, with a large amount of salt. They are the accompaniment to many dishes and are eaten with mojo picón or mojo verde.*

Mojo picón

Mojo, a pounded sauce that varies in its taste and colour depending on whether it is made with coriander or paprika, is used as a dip with pretty much anything. *Papas arrugadas* (wrinkly potatoes) are another local speciality.

Potaje de berros, *a thick soup containing watercress, potatoes, corn on the cob, pork, beans and cumin.*

Caldo de pescado, *a type of fish soup. Fish is sometimes served separately, accompanied by potatoes, bouillon and bread.*

Puchero, *a saffron-flavoured stew consisting of chorizo, beans and vegetables, seasoned according to local traditions.*

Rancho canario *consists of many types of meat, chickpeas, potatoes and noodles, which are slowly stewed together.*

Arroz con verduras *is a light and colourful mixture of rice, chopped peppers, sweetcorn and tomatoes.*

Ropa vieja *is a type of thick vegetarian stew made with chickpeas, onion, tomatoes and fried potatoes.*

FRUIT

The mild climate of the Canary Islands is conducive to the growth of numerous varieties of fruit, and locally grown fresh fruit is available all year round. The most popular varieties include Canary bananas, prickly pears, papayas and pineapples. These are the basis of many tasty desserts.

Pineapple

Prickly pear

Pomegranate

Bananas

Papaya

Dates

Grapes

Churros de pescado *are fishcakes made of minced fish, coated with salty batter and fried in oil.*

Morena frita *is one of the most popular fish dishes. Fried* morena *is served with sauces and* papas arrugadas.

Sancocho de pescado *is fish with potatoes and vegetables. Individual ingredients are served separately.*

Conejo al salmorejo, *an appetizing stew made with rabbit and tomatoes, is best eaten with* papas arrugadas.

Carne de cabra en salsa *is a typical Canary meat dish. Pieces of goat meat are stewed in a wine-based gravy, with added herbs and seasoning. The dish may be served with potatoes and* papas arrugadas.

Stewed pieces of goat meat

Stewed vegetables

Red peppers

Mojo verde, made of oil, coriander and garlic

Sama frita con mojo verde *is one of the islands' typical fish dishes. Fried fish is served with* papas arrugadas *and accompanied with sauce.*

Papas arrugadas

Fried pieces of sama

DESSERTS

The islands' desserts are not sophisticated but delicious all the same. They consist mainly of sweets made with *gofio* and a variety of fruit.

Gofio de almendras, a rich dessert made with almonds

Rapaduras, dessert made of sugar, milk and almonds

RUM AND MALVASÍA

The Canary Islands are famous for two types of drinks – rum and Malvasía. Rum is produced in several varieties. The most typical is *ron miel* – mead rum – which is made with palm honey, and contains 35 per cent alcohol. There are also several brands of wine produced on the islands. Once red wines from Tenerife were famous. Today Malvasía is more popular. Produced on Lanzarote, particularly sought-after brands come from the region of La Geria.

Dark Canary rum

Malvasía from Lanzarote

Choosing a Restaurant

THE FOLLOWING RESTAURANTS have been chosen for their fine food, with particular emphasis on regional cuisine, as well as for the quality of their location and décor. Establishments are listed in the order in which the islands appear in the guide, and then in alphabetical order according to location. For more details on food and restaurants, see pages 164–167.

	CREDIT CARDS	REGIONAL CUISINE	AIR CONDITIONING	GARDEN OR TERRACE	PARKING
GRAN CANARIA					
AGAETE: *Casa Pepe* €€ C/Alcalde Armas Galván, 5. (928 898 227. This restaurant prides itself on its variety of fish and shellfish dishes. It also serves typical local *papas arrugadas* and *mojos*. ○ Thu–Tue. ● 15–30 Oct.		●	■		
AGAETE: *Puerto Laguete* €€ Nuestra Señora de las Nieves, 9. (928 554 001 This is an excellent place to sample typical Canary cuisine. ○ daily.		●			
AGAETE: *La Palmita* €€€ Ctra. de Las Nieves, s/n. (928 898 704. The restaurant specializes in fish and Canary cuisine. A dish particularly recommended is the *venison à la espalada*. ○ 11am–11pm Wed–Mon.	■	●		●	■
AGÜIMES: *La Farola* €€€ Puerto de Arinaga. (928 180 410. Canary-style fresh fish dishes are the speciality in this charming restaurant. ● Sun evening & Mon. 🅰	■	●	■		
ARUCAS: *Meson de la Montaña* €€€ Montaña de Arucas, s/n.(928 601 475. @ mesonarucas@hvsl.es One can find here Canary cuisine at its best. All the dishes are varied and beautifully presented. ○ noon–midnight daily. 🅰	■	●	■	■	
LAS PALMAS DE GRAN CANARIA: *Chacalote* €€ C/Proa, 3. (928 312 140. With a décor that resembles a ship's interior, this restaurant has a delightful atmosphere. It serves good food, and the fish dishes are exceptional.	■		■		
LAS PALMAS DE GRAN CANARIA: *El Novillo Precoz* €€€ C/Portugal, 9. (928 221 659. Situated near the beach, this restaurant serves delicious meat that has been grilled on glowing embers. ○ Tue–Sun. ● 2 weeks in May & Aug.	■				
LAS PALMAS DE GRAN CANARIA: *Mesón La Cuadra* €€€ C/General Mas de Gaminde 32. (928 243 380. Relish the tempting variety of tapas at the bar or choose from the "home-grown menu". The owner's own farm produces many of the ingredients for this restaurant. ● Mon.	■				
LAS PALMAS DE GRAN CANARIA: *Asturias* €€€€ C/Capitán Lucena, 6. (928 274 219. Situated in a maze of small streets near the beach, this restaurant specializes in Asturian dishes. ● 1–15 Sep.	■		■		
LAS PALMAS DE GRAN CANARIA: *Felo Botello* €€€€ C/León y Castillo, 274. (928 296 840. Felo Botello serves mainly creative cuisine, although you can also sample some more traditional local dishes. ○ Mon–Sat. ● Sat evening. 🅰	■		■		
LAS PALMAS DE GRAN CANARIA: *La Cabaña Criolla* €€€€ C/Los Martínez de Escobar, 37. (928 270 216. Meat dishes are the speciality, and are prepared in a variety of ways. Prices reflect the quality of the food. ● Mon.	■		■		
LAS PALMAS DE GRAN CANARIA: *La Dolce Vita* €€€€ C/Agustín Millares, 5. (928 310 463. This is an upmarket restaurant, serving authentic Italian food and wines. ○ Mon–Sat. ● Jul.	■				

	CREDIT CARDS	REGIONAL CUISINE	AIR-CONDITIONING	GARDEN OR TERRACE	PARKING

Price per person for a three-course meal, including wine and tax (without tip).
€ up to 15 euros
€€ 15–20 euros
€€€ 20–25 euros
€€€€ 25–30 euros
€€€€€ over 30 euros.

CREDIT CARDS
Eurocard, MasterCard, Visa, Diners Club all accepted.

REGIONAL CUISINE
Menu includes choice of Canary cuisine.

AIR-CONDITIONING
Restaurant with air-conditioning.

GARDEN OR TERRACE
Meal can be served on a terrace, in a garden or courtyard.

PARKING
Restaurant has its own parking.

LAS PALMAS DE GRAN CANARIA: *La Marinera* €€€€
C/Alonso de Ojeda, s/n. 928 461 555.
A full and varied selection of cuisine is on the menu, with the emphasis on fresh ingredients. The fish dishes, cooked according to local recipes, are particularly tasty.

■	●		●	

LAS PALMAS DE GRAN CANARIA: *La Sama* €€€€
C/Marina, 87. 928 321 428.
This restaurant specializes in fish and seafood, which is always fresh and well prepared.

■			●	

LAS PALMAS DE GRAN CANARIA: *Amaiur* €€€€€
C/Pérez Galdós, 2. 928 370 717.
This is one of the town's best restaurants, boasting a good selection of wines and Basque cuisine at its best. ☐ Mon–Sat. ● Aug.

■		■		■

LAS PALMAS DE GRAN CANARIA: *Casa de Galicia* €€€€€
C/Salvador Cuyás, 8. 928 279 855.
This restaurant gives you the choice of two settings to enjoy your meal as it consists of two areas. At No. 8 is the Galician restaurant, serving the traditional cuisine of that region. The Anexo restaurant, at No. 10, specializes in rice dishes.

■		■		

LAS PALMAS DE GRAN CANARIA: *El Cucharón* €€€€€
C/Reloj, 2. 928 333 296.
A smart restaurant, serving creative cuisine. All the dishes are sophisticated and elaborately prepared. ☐ Mon–Sat. ● Sat afternoon & 15 Aug–15 Sep.

■		■		

LAS PALMAS DE GRAN CANARIA: *Las Trébedes* €€€€€
Avda. José Mesa y López, 18. (El Corte Inglés). 928 263 000.
Typical Spanish dishes are on offer at this restaurant, with particular emphasis on Canary cuisine. ☐ Mon–Sat.

■	●	■		

LAS PALMAS DE GRAN CANARIA: *Portovigo* €€€€€
C/General Vives, 90. 928 279 276.
Exclusive and sophisticated cuisine, inspired by Galician traditions.
☐ 1–4pm & 8–midnight Mon–Sat. ● Aug.

■		■		

MASPALOMAS: *Chilis* €€€€
Avda. de Tenerife, 17. 928 770 047.
A rich array of Mexican dishes are on offer in this bright and cheerful restaurant, with a modern interior décor. Particularly recommended is the spectacular flaming Mexican coffee. ☐ 7pm–1am.

■		■		

MASPALOMAS: *El Portalón* €€€€
Avda. Tirajana, 27. 928 772 030. @ sol.barbacon@solmelia.es
An excellent place for sampling a selection of Basque dishes, all of which are splendidly prepared and served.

■		■	●	

MASPALOMAS: *Orangerie* €€€€
Hotel Palm Beach, Avenida Oasis. 928 140 806.
A restaurant of creative and upmarket cuisine, which offers diners a choice of eating indoors or outside. ● Thu, Sun, Jun & Jul.

■		■	●	

MOGÁN: *Tu Casa* €€
Avda. de las Artes, 18. 928 565 078.
The secret of this restaurant's success is its unfailingly fresh ingredients, prepared by the chef. The dishes are based on Canary cuisine.

■	●	■	●	

MOGÁN: *Acaymo* €€
El Tostador, 14. 928 569 263.
A restaurant specializing in traditional Canary cuisine, which includes fish and meat dishes. ☐ noon–11pm Tue–Sun. ● 15 Jun–15 Jul.

■	●		●	■

For key to symbols see back flap

Price per person for a three-course meal, including wine and tax (without tip).
€ up to 15 euros
€€ 15–20 euros
€€€ 20–25 euros
€€€€ 25–30 euros
€€€€€ over 30 euros.

CREDIT CARDS
Eurocard, MasterCard, Visa, Diners Club all accepted.

REGIONAL CUISINE
Menu includes choice of Canary cuisine.

AIR CONDITIONING
Restaurant with air conditioning.

GARDEN OR TERRACE
Meal can be served on a terrace, in a garden or courtyard.

PARKING
Restaurant has its own parking.

	CREDIT CARDS	REGIONAL CUISINE	AIR CONDITIONING	GARDEN OR TERRACE	PARKING
SAN AGUSTÍN: *Anno Domini* €€€€€ Centro Comercial, local 82–85. 928 762 915. A comfortable and pleasant restaurant, specializing in French and international cuisine. ☐ Mon–Sat. ● 1 Oct–30 Apr.	■		■	●	
SAN BARTOLOMÉ DE TIRAJANA: *Rias Bajas* €€€€ Avda. Tirajana and Avda. EE.UU. 928 764 033. Galician regional restaurant, serving very tasty and well-prepared food.	■		■		■
SAN FERNANDO: *Casa Wences* €€€ Secundino Delgado. Ed. Jovimar. 928 761 700. Cantabrian regional cuisine serving traditional dishes, all of which are splendidly prepared. ☐ 12–4pm & 8–midnight. ● Mon.	■		■	●	
SAN FERNANDO: *Mallorca* €€€ C/Alcalde Santos González, 11. 928 770 516. As the name suggests, the restaurant specializes in a variety of dishes from Majorca.	■		■	●	
SANTA BRÍGIDA: *Las Grutas de Artiles* €€ Las Meleguinas. 928 640 575. Set in caves, this restaurant has authentic Canary Island specialities on the menu as well as a selection of grilled meat. There is a swimming pool and garden, which makes it ideal for families.	■			●	
SANTA BRÍGIDA: *Mano de Hierro* €€€€ Vuelta del Pino, 25. 928 640 388. Serving mainly traditional German cuisine, this restaurant also offers a variety of international dishes. If this fails to tempt the taste buds, a selection of local delicacies is also on the menu. ● Jul.	■			●	■
SANTA BRÍGIDA: *Satautey* €€€€ Real de Coello, 2. Monte Lentiscal. 928 355 511. Excellent upmarket restaurant, situated in Santa Brigida hotel. It specializes in local and international cuisine.	■	●			
VEGA DE SAN MATEO: *Cho-Zacarías* €€€ Avda. Tinamar, s/n. 928 661 796. Uniquely set in old farmers' cottages, this delightful restaurant serves Canary homemade dishes such as *cherne* (a local fish) in coriander sauce. ☐ 1–6pm & 8–midnight. 🔧		●		●	
VEGA DE SAN MATEO: *La Veguetilla* €€€ Ctra. General del Centro, 20. km. 928 660 764. Local and Spanish cuisine. ☐ Wed–Mon.	■	●		●	■
FUERTEVENTURA					
BETANCURIA: *Casa Santa Maria* €€€ Plaza de la Concepción, s/n. 928 878 282. @ rloos@lix.intercom.es The food is always prepared from fresh produce of the highest quality. The restaurant offers painstakingly prepared dishes, inspired by traditional Mediterranean cuisine. ☐ 11am–6pm daily. 🔧	■			●	
BETANCURIA: *Valtarajal* €€ Roberto Roldán, s/n. 928 878 007. This restaurant offers typical Canary cuisine in pleasant surroundings. ☐ 9am–5pm daily.	■	●		●	■
CORRALEJO: *La Marquesina* €€€ Muelle Chico. 928 535 435. Specializing in fish, prepared according to traditional recipes, this restaurant also serves a variety of international dishes. ☐ 10am–11:30pm daily.	■	●	■		

CORRALEJO: *Siño Juan* €€€
Placita Félix Estévez, s/n. 928 867 000.
Excellent international cuisine is served at this restaurant, with dishes
prepared from the finest ingredients.

COSTA CALMA: *Don Quijote* €€€
C/Tenerife, s/n. Apartamento Santa Ursula. 928 875 158.
The best dishes on offer here are definitely the roast suckling pig and roast
lamb, although other dishes are also worth a try. ☐ *noon–midnight daily.*

JANDIA-PAJARA: *El Marinero Esquinzo* €€€€
Montaña de la Muda, 2. 928 544 075.
Smart restaurant, specializing in international cuisine. The dress code is
obligatory. ☐ *noon–10pm daily.*

PUERTO DEL ROSARIO: *La Casa del Jamón* €€€
La Asomada, s/n (junto al Aeropuerto viejo). 928 530 064.
Resembling a traditional Spanish *mesón*, there is a mix of Basque and
regional dishes (including roast kid, Iberian cold meats and a variety of
delicious cheeses) at this family-run restaurant. ☐ *Tue–Sun.* ● *Sun night.*

PUERTO DEL ROSARIO: *Benjamin* €€
C/León y Castillo 139. 928 851 748.
Local produce is used almost exclusively for this traditional Canary
restaurant, which serves authentic dishes such as potatoes with *mojo* (a
spicy sauce). Also to be recommended are the cheeses and desserts such as
a sorbet made from prickly pear. ● *Sun & public holidays.*

LANZAROTE

ARRECIFE: *Leito de Proa* €
Avenue César Manrique. 928 802 066.
Beautifully situated on a lagoon – El Charco (the puddle), this restaurant
serves *tapas* and full portions of typical Canary food.
☐ *noon–4:30pm & 7–11pm.* ● *Sun.*

ARRECIFE: *Mesôn Trasgu* €€
C/José Antonio, 98. 928 806 676.
This is an Asturian restaurant, with especially delicious, inexpensive and
varied *tapas* on the menu.

ARRECIFE: *A. Colon* €€€€€
C/Cactus, s/n. Playa del Cable. Ciudad Jardín.
928 805 649. @ colons@jet.es
Decorated in a nautical style, this restaurant serves sophisticated and
expertly prepared dishes, including duck foie gras. Menu varies with the
seasons of the year. Also with an excellent wine list, this is far and away
the best restaurant on the island.
☐ *Mon–Sat.* ● *15 Aug–15 Sep.* ♿

COSTA TEGUISE: *Chu-Lin III* €€
Centro Comercial Tandarena, local 8. 928 592 011
As the name suggests, this is a Chinese restaurant, offering a surprisingly
good selection of wines. ☐ *1pm–midnight daily.*

COSTA TEGUISE: *Neptuno* €€€
Avda. del Jablillo, s/n. Centro Comercial Neptuno, local 6. 928 590 378.
A restaurant serving mainly international cuisine, although the menu
includes a number of local specialities. ☐ *Mon–Sat.* ● *10 Jun–20 Jul.*

COSTA TEGUISE: *La Jordana* €€€€
Los Geranios, s/n. Centro Comercial Lanzarote Bay. 928 590 328.
Simple, inexpensive, tasty fare, prepared using Mediterranean produce and
recipes. ☐ *Mon–Sat.* ● *Sep.*

HARÍA: *Casa'l Cura* €€€
C/Nueva, 1. 928 835 556. FAX 928 821 442.
The Casa'l Cura is a reliable restaurant, offering a wide variety of dishes.
☐ *noon–5pm daily.*

NAZARET: *Lagomar* €€€€
C/Los Loros, 6. 928 845 665.
The restaurant occupies a villa that was designed by César Manrique for
Omar Sharif. The talented chef uses only fresh produce.
☐ *noon–midnight Tue–Sat, Sun noon–6pm.*

For key to symbols see back flap

Price per person for a three-course meal, including wine and tax (without tip).
€ up to 15 euros
€€ 15–20 euros
€€€ 20–25 euros
€€€€ 25–30 euros
€€€€€ over 30 euros.

CREDIT CARDS
Eurocard, MasterCard, Visa, Diners Club all accepted.
REGIONAL CUISINE
Menu includes choice of Canary cuisine.
AIR CONDITIONING
Restaurant with air conditioning.
GARDEN OR TERRACE
Meal can be served on a terrace, in a garden or courtyard.
PARKING
Restaurant has its own parking.

	Price	CREDIT CARDS	REGIONAL CUISINE	AIR CONDITIONING	GARDEN OR TERRACE	PARKING
PLAYA BLANCA: *El Marisco Casa Brígida* C/El Palangre, 1. 928 517 385. An inexpensive restaurant, serving delicious fish and seafood. Tue–Sun. 15 Jun–15 Jul.	€€€	■			●	
PLAYA BLANCA: *Almacén de la Sal* Marítimo, 12. 928 517 885. Occupying a former salt storehouse, this restaurant specializes in traditional Spanish cuisine. Tue.	€€€€	■			●	
PARQUE NACIONAL DE TIMANFAYA: *El Diablo* 928 840 057. The restaurant commands a magnificent view over the national park, the volcanic rocks and the ocean. One of its curiosities is to prepare dishes on a "volcanic grill". during park opening hours.	€€					■
PUERTO DEL CARMEN: *La Dolce Vita* Avda. Playas, 31 (junto al Centro Comercial Atlas). 928 513 231. An Italian restaurant, offering a wide selection of dishes. 6pm–midnight.	€	■		■		■
PUERTO DEL CARMEN: *La Cañada* C/César Manrique, 3. 928 512 108. It is definitely worth a visit to this typical Canary restaurant, which serves excellently prepared food. 12:30pm–midnight Mon–Sat.	€€€€	■	●	■	●	
PUERTO DEL CARMEN: *O Botafumeiro* C/Alemania, 9. Centro Comercial Costa Luz. 928 511 503. You can find genuine Galician cuisine at this restaurant. Tue.	€€€€	■				
TEGUISE: *Ikarus* Plaza 18 de Julio, s/n. 928 845 332. A restaurant serving excellent international cuisine, with prices that reflect the quality of the food. 9am–10:30pm Tue–Sun. Sun and Jul.	€€€	■				
YAIZA: *La Era* El Barranco, 3. Trasera del Ayuntamiento. 928 830 016. info@la-era.com. Occupying a historic building, this restaurant is decorated in a rustic style and provides traditional Canary cuisine. 1pm–11pm. Mon.	€€€	■	●	■	●	■

TENERIFE

	Price	CREDIT CARDS	REGIONAL CUISINE	AIR CONDITIONING	GARDEN OR TERRACE	PARKING
ARONA: *Mesón Las Rejas* Ctra. General del Sur, 1. 922 720 894. This restaurant specializes in roast-meat dishes. Mon–Sat. Jul.	€€€	■		■		
BUENAVISTA: *El Burgado* Avenida Playa de las Arenas s/n. 922 127 831. Sample fresh fish and Canary desserts on the terrace of this seaside restaurant.	€€€	■	●		●	
CANDELARIA: *El Archete* Aroba, 2. 922 500 115. The order of the day at this restaurant is to provide exquisite food, based on traditional Canary cuisine. Tue–Sat. 1–15 Oct.	€€€€			■		■
EL SAUZAL: *Casa Del Vino* Autopista del Norte, 21. km. La Baranda. 922 563 886. amos@jet.es A good selection of modern Canary dishes, which are yet based on traditional ingredients and recipes. Tue–Sun. Sun evenings & Mon.	€€€	■	●		●	■
LA LAGUNA: *El Principito* C/Santo Domingo, 26. 922 633 916. This restaurant specializes in French cuisine, and its interior evokes the atmosphere of an authentic French eatery. Sun & Mon.	€€€€€	■				

LA MATANZA: *Casa Juan* €€€
C/Acentejo, 77. 922 577 012. @ casajuan@arrakis.es
The emphasis is on German food, but the restaurant also serves
international cuisine. ☐ Tue–Sat. ● 15 Apr–15 May. &

LOS REALEJOS: *La Finca* €€€
El Monturio, 12. 922 340 143. @ dreisorner@teleline.es
Inspired by North-European cuisine, this restaurant serves excellent food,
which is exquisitely prepared and presented. ☐ Tue–Sat. ● Jul. &

PLAYA DE LAS AMÉRICAS: *Bleu de Toit* €€€€€
Torviscas – Centro Comercial Río Center. 922 714 938.
Exclusive, sophisticated French cuisine is served in this restaurant. It is only
open in the evening. ☐ Mon–Sat. ● May.

PUERTO DE LA CRUZ: *La Gañania* €€
Camino del Durazno, s/n. 922 371 000.
This restaurant offers various dishes, ranging from local Canary food to
international cuisine, not forgetting traditional Spanish dishes.
☐ Tue–Sat. &

PUERTO DE LA CRUZ: *Magnolia* €€€€€
Avda. Marqués de Villanueva del Prado. 922 385 614.
Catalonian regional cuisine, combining produce typical of the coastal and
mountain regions, so providing something a little different. ● Tue. &

SAN ISIDRO: *Bodega el Jable* €€€€
Bentejúi, 9. 922 390 698.
Excellent local cuisine, including all the most popular dishes.
☐ Mon–Sat. ● Mon lunchtime.

SAN JUAN DE LA RAMBLA: *Las Aguas* €€€€
La Destila, 20. 922 360 428.
The restaurant offers typical homemade Spanish food, exquisitely prepared.
● Sun night & Mon.

SANTA CRUZ DE TENERIFE: *Cofradía de Pescadores* €
Playa de Teresitas. 922 549 024.
One of the best places in town, which specializes in fish. ☐ daily.

SANTA CRUZ DE TENERIFE: *Marisquería de Ramón* €€
C/Dique 23. 922 549 308.
An inexpensive place, where you can try fresh seafood and fish.

SANTA CRUZ DE TENERIFE: *Da Gigi* €€€
Avda. de Anaga, 43. 922 274 326.
Italian restaurant, serving a wide variety of pasta and other Italian dishes.

SANTA CRUZ DE TENERIFE: *Viva México* €€€
C/Santa Clara, 8. 922 296 088.
A wide selection of Mexican cuisine. ● Sun & Mon.

SANTA CRUZ DE TENERIFE: *El Líbano* €€€
C/Santiago Cuadrado, 26. 922 285 914.
A perfect opportunity to try Middle Eastern cuisine. The menu
includes the most typical and traditional Arabian dishes.

SANTA CRUZ DE TENERIFE: *El Principado* €€€€
C/General Antequera, 17. 922 281 263.
A good range of international and local cuisine, which is both appetizing
and attractively presented. ● Sun and evenings.

SANTA CRUZ DE TENERIFE: *La Cazuela* €€€€
C/Robayna, 34. 922 272 300.
Creative cuisine, inspired by Mediterranean traditions. ☐ Mon–Sat.

SANTA CRUZ DE TENERIFE: *La Hierbita* €€€€
El Clavel, 19. 922 244 617.
Traditional local dishes based on regional products and excellent local
wines, served in a family atmosphere. ● Sun.

SANTA CRUZ DE TENERIFE: *Mesón Castellano* €€€€
C/Callao de Lima, 4. 922 271 074.
An excellent restaurant, specializing in Castilian cuisine. The marvellous
meat dishes are particularly recommended. ● Sun.

	CREDIT CARDS	REGIONAL CUISINE	AIR CONDITIONING	GARDEN OR TERRACE	PARKING
Price per person for a three-course meal, including wine and tax (without tip). **€** up to 15 euros **€€** 15–20 euros **€€€** 20–25 euros **€€€€** 25–30 euros **€€€€€** over 30 euros. **CREDIT CARDS** Eurocard, MasterCard, Visa, Diners Club all accepted. **REGIONAL CUISINE** Menu includes choice of Canary cuisine. **AIR CONDITIONING** Restaurant with air conditioning. **GARDEN OR TERRACE** Meal can be served on a terrace, in a garden or courtyard. **PARKING** Restaurant has its own parking.					
SANTA CRUZ DE TENERIFE: *Amos* €€€€€ C/Poeta Tomás Morales, 2. (922 285 010. @ amos@jet.es The restaurant offers international cuisine, as well as local specialities, with a wide selection of dishes to suit all tastes. ○ Mon–Sat. ● Aug.	■		■	●	■
SANTA CRUZ DE TENERIFE: *Los Menceyes* €€€€€ Avda. Dr. José Naveiras, 38. (922 609 900. @ mencey@ctv.es An excellent restaurant, situated in the luxury Mencey Hotel, belonging to the Sheraton chain. The sophisticated dishes are based on traditional Spanish cuisine. &	■		■	●	■
SANTIAGO DEL TEIDE: *Pancho* €€€€ Playa de la Arena, s/n. (922 861 323. @ fraro@abaforum.es Exquisite Canary cuisine, which is both sophisticated and well prepared. All dishes are attractively presented. ● Mon.	■	●		●	
TACORONTE: *Los Limoneros* €€€€€ Ctra. General del Norte, 15.5 km. Los Naranjeros. (922 636 637. International cuisine, with Spanish and Canary accents, and excellent seafood. ○ 1pm–11pm Mon–Sat. ● 15 days in Aug. &			■	●	■

LA GOMERA

	CREDIT CARDS	REGIONAL CUISINE	AIR CONDITIONING	GARDEN OR TERRACE	PARKING
PLAYA DE SANTIAGO: *Avenida* €€ Avda Marítima, Playa de Santiago. (922 895 498. This restaurant has a particularly varied menu and is popular with tourists. Tasty dishes include fish and homemade pizza.	■				
PLAYA DE SANTIAGO: *Playa* €€ Avda. Marítima. (922 895 147. Typical seaside restaurant, offering mainly freshly caught fish.	■		■	●	
PLAYA DE SANTIAGO: *El Laurel* €€€€ Lomada de Tecina. (922 145 850. Belonging to the Jardín Tecina hotel chain, this restaurant offers creative cuisine, based on traditional local recipes and a standard of service that you might expect. ○ 7pm–10pm daily.	■			●	■
PLAYA DE SANTIAGO: *Tagoror* €€€€ Lomada de Tecina. (922 895 425. This restaurant specializes in local cuisine, based on fresh produce and recipes particular to La Gomera. It also has a good range of international dishes on offer. ● Thu.	■	●			
SAN SEBASTIÁN DE LA GOMERA: *Casa del Mar* € Avda. Fred Olsen 2. (922 871 219. Family-style restaurant close to the harbour, serving simple seafood dishes. ● Sun.	■				
SAN SEBASTIÁN DE LA GOMERA: *El Pajar* €€ C/Ruiz de Padrón, 26. (922 870 355. Excellent and inexpensive restaurant, serving mainly local cuisine.	■	●			
SAN SEBASTIÁN DE LA GOMERA: *Mesón el Pejín* €€ Avda. Colón, 26. (922 870 033. This restaurant serves a particularly varied menu. The beautifully prepared fish and seafood dishes are especially good.					
SAN SEBASTIÁN DE LA GOMERA: €€€€ Llano de la Horca, 1. (922 871 100. The restaurant is situated in a smart *parador*. As is the case with most of the state-run hotels, its décor and menu reflect the local traditions. Particularly worth recommending are the fish dishes.	■	●			■

VALLE DEL GRAN REY: *El Palmarejo*　　€€
Ctra. Gral. de Arure, s/n. **♩** 922 805 868.
The food on offer represents Canary Island cuisine, although
the menu also includes a number of international dishes.

EL HIERRO

ECHEDO: *La Higuera de Abuela*　　€€
Tajiniscoba, s/n. **♩** 922 551 026.
Simple, traditional Canary Island cuisine is served here, with a good
selection of local wines. ◯ *Wed–Mon* . ▼

LA RESTINGA: *Casa Juan*　　€
Juan Gutiérrez Monteverde, 23. **♩** 922 557 102.
The Casa Juan offers a wide selection of simple and tasty fish dishes.
All the food is prepared using freshly caught fish. ● *Wed.*

LAS PLAYAS: *Parador del Hierro*　　€€€€
♩ 922 558 036.
A *parador* restaurant, serving local and Spanish food. The cheese
soup is particularly delicious.

VALVERDE: *Mirador de la Peña*　　€€
Ctra. de Guarazoca, 40. **♩** 922 550 300.
One of the Hacensa chain of training restaurants, which
organizes catering weeks, competitions and courses. There's nothing
unprofessional about the food here though. ◯ *Tue–Sun.*

LA PALMA

BARLOVENTO: *La Palma Romántica*　　€€€€
Ctra. Gral. Las Llanadas, s/n. **♩** 922 186 221.
The restaurant is situated in the hotel of the same name. It offers
a wide choice of dishes, ranging from Canary through Spanish, to
international cuisine. ♿

BREÑA BAJA: *La Fontana*　　€€
Los Cancajos. **♩** 922 434 729.
Next to the beach, the restaurant offers excellent meat and fish dishes.

BREÑA ALTA: *Las Tres Chimeneas*　　€€€
C/Buenavista de Arriba, 82. **♩** 922 429 470.
A pleasant restaurant, offering food based on traditional island cuisine.
◯ *Wed–Mon.* ● *Mon night & 19 Aug–25 Sep.*

GARAFÍA: *El Bernegal*　　€€
C/Díaz y Suárez, 5. **♩** 922 400 480.
This restaurant serves excellent home-cooked Canary and Spanish
cuisine, and it also has a good range of vegetarian dishes.
◯ *noon–5pm Tue–Sun.* ● *Mon & Jun.*

LOS LLANOS DE ARIDANE: *San Petronio*　　€€
C/Pino de Santiago, 4. **♩** 922 462 403.
A good Italian restaurant. ● *Sun & Mon.*

LOS LLANOS DE ARIDANE: *La Casona de Argual*　　€€€
Plaza Sotomayor, 6. **♩** 922 401 816. **FAX** 922 401 816.
@ casonaargual@atensis.com.
A smart restaurant with a unique atmosphere, serving sophisticated
dishes of international and French cuisine. ◯ *Fri–Wed.* ● *3 weeks in Jun.*

SANTA CRUZ DE LA PALMA: *Pizzeria Alameda*　　€
C/Pérez Camacho, 3. **♩** 922 420 865.
This restaurant offers a wide selection of dishes, from both Italian and
Canary cuisine.

SANTA CRUZ DE LA PALMA: *El Faro*　　€€€€
Avda. Marítima, 27. **♩** 922 412 890
One of the most popular restaurants in town. It offers mainly creative
cuisine, made with local produce according to traditional recipes.

TAZACORTE: *Playa Mont*　　€€
El Puerto, s/n. **♩** 922 480 045.
This restaurant specializes in fresh fish, prepared Canary style.
◯ *Fri–Wed.* ● *Jul.* ♿

For key to symbols see back flap

SHOPPING IN THE CANARY ISLANDS

As with Spain's other regions, the Canary Islands boast their own culinary specialities. Many tourists buy local delicacies including goat's cheese, rum, wine, palm mead and the delicious *mojo* (ready-made sauce). Potted plants have also recently become popular presents from the islands. These may even include small banana trees, palms and dragon trees. Other souvenirs, such as

Label for Malvasía wine

handicraft products, embroidery and lace, leather goods and pottery, are likewise snapped up as mementos. Some visitors notice a price difference – a remnant of the days when the islands were a duty-free zone. Products such as alcohol, cigarettes, perfumes, sunglasses and electronic equipment are generally cheaper than in mainland Europe and are among the most easily purchased items.

Entrance to the shopping centre at Playa de las Américas

WHERE TO BUY

THERE ARE MANY shopping centres in large towns and around resorts. They offer practically every essential food product and manufactured item, and are less imposing than the megastores you find in Spain and elsewhere. They often include bars and restaurants.

Apart from the large department stores, the resorts have many small shops, offering souvenirs, clothes and cosmetics. They can be found along the main streets and seafront boulevards. There are many electronic equipment shops too. Fixed prices are not set in stone on the islands and it is well worth haggling. Just as numerous as the electronic shops are the *artesanía* shops, selling souvenirs and handicraft items. Here, too, haggling over the price is

almost expected. The local shops in smaller towns and villages are worth checking out, particularly when shopping for food, as they may sell products that do not reach larger towns.

Those wishing to buy local handicraft products might try buying directly from the local artists who made them. Cutting out the middle man means prices will be lower than those charged by the seaside shops.

OPENING HOURS

LARGE shopping centres in big towns are generally open from 9am until 9pm Monday to Saturday. Some of the smaller ones may close for siesta, i.e. between 2pm and 5pm and then stay open for another few hours. Many

shops, particularly food stores in tourist centres, are open non-stop, until late at night.

Most smaller shops and boutiques do not have such regular opening hours and may close without warning. Also, afternoon closing hours are not fixed. In small towns and villages, where the pace of life is slower, siesta breaks are longer, and shops may close earlier.

Traditionally decorated pot from La Orotava

HOW TO PAY

MOST SHOPS accept major credit cards. The most popular are Visa and MasterCard. When shopping in small provincial shops and bazaars, you should bear in mind that credit cards may be of no use. When venturing outside large towns it is best to carry a certain amount of cash.

African carvings on sale at Teguise market

MARKETS AND BAZAARS

MARKETS AND BAZAARS are an inherent feature of the Canary Islands' scenery. Markets are held at regular intervals in small towns and generally serve the local population. The articles on offer include food and items of everyday use (at home and on the farm). Prices are usually low; the olives and cheeses are exceptionally tasty.

Bazaars are organized in larger towns, with tourists in mind. They sell mainly handicraft products and island souvenirs. Prices are relatively high, but you can always haggle. A number of the bigger towns also have flea markets once a week, which can sometimes be a good place to pick up a curiosity.

In Gran Canaria and Lanzarote, the bazaar vendors include African traders. They sell goods that have nothing to do with the islands, but are attractive and eye-catching nevertheless.

Stalls at a weekly bazaar in Puerto de Mogán

ART AND HANDICRAFTS

AMONG THE MOST popular island handicraft products has been the Canary knife (*Cuchillo Canario*). It is not advisable to purchase these, however, as increased airport security means you may not be able to take them home.

The most popular product made of wood is undoubtedly the *timple* – a kind of ukulele. It is also worth taking a look at other products made of wood, such as small boxes, bowls and smoking pipes. Wooden castanets are an especially popular souvenir. Wickerwork is also worth seeking out. Traditional woven baskets and other knick-knacks are on sale virtually everywhere.

Ceramic items on sale are often based on traditional Guanche designs. They include statuettes, beads and countless vessels, including bowls, pots, jugs and vases. They are often decorated in traditional geometric patterns,

A jar of palm honey

typical of the first inhabitants of the islands.

Popular among textiles are embroidery, woollen hand-woven cloths and lace. Many shops offer textile products such as tablecloths, shawls and napkins, which can also be found in bazaars. Some shops have their own workshops, where you can see the products being made. Those interested in ethnography can take home the traditional folk costume.

FOOD AND DRINK

GOAT'S CHEESE IS one of the traditional Canary food items. The best known are *majorero*, from Fuerteventura, and *herre*, from El Hierro. In small villages you can often

buy locally made cheese. Here, preference is given to neighbours, with tourists only being offered the surplus.

Popular among alcoholic beverages are rum and its mead version – *ron miel* – as well as Malvasía *(see p167)*. Other wines have not gained such recognition with the Spaniards, although the locals are very keen on wines made on Tenerife.

Another speciality is palm mead, known as *guarapo*, from La Gomera. It is made from palm juice, thickened through boiling.

Many tourists like to take home Canarian sauces – *mojos*. There are several types of them and they can be found in every supermarket.

The Canary Islands are also famous for the production of *puros palmeros* – cigars from La Palma. Although not as well known as the Havana cigars, they are nevertheless highly valued for their flavour and are even purchased for the Royal Court in Madrid.

Supermarkets are often the best place to buy food. They offer a wide variety, at moderate prices.

Another popular gift item is flowers, especially *estrelitsia*, the bird-of-paradise plant. You can buy them on departure ready-packed, from a flower shop or at the airport.

Main shopping precinct in Las Palmas

ENTERTAINMENT IN THE CANARY ISLANDS

THE CANARY ISLANDS offer seemingly endless forms of entertainment to tempt tourists. There are plenty of demonstrations of traditional skill on offer, from Spanish and local dancing, to the old custom of *lucha canaria* – wrestling. Typical modern attractions, including bars, nightclubs, casinos, cinemas, theatres and concerts, are likewise much in

Logo of Parque Las Aguilas

evidence. A wide variety of holiday entertainment is also on offer. The islands feature many small parks and botanical gardens, with tropical plants and wild animals. A trip in a glass-bottomed boat to see the marine fauna, including dolphins and whales, is a memorable experience, while the many water-parks, with their slides and splash pools, will have children squealing with delight.

Casino in Santa Catalina hotel

INFORMATION

INFORMATION regarding cultural events and concerts may often be found in the local press, which advertises them some days in advance. Keep your eyes peeled, too, as many interesting events are advertised on street posters. Other good sources of information are hotel reception foyers and tourist information centres.

NIGHTLIFE

THERE IS A vast selection of nightclubs. Discos, pubs, bars, karaoke bars and casinos tempt visitors with their neon signs and music. In recent years, some larger towns have started imposing severe night-time noise level restrictions, which has done little to curb the number of pubs, clubs and bars.

There is a basic difference between bars and pubs on the islands. Bars *(tabernas)* are open all day, serving mostly beer and wine as well as snacks. This is often the first stop before the evening "ruta", where you can have a drink and a quiet conversation. They close around 1am.

Pubs *(cervecerías)* provide more typical evening entertainment. They also serve alcohol, but wine is not very common. The music is loud, and those wishing to dance can do so. Discos open late and close around 5am. They become crowded around 1am, or later, when other places close.

DAYTIME ENTERTAINMENT

DURING THE DAYS the entertainment on offer includes glass-bottomed boat and submarine trips. There are also dolphin and whale-watching trips (prices usually include lunch on board).

For the benefit of younger guests, the islands have developed numerous water-parks with merry-go-rounds, slides and swimming pools. Gardens such as **Palmitos Parque** and **Loro Parque** stage parrot and dolphin shows, specifically aimed at children. Another fun way to spend the day is to take one of the numerous safaris over wilderness areas, on camel-back or by jeep.

THEATRE AND CINEMA

IT IS ONLY the large towns that have cinemas, theatres and concert halls. New films come to the screen with minimum delay. However, films are usually dubbed (except for a few cinemas) and therefore incomprehensible to non-Spanish speakers.

Trained sea-lion show in Loro Parque on Tenerife

Las Palmas Film Festival

MUSIC AND CONCERTS

THE BIGGEST MUSICAL event on the islands is the annual **Womad** concert. This ethnic music extravaganza is organized by former *Genesis* band member, Peter Gabriel, in Las Palmas de Gran Canaria. Gran Canaria is also the venue of **Atlantida** – a lively annual pop music concert that takes place in February on Playa del Inglés.

Fans of jazz music can enjoy the **International Canarias Jazz & Heineken** festival. It is organized each year, with concerts held on all the islands, except La Gomera and El Hierro.

Lovers of classical music can visit the concert halls in Las Palmas de Gran Canaria and Santa Cruz de Tenerife. At the end of January and the beginning of February there is a classical music festival. Concerts are held in the **Auditorium Alfredo Kraus** in Las Palmas de Gran Canaria, and **Teatro Guimerá** in Santa Cruz de Tenerife, as well as on other islands.

Hotels often organize their own concerts and shows of flamenco dancing, as well as Spanish and local folk dances. These shows are very popular with tourists.

FESTIVALS

THE BEST-KNOWN event on the Canary Islands is, of course, the carnival (Feb/Mar). The biggest and wildest one, held in Santa Cruz de Tenerife, is often compared to the famous carnival in Rio de Janeiro.

The theatre festival in Agüimes on Gran Canaria is the only one of its kind in Spain. This prestigious event is held in September and it attracts a wide range of theatre groups from Europe, Latin America and Africa.

The film festival held on Gran Canaria (Oct/Nov, every two years) includes works of international cinema, with special emphasis placed on European, African and Latin American movies. One category is reserved for Canary films, or films thematically linked with the archipelago.

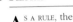

Tiles commemorating the 1981 carnival

FIESTAS

AS A RULE, the religious festivals are an opportunity for the islanders to let their hair down. The central activity of most fiestas is the statue-carrying processions but they may also include fancy-dress parades and street decorations. Fiestas can easily last several days, during which time town life comes to a virtual halt: all public places, including shops, bars and restaurants, are closed.

Folk dancers on Gran Canaria

OUTDOOR ACTIVITIES

BECAUSE OF THEIR superb climate, the Canary Islands are an excellent place for all types of sport. Visitors seeking to combine lounging on the beach with something more strenuous can come here at any time of the year, sure to find professional help and guidance. The most popular are, of course, water sports. Pozo Izquierdo on Gran Canaria is one of the world's best beaches for windsurfing. The coastal waters are considered some of the most attractive diving sites. Tenerife and the remaining islands offer excellent conditions for paragliding and hang-gliding. Anyone interested in golf, tennis, horse riding, hiking or cycling will also find plenty of opportunities to indulge in their favourite pastimes.

Windsurfer on Fuerteventura

Caldera de Bandama golf course on Gran Canaria

JOGGING

THERE ARE EXCELLENT conditions for running. Seaside promenades and sandy beaches, such as the ones on Fuerteventura, are ideal places for burning off the calories.

In the rugged central regions of the islands, small villages offer less favourable conditions for jogging. The best times to take a run are mornings and evenings, when temperatures are lower and the crowds thinner.

HIKING

THE ISLANDS, with their pleasant climate, diverse landscape and numerous national parks and nature reserves, present many opportunities for hikers. Tourist offices on all the islands can offer advice as to the best walking trails.

The national park areas, including Garajonay on La Gomera, are particularly attractive and feature many marked trails, but walkers should bear in mind the obligatory rules and restrictions. Walking trips around the islands are often the best method of exploring. The routes are not too difficult or arduous, though most footpaths are rocky.

Many routes lead over high ground along mountain ridges. Temperatures here can be low, even in the summer when the sun's rays still do not generate much heat. You should always make sure to bring warm clothing and do not forget to pack sunscreen, water and something to eat.

GOLF

GOLF COURSES CAN be found on Gran Canaria, La Gomera, Lanzarote and Tenerife. The best known are the Maspalomas Golf Club on Gran Canaria and Golf del Sur on Tenerife. Real Club de Golf de Las Palmas, founded in 1891, is one of the oldest golf clubs outside Britain.

The mild climate makes it possible to play the game all year round. Most clubs can offer equipment hire, beginners' courses and, naturally, excellent conditions for more advanced players.

TENNIS

GOOD QUALITY TENNIS courts, some of them floodlit, can be found in the grounds of many hotels and apartments. These can often be hired out, even if you are not a resident. Instructors and equipment hire are easy to organize. More information about holidays combined with tennis lessons can be obtained from the Real Federación Española de Tenis. Those longing for a game of squash will also find appropriate facilities, mainly within the hotel complexes.

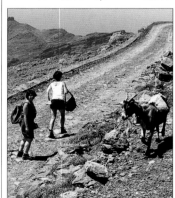

Hikers on La Gomera

HORSE RIDING

THERE ARE SEVERAL riding centres on the islands, offering facilities for beginners as well as for advanced riders.

In the main, however, the islands do not offer attractive riding opportunities. The rocky and uneven terrain and the hard surfaces mean that there is a lack of routes suitable for galloping. The latter can only be done on some sandy beaches.

Among the most interesting trips on horseback are the sightseeing tours of the national parks, including Garajonay on La Gomera.

All horse-riding outings, performed individually or in groups, are always supervised by the owner of the stable or an instructor who knows the area well.

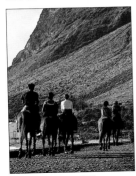

Riders at sunset on Valle Gran Rey beach

CYCLING

THE MOUNTAINOUS character of the islands creates excellent conditions for riding mountain bikes or racers. On steep, winding roads you can often encounter groups of cyclists whizzing past. Cycling, however, given the nature of the terrain you are likely to encounter, requires much care. Traffic, too, presents a serious danger.

More ambitious cyclists can undertake a guided tour. These usually lead over areas of wilderness and require a lot of stamina. The best places for this type of adventure are the national

Yachts moored in Puerto de Mogán harbour

parks. There are many agents offering such tours. They organize transport for cyclists and their equipment to the starting point and collect them at the end. Some firms also include a picnic lunch in the price of the outing.

Bicycles are an excellent means of transport around the islands. Many tourists use touring bikes to reach distant beaches, for shopping trips or just to escape from the crowds.

SAILING

ALMOST EVERY LARGE coastal town or village has a marina. These have been an important call for transatlantic sailors since the time of Columbus, and are visited by yachts from all over Europe. Modern marinas have facilities for yacht repair. Food supplies are available in local shops, while harbour restaurants tempt hungry sailors. In smaller places, yacht harbours are usually combined with fishing harbours.

Conditions for sailing are good the whole year through, and you can charter a yacht or catamaran for a day or longer, provided you have the relevant qualifications. Those who do not can go on a cruise. These, too, can last a day or longer. Many of the cruises offer food, and even drink, as part of the price.

Everybody has the chance to learn the basic skills of sailing in the Canary Islands. All islands have sailing centres, offering short sailing courses for all ages.

FISHING

THE CANARY ISLANDS' waters are packed with fish that attract anglers, but due to depleted stocks there are now more restrictions in place. Almost every island offers sea trips combined with marlin fishing. One of the best places for trying to catch this fish are the waters around Isla Graciosa, off the north coast of Lanzarote.

Tourists can hire a boat or join an organized expedition. Fishing equipment is generally provided by the organizer.

NATURISM

NATURISM IS LEGAL on all the islands' beaches. There are, however, some beaches which are more popular with nudists, such as Le Tejita to the south east of Tenerife, and Playa Guasimeta near Arrecife airport in Lanzarote. These beaches, however, may also be used by non-nudists.

Cyclists by Castillo Santa Barbara, near Teguise

HANG-GLIDING AND PARAGLIDING

HANG-GLIDING and paragliding (similar to hang-gliding but using a parachute-type wing) offer an unforgettable way to see the islands. The large islands, such as Gran Canaria, have particularly favourable weather for this sport. Tenerife alone has more than 40 centres for hang-gliding.

Many centres offer hanggliding courses. They are held in the island's interior regions, which feature the best lifting currents. When the weather is right, it is possible to fly over an entire island by hangglider. Those wanting a less risky taste of gliding can try their hand at paragliding behind a motorboat.

WATER MOTORSPORTS

MOTORBOAT RACES AND other similar events are a rare sight on the islands. However, many people take the opportunity to try jet-ski rides. Equally popular are water-skiing and bumping along in rubber rafts towed by a speeding boat.

DIVING

SNORKELLING and scuba diving are both well catered for on the islands and provide the opportunity to see rays, barracuda, turtles and a variety of tropical fish. You might even see a shark! There are many diving centres (centro de buceo) where you can hire equipment, go for a test dive with an instructor or join

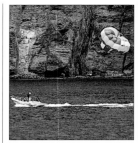
Parachute towed by a motorboat near Los Gigantes cliffs

courses, for all levels of proficiency. In order to go scuba diving in Spain, you must have a proper diving certificate. The recognized ones include PADI, CUC, CMAS/FEDAS and SSI.

Holders of these certificates can join underwater expeditions. Diving around Famara, on Lanzarote, or La Restinga on El Hierro, provides an unforgettable experience. Underwater spearfishing is permitted only to snorkellers.

WINDSURFING

HITCHING YOURSELF to a windsurfing board is undoubtedly one of the islands' most popular sports. The strong winds on many beaches, combined with the sunshine, create excellent conditions for this sport.

There are several schools that can teach you how to do it. They also rent sailboards to stronger swimmers.

Advanced windsurfers (or windsurfistas as they are known to the locals) should definitely try the beaches at Playa de la Jacite on Tenerife, Playa de Sotavento on

Fuerteventura and Pozo Izquierdo on Gran Canaria. These also play host to a number of international windsurfing events.

It should, however, be remembered that along beaches where top international events take place, the conditions can be very treacherous. Winds are strong and variable and the waves are big. The winds are particularly strong from April until the end of summer, while in the winter months the Atlantic waves are bigger and more dangerous to inexperienced windsurfers.

Windsurfer off the coast of Fuerteventura

SURFING

YOU WILL FIND surfers or people playing with boogie boards on practically all Canary Island beaches. Surfing schools are thin on the ground, however, but there are a number of hire shops in places that have particularly favourable sea conditions such as Gran Canaria's Maspalomas Beach.

Surfing is popular with the locals but it can be extremely dangerous and you should exercise great caution, particularly around the northern shores, where waves are much stronger than they seem from the shore. In many places, eddies and currents make the conditions even more treacherous. Another hazard is the rocky seabed, so before entering the water you should find out whether the beach is safe.

Diving – one of the most popular island sports

DIRECTORY

GOLF

Amarilla Golf & Country Club
Urb. Amarilla Golf.
San Miguel de Abona.
☎ 922 730 319.
FAX 922 785 557.

Campo de Golf Maspalomas
Avda. Touroperadores
Neckermann, s/n.
Maspalomas.
☎ 928 762 581.
FAX 928 768 245.

Golf Costa Teguise
Urb. Costa Teguise.
☎ 928 590 512.
FAX 928 592 337.
@ golflanzarote@step.es

Golf del Sur
Urb. Golf del Sur.
San Miguel de Abona,
Autopista del sur.
☎ 922 738 170.
FAX 922 738 272.

Golf las Américas
Playa de las Américas.
☎ 922 752 005.
FAX 922 795 250.
@ info@golf-
tenerife.com

Real Club de Golf de Las Palmas
Ctra. de Bandama.
Santa Brígida.
☎ 928 350 104.
FAX 928 350 110.
@ rcglp@step.es

HORSE RIDING

Association of Gran Canaria Riding Clubs
C/León y Castillo, 47.
Las Palmas de Gran Canaria.

Centro Hípico Los Brezos
Camino Candelaria Monte,
Tacoronte.
☎ 922 567 222.

Círculo Hípico Manivasán
C/Terra, 5. El Paso.
☎ 922 486 312.

Lanzarote a Caballo
Ctra – Arrecife – Yaiza, 17 km.
☎ 928 830 314.
FAX 928 813 995.

Mamio Verde
Cuadras de Pino Alto, 39.
La Orotava.
☎ 922 333 508.
FAX 922 322 504.

Sociedad Hípica Miranda
Miranda de Abajo.
Breña Alta.
☎ 922 437 696.
FAX 922 181 392.

CYCLING

Bike Station Gomera
La Puntilla, 7.
San Sebastián de La Gomera.
☎ 922 805 082.

Bike'n Fun
C/Calvo, 20.
Los Llanos de Aridane.
☎ 922 401 927.

Pemai
Avda. Marítima, 9.
Tazacorte.
☎ 922 408 106.

Tommy's Bikes
C/Goleta, 16. Costa Teguise.
☎ 928 592 327.
FAX 928 592 220.

SAILING

Club de Deportes Naúticos Barlovento
Puerto Deportivo "San
Miguel", San Miguel.
Las Palmas de Gran Canaria.
☎ 922 691 482.
FAX 922 691 492.
@ barlo@idecnet.com

Club de Mar de Radazul
Avda.Marítima, Radazul
– El Rosario.
☎ 922 681 099.
@ radazul
@clubmradazul.com

Real Club Naútico de Gran Canaria
C/León y Castillo, 308.
Las Palmas de Gran Canaria.
☎ 928 234 566.
FAX 922 273 117.
@ rcng@rcng.com

Real Club Náutico de Tenerife
Avda. Francisco La Roche,
s/n. Santa Cruz de Tenerife
☎ 922 273 700.
@ rcnt@rcnt.com

FISHING

Anglers' Association
C/San Sebastian, 76.
Santa Cruz de Tenerife.
☎ 922 226 771.

NATURISM

Federación Española de Naturismo
(Nudist beach listings)
W www.naturismo.org

HANG-GLIDING AND PARAGLIDING

Aeroclub Maspalomas
☎ 922 762 447.

Escuela de Parapente "IZAÑA"
Güimar.
☎ 922 524 526.

Escuela Parapente Palmasur
C/La Cruz, 2. Los Quemados.
☎ 922 444 034.

Guelillas de el Hierro
C/Doctor Quintero, 23.
Valverde.
☎ 922 551 824.

Libertad Tacoronte
Pabellón de Deportes.
C/Perez Reyes, Tacoronte.
☎ 922 563 251.

Paraclub of Gran Canaria
C/León y Castillo, 244. Las
Palmas de Gran Canaria.
☎ 928 157 000.
FAX 9º28 157 073.

DIVING

Blue Explorers Dive Centers
Avda. de Tirajana, 24.
Playa del Inglés.
☎ 928 774 539.
W www.blue-explorers.com

Centro de Buceo las Toninas
Aptos. Playa Flamingo,
Playa Blanca.
☎ 928 517 300.
FAX 928 517 490.
@ divingtoninas@arraks.es

Club Barakuda
Playa Paraíso. Adeje.
☎ 922 741 881.
@ barakuda@arrakis.es

Club Manta Sub
Puerto Colón, 125.
Playa de las Américas.
☎ 922 715 873.
FAX 922 715 098.
@ mantasub@ctv.es

Dive Center
C/Nuestra Señora del Pino,
22. Corralejo.
☎ 928 535 906.
@ buceodcc@ecomix.es

El Submarino
Avda. Marítima, 2.
La Restinga.
☎ 922 557 068.

WINDSURFING

Centro Insular de Deportes Marítimos de Tenerife
Ctra. a San Andrés.
☎ 922 240 945.

Fanatic Fun Center
Caleta de Fuste.
☎ 928 535 700.

Flag Beach Windsurf Centre
General Linares, 31.
Corralejo.
☎ 928 866 389.

Pro Center René Egli – Windsurf & Kiteboarding
Hotel Sol Los Gorriones.
Sotavento.
☎ 928 547 483.
@ info@rene-egli.com

Sport Away Lanzarote
Calle de las Olas – Plaza
de Tenerife. Puerto
de Tahiche.
☎ 928 590 731.
@ sportaway@
interlan-stc.es

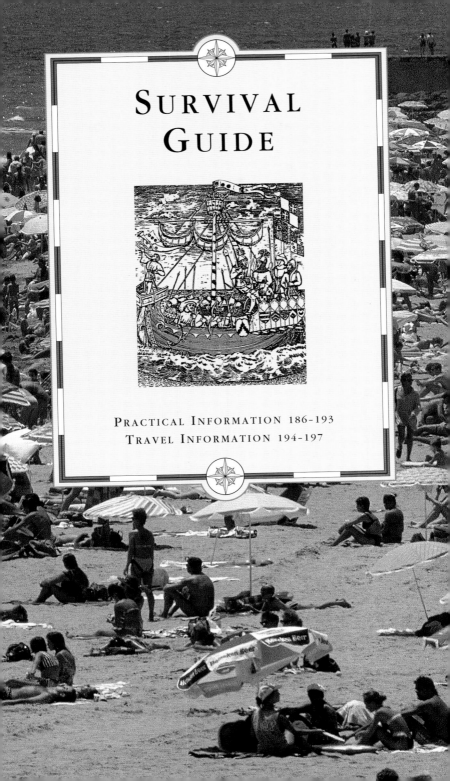

SURVIVAL
GUIDE

PRACTICAL INFORMATION

THE CANARY ISLANDS' warm climate means that the tourist season here lasts the whole year. The huge investment in the tourist infrastructure means that the islands are well prepared to receive multitudes of visitors and have extensive hotel and catering facilities, as well as numerous attractions and things to do. Frequent charter flights to the islands plus a very well-developed information

Logo of the island of Lanzarote

service, particularly on the Internet, makes planning a holiday here a reasonably straightforward business. Those intending to visit can easily find all the necessary information and organize the necessary hotel bookings well in advance. This is important since, particularly in summer and winter, the islands can get extremely crowded, and it can be very difficult to find accommodation without prior booking.

WHEN TO VISIT

THE HOLIDAY SEASON lasts practically all year round on the Canary Islands. Thanks to their magnificent weather, the beaches can be used almost from January until December. The islands are particularly popular with visitors during winter months. Many decide to spend a balmy Christmas on the islands, rather than huddled round a fire in Europe.

The second most popular season is summer, particularly July and August, when the islands are packed, and early spring is also very busy. Late autumn has fewer visitors.

The islands are not only attractive for their sunshine and beaches. One local event that attracts crowds of tourists is the carnival. Visitors from Spain, and further afield, come mainly to Santa Cruz de Tenerife or Las Palmas de Gran Canaria to join the carnival celebrations. Magnificent fiestas, including

the Bajada de la Virgen de las Nieves in Santa Cruz de La Palma, provide another reason to visit the islands.

VISAS

REGULATIONS COVERING admission to the Canary Islands are exactly the same as for the rest of Spain. Nationals of all the European Union member states do not require a visa to enter the Canary Islands for tourist visits of up to 90 days. Other non-EU countries including Australia, Canada, Ireland, Israel, Japan, New Zealand and the USA are likewise not required to obtain a visa before entry. When in doubt, you should contact the Spanish Embassy or seek advice from a travel agent. Anyone who does require a visa must apply in person at the consulate in their own country.

Tourists at a viewpoint

CUSTOMS REGULATIONS

WHEN SPAIN JOINED the European Union, the Canary Islands lost their status as a duty-free zone. For customs purposes, however, the islands are still not considered to be part of the EU and there are detailed regulations as to the amount of goods permitted for export. They include 200 cigarettes or 50 cigars, two litres of wine and one litre of alcohol over 22 per cent or two litres of sparkling wine.

In addition, visitors are allowed 250 ml of eau de toilette and up to 162 euros worth of souvenirs. Tobacco and alcohol allowances apply only to adults.

Specific cases may be referred to the *Departamento de Aduanas e Impuestos Especiales* (Customs and Excise Department) in Madrid. Travel agents and tour operators can provide further information.

Resting on a colourful bench in Santa Cruz de Tenerife

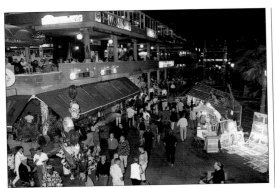

Maspalomas' centre, on Gran Canaria, at night

LANGUAGE

THE OFFICIAL LANGUAGE of the Canary Islands is Spanish. Local accents differ from those of mainland Spain, but apart from this and a few words particular to the islands, there are no major differences.

Apart from Spanish, it is possible to communicate in various foreign languages in all the tourist resorts, where you could get by without any Spanish at all. The second language is German, but most people also speak English. Information signs and restaurant menus are generally multilingual. The most frequent combination is Spanish, German and English.

Communication problems may arise while away from the major tourist centres. Here most people speak only Spanish, though the younger population may be able to understand German or English.

TOURIST INFORMATION

TOURIST INFORMATION on the Canary Islands is a well-oiled machine. Bigger towns and tourist centres have an *oficina de turismo* (information office). These provide information about the locality, accommodation (including staying on a farmstead or in a converted village house), events and tourist attractions.

Tourist offices can also provide visitors with free information packs and maps and can offer advice regarding the best walking routes, nearby historic sights and a variety of day trips.

The information packs are an excellent point of reference. They are illustrated with colour photographs and issued in several languages.

Outside Spain, there are plenty of Spanish information offices, which are usually attached to the embassies, where you can obtain all the necessary information prior to visiting the islands.

The Internet is another free source of information, but often official sites are not updated as often as they should be. Every island and many individual regions have their own websites that are nevertheless worth visiting. The Spanish Tourism Institute – *Turespaña* – has its own site, which provides information about hotels, camping sites and tourist attractions throughout Spain. Various travel agents, hotels, restaurants, car hire firms and other establishments also advertise their services on the Internet. Their pages generally include many photographs, which can be helpful when choosing a hotel.

Information packs promoting tourism

Paseo de las Canteras in Las Palmas de Gran Canaria

YOUTH/STUDENTS

H OLDERS OF THE
International Student
Identity Card (ISIC) and the
Euro under-26 card are
entitled to many benefits
when visiting the Canary
Islands. They can get
discounts on ferry travel,
entrance charges to museums
and galleries and tickets to
many other tourist attractions.
Many travel agents offer
cheap flights to cardholders.

Under-26 cards can be
obtained on Tenerife or Gran
Canaria with a passport. To
get an ISIC card you will
need to provide proof that
you are a full-time student.

CHILDREN

T HE CANARY ISLANDS are
geared up for family
holidays and, as with most of
Europe, children are welcome
almost everywhere. The
beaches provide a safe
playground all year round.
The numerous water parks
and the zoos, which stage
trained parrot and dolphin
shows, are a big draw and are
aimed, to a large extent,
squarely at kids.

Many travel agents
specialize in arranging family
holidays. They provide all-day
childcare, giving parents a
chance to take a well-earned
rest. They also organize
competitions, games and trips
for their younger guests.

There is no problem
feeding young children.
Children's portions, high-

chairs, activity packs and
outside seating are the norm
rather than the exception in
most restaurants.

FACILITIES FOR
THE DISABLED

T HE ISLANDS ARE not
particularly hospitable
to disabled people.
The majority of
restaurants and
hotels are not
adapted to serve
guests who use
wheelchairs. Moving
around some of the
towns is also very
difficult, and taking
part in events or going on
organized trips is practically
impossible.

When planning a visit to the
islands, a disabled tourist
should check the travel

**Parking for the
disabled sign**

conditions and hotel facilities
with their travel agent. The
organization which helps
disabled people to plan their
holiday on the Canary Islands
is the Confederación
Coordinatora Estatal de
Minusválidos Físico de
España (COCEMFE) – The
Spanish Association for the
Disabled. There are also
special guides published.
Another helpful agency is
Viajes 2000.

SIGHTSEEING TOURS

A WIDE RANGE of sightseeing
tours are is available for
tourists throughout the
islands. Most organizers and
travel agents offer a variety of
types. These may include
desert safaris by jeep or on
the back of a camel, fishing
trips, organized walks,
submarine cruises, trips in a
glass-bottomed boat, and
visits to one of the islands'
parks, including Palmitos
Parque or Loro
Parque. People tend
to see only one or
two islands when
they visit the Canaries
but there are day
trips to small
islands, such as the
Isla de Lobos, close
to Fuerteventura.

Those not wishing to join a
trip organized by a hotel or
travel agent can find many
other alternatives. Hotel
reception desks and tourist
offices carry a range of
colourful leaflets with
relevant information.
The tours are mainly
reasonably priced
daytrips though some
can last overnight
or even longer. Most
of them start after
breakfast and the price
includes lunch on
board a boat or in
a friendly restaurant
catering for groups of
tourists. Visitors living
away from the large
towns are offered
trips to city nightclubs.
Shows, dancing and
karaoke are the most
common features
of these forms of
evening entertainment.

Minigolf for children and adults

OFICINA DE TURISMO

Tourist information sign

TIME

THE CANARY ISLANDS are on GMT, the same as the UK and Ireland, and an hour behind mainland Spain. In summer, to make better use of the sunshine, the clocks go an hour forward. The changeover takes place on the last Sunday in March. The clocks are put back again on the last Sunday in October.

2,6 Las Creces

3,3 Carretera dorsal

Road sign for visitors to Parque Nacional de Garajonay

ELECTRICAL EQUIPMENT

THE MAINS VOLTAGE on the islands is generally 220 V. A readily available three-tier standard travel converter will enable you to use foreign equipment. Mains sockets require round-pin plugs.

RELIGION

SIMILAR TO THE rest of Spain, the Canary Islands are Roman Catholic. Religion plays an important role in community life. All religious festivals are lavishly celebrated, and many **fiestas** are of religious origin. Most of the islands' churches are Roman Catholic. Their opening hours differ; some are open only during services.

There are also churches of other denominations. Services are held in various languages, and their times change frequently. Hotel reception desks and tourist information centres can usually provide details. A multi-denominational church – Templo Ecuménico – has recently opened on

Gran Canaria, in Playa del Inglés. A similar one can be found in Puerto de la Cruz, on Tenerife.

OPENING HOURS

MOST MONUMENTS and museums are open from Tuesday to Sunday. The hours are generally from 10am to 2pm. They close for the siesta and reopen from 5pm to 8pm. They generally close for public holidays and fiestas, similar to all offices. The hours for museums in smaller towns are more unpredictable and it is best to phone ahead. Outside of the major tourist resorts, shops close on Sundays. Church opening hours also vary. The best time to visit is during morning or evening services.

Theme parks and gardens are generally open seven days a week, but even these close for public holidays.

WATER

TAP WATER ON the Canary Islands is suitable for drinking, although it does not taste very good as it tends to be desalinated sea water. It is generally recommended that you drink bottled water and use tap water for cooking. You should remember to drink a lot of liquid, to prevent dehydration.

Shops offer a large variety of bottled waters, mainly from local wells. Particularly good are the sparkling waters, including those from Firgas, on Gran Canaria.

Jardin Canario

Sign for Gran Canaria's botanical garden

Personal Security and Health

Visitors to the Canary Islands can generally feel safe. Thefts do occur in the most crowded places and even in hotels, but they can be minimized by taking sensible precautions. Credit cards and money are best hidden away or carried in a belt. Never leave anything visible in your car when you park it. It is also advisable to avoid carrying excessive amounts of cash. When in need, you can always ask a policeman for help. Basic medical help and advice is usually provided by a pharmacist. Holders of valid medical insurance can receive treatment in public hospitals and clinics.

Information board at Amadores beach on Gran Canaria

PERSONAL PROPERTY

Before going away it is necessary to make sure you have adequate holiday insurance in order to protect you financially from the loss or theft of your property.

Even so, it is advisable to take common-sense precautions against loss or theft in the first place. Traveller's cheques are a far safer option than cash. If you have two credit cards, do not carry them together. Particular care should be exercised in crowded places, such as airports or bus stations, as well as inside tourist attractions, which are always full of people. Patrolling policemen often remind visitors about the need to be careful. There are also cases of tourists falling victim to theft when drunk. Never leave a bag or handbag unattended and do not put down a purse or wallet on the tabletop in a café. The moment you discover a loss or theft, report it to the local police station. The police will give you a *denuncia* (written statement), which you will need to make an insurance claim. If you have your passport lost or stolen report it to your consulate.

SPANISH POLICE

In the canary islands, as in the rest of Spain, there are essentially three types of police. The *Policía Nacional* (state police), the *Policía Municipal,* also known as the *Policía Local* (local police), and the *Guardia Civil* (National Guard).

The *Policía Nacional* wear blue uniforms and drive white cars with navy-blue doors. These operate in towns with a population of more than 30,000.

The uniform of the *Policía Local* varies depending on the locality. Their officers are mostly encountered in small towns, and patrol the streets of crowded tourist resorts; they have a separate branch for traffic.

The *Guardia Civil* wear green uniforms and generally drive white-and-green four-wheel drive vehicles. They mainly patrol the open roads.

The islands' police are friendly towards tourists. They are, however, very firm with those who commit traffic offences. All three services will direct you to the relevant authority in the event of an incident requiring police help.

Uniform of the Guardia Civil

SUNSHINE

Though it is, of course, one of the attractions, the sun should be taken seriously in the Canary Islands. The archipelago lies in the tropical zone where the sun is much stronger that in the rest of Spain. People with pale skin should always use sun block creams to avoid burning. Many people tend to forget that creams do not remain active throughout the entire day and should be reapplied every few hours.

When going to the beach try to avoid the hottest hours of the day. Between 1pm and 4pm it is best not to stay in the sun for too long. The sun is also strong in the mountains, above the clouds. The somewhat cooler air makes it feel less hot, but the results can be just as unpleasant. When sitting out in the sun you should remember to wear a hat, to prevent sunstroke.

OUTDOOR HAZARDS

Another potential problem on the islands, besides the sunshine, is the ocean. Many people do not realize the strength of the ocean waves.

In order to avoid any unpleasant surprises, you should always swim where there are lifeguards. Always take note of warning signs. The currents can be particularly powerful around the Canary Islands. If you cannot see plenty of other people swimming in the water then the chances are that it may not be safe. Never bathe where there are surfers or windsurfers. These are a

Local police four-wheel drive car, a common sight on the islands

potential hazard, especially when beginners come too close to the shore. Surfers and divers using unguarded beaches should be aware of the rocky ocean bottom. A violent wave can sometimes throw a person against the rocks, causing serious injuries.

When diving near the shore, it is always advisable to have another person with you for protection. The marine fauna do not present a danger to swimmers, although jellyfish can inflict a painful sting.

MEDICAL CARE

BOTH NATIONAL AND private healthcare is available in Spain. Visitors from EU countries are entitled to free national health treatment. They must, however, remember to travel with a certified copy of an E111 or E112 form (the latter applies to chronic conditions). These can be obtained in the UK from the Department of Health or from a post office before you travel. Please note that Spanish healthcare does not cover all expenses, such as the cost of dental treatment. Visitors from outside the EU should always carry valid insurance.

In case of illness, you should report to the nearest hospital or clinic. At night, you should contact the emergency service (*Urgencias*) and in case of an accident call for a Red Cross ambulance (*Cruz Roja*).

Ambulance in Las Palmas de Gran Canaria

PHARMACIES

PHARMACISTS CAN OFFER help and advice. In some cases, they can also prescribe medicines. If you have a non-urgent medical problem the *farmacia* is a good place to start. Most pharmacists will speak English. They are open during the same hours as other shops and carry a green cross sign, often with the word *farmacia*. Details about those open at night and on public holidays can be found in the windows of all pharmacies.

Illuminated Spanish pharmacy sign

FIRE HAZARDS

THE HIGH TEMPERATURES on the islands make them very dry. This should be remembered, particularly when travelling by car. At woodland camp sites and picnic spots, great care must be taken to prevent fire. When leaving, check carefully the remains of any bonfires and pick up glass, particularly empty bottles, which can cause fires. It goes without saying that you should be especially careful with cigarettes.

Sign warning of the risk of forest fires

OUTDOORS

VISITORS TOURING THE islands may see various signs written only in Spanish, as well as warning and information notices.

Coto de caza or *vedat de caça* means a hunting ground. *Camino particular* means a private road, while *privado* informs you that the area is private property.

Hiking routes on the islands can be difficult. When setting off you should take the right equipment and plenty of water. Tell someone where you are going and when you intend to return.

DIRECTORY

EMERGENCY NUMBERS

Police, ambulance, fire brigade
📞 112.

Policía Nacional
📞 091.

Policía Municipal
📞 092.

Guardia Civil
📞 062.

Ambulance
📞 061.

Sea Rescue
📞 900 202 202.

Fire Brigade
📞 080.

INFORMATION ON PHARMACIES

w www.farmaciasde-guardiacanarias.com

Tenerife
📞 922 282 424.

Communication and Banks

LA CAJA DE CANARIAS

Logo of a local bank

MOST PUBLIC TELEPHONES are served by the Spanish company Telefónica. There are plenty of public telephones and no problems in finding them. Thanks to the transfer to digital technology in 1998, the line quality is generally good. The Spanish postal system is not among the best. When exchanging messages with Spanish firms it is best to use fax or e-mail. There are several banks on the islands. These generally offer the best exchange rates. The major Spanish and foreign banks, including Deutsche Bank and Banesto, have branches here. There are also many local banks.

Typical post box belonging to the Spanish *correos*

TELEPHONING

THERE ARE TWO types of payphone on the island: card- and coin-operated, and card-operated (which do not accept coins). Some phones are equipped with multi-lingual electronic displays.

Phonecards are very convenient and can be purchased at newsstands and *estancos* (tobacconists). There are two types of telephone cards. One has a magnetic strip with an encoded value, the other has a PIN number that is entered before a connection is made.

When dialling a number you should remember that in Spain the area code is a permanent part of the number, which consists of nine digits in total. For Tenerife and its dependent islands, El Hierro, La Palma and La Gomera the area code

is 922. For Gran Canaria province and islands, Lanzarote and Fuerteventura, the number is 928. Calls between islands of the same province are charged at the same rate as long-distance calls within the island. Other calls are charged at the inter-provincial rate.

When calling Spain from abroad you should dial 34, followed by the subscriber's number, including the area code. When calling a mobile phone number you should dial the country code followed by the subscriber's number.

International calls are cheapest at night (after 8pm) and on Sunday. A call from a public telephone box costs 35

per cent more than one made from a private phone in someone's home. Using public telephones is always cheaper than making calls from a hotel, however.

POSTAL SERVICE

POST OFFICES ARE open between 9am and 7pm. Postage stamps can be bought at post office desks or any of the kiosks displaying the word *timbre*. Letters should be posted in yellow post boxes, marked *correos*. The Spanish *correos* (post office) is the only institution authorized to handle mail, so it is not recommended that you leave your letters in shops or hotels, which sometimes offer this service.

One of the many Spanish phonecards

The postal system works at its own pace. You should therefore not be surprised if a letter or postcard takes a week or more to reach its destination.

Postal charges depend on where the item is being sent and fall into bands that include the EU, the rest of Europe, the USA and the rest of the world. Post offices also accept telegrams, registered mail and parcels.

CURRENCY

IN MARCH 2002, the Spanish peseta was fully replaced by the common EU currency – the euro. Notes have several denominations, ranging from 5 to 500 euros.

USING A COIN AND CARD TELEPHONE

1 Lift the receiver and wait for the dialling tone and for the display to show *Inserte monedas o tarjeta*.

2 Insert either coins *(monedas)*, using the button on the top if there is one or a card *(tarjeta)*.

3 Key in the required number firmly, but not too fast – Spanish phones require a slight pause between each digit.

4 As you press the digits, the number you are dialling will appear on the display. You will also be able to see how much money or how many units are left.

5 When you finish your call, replace the receiver. The phonecard will re-emerge or any excess coins will be returned.

CHANGING MONEY

ALL MAJOR CURRENCIES can be exchanged without problem in bureaux de change or banks.

Bureaux de change charge higher rates than banks, but even banks charge a few per cent commission. You can draw up to 300 euros on major credit cards at a bank.

In smaller towns and on islands, such as El Hierro, you may have problems with exchanging money. When travelling to some of the more remote places you should carry enough cash. *Cajas de Aborro* (savings banks) can also exchange money. They open from 8:30am to 2pm on weekdays and also on Thursday afternoons from 4:30pm to 7:45pm.

Logo of one of the islands' most popular banks

BANKS AND CASH DISPENSERS

IT IS USUALLY easy enough to find a bank or cash dispenser on the islands. Most banks are open from 9am until 1pm or 2pm. Some change their opening hours once a week and open in the afternoon instead.

Cash dispensers can be found on almost every street corner. They all dispense money and accept all major credit cards. Some charge a commission on withdrawals with cards issued by other banks. If you want to avoid this, you should find out if any Spanish bank has an agreement with your own bank before travelling.

CREDIT CARDS

CREDIT CARDS ARE generally accepted, particularly in the tourist resorts, where every effort is made to make it easy for visitors. In less-frequented places, small shops and local bars it is sometimes necessary to pay in cash, and it is always worth carrying some cash to pay for small items. The most widely accepted card in Spain is Visa. MasterCard and American Express are also generally accepted. When you pay with a card, cashiers will usually pass your card through a reading machine. Sometimes you may be asked to punch in your PIN number.

NEWSPAPERS

EACH OF THE islands of the archipelago publishes its own newspaper, dealing mainly with local issues. These are an excellent way to find out about any local events. There are also newspapers common to all the islands, including *Canarias 7*.

In many towns, kiosks and hotels sell Spanish national papers and also foreign newspapers, including a number of German and English language titles.

RADIO AND TELEVISION

THERE ARE SEVERAL local radio stations on the islands. Reception quality varies because of the mountainous character of the area. Similar to the mainland stations they broadcast mainly Spanish music and news. There are also some foreign language stations.

You can receive Spanish television programmes, such as TVE1, without any problem. Hotels often also offer a number of foreign satellite channels such as CNN, Eurosport and Cinemania.

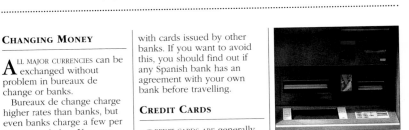

One of the many cash dispensers available on the islands

Popular dailies published on the Canary Islands

DIRECTORY

LOST OR STOLEN CREDIT CARDS

Visa
915 196 000.

American Express
902 375 637.

MasterCard
915 192 100.

Diners Club
915 474 000.

POST OFFICES

Gran Canaria
C/Primero de Mayo, 62,
Las Palmas de Gran Canaria.
928 361 320.

Fuerteventura
C/Primero de Mayo, 58–60,
Puerto del Rosario.
928 850 412.

Lanzarote
C/General Franco, 8,
Arrecife.
928 800 673.

Tenerife
Plaza de España,
Santa Cruz de Tenerife.
922 259 605.

La Gomera
C/del Medio, 68,
San Sebastián de La Gomera.
922 871 081.

El Hierro
Correo 3,
Valverde.
922 550 291.

La Palma
Plaza de la Constitución,
Santa Cruz de La Palma.
922 411 702.

TRAVEL INFORMATION

AIR LINKS WITH most of Europe and the Canary Islands are extremely efficient. Each island has an airport. Tenerife, Gran Canaria and Lanzarote take in most of the international flights as well as those from mainland Spain, while the other smaller airports are principally for hopping from island to island. Most of the air transport to and from the islands is by charter flights. Air links between the islands are provided mainly by Binter Canarias Airlines. You can also travel to the Canary Islands by ship. Most boats sail from harbours on mainland Spain or the West African coast. Ferries and fast catamarans provide regular links between the islands.

Airport sign

Attended car park at Gran Canaria airport

GETTING THERE

THERE ARE SCHEDULED flights to the islands from all major Spanish towns. Flights from Madrid to Gran Canaria run almost every hour. These routes are served by three airlines: Iberia, Spanair and Air Europa. Iberia planes fly to all the islands of the archipelago, while the other two airlines fly only to Tenerife, Gran Canaria and Lanzarote.

The Canary Islands also have scheduled flights to and from many European cities. Air links with Africa are provided by three airlines – Air Maroc, Air Mauritanie and Air Atlantic. These connect the islands with the towns of Morocco and the former Spanish Sahara.

Apart from scheduled flights, all airports operate hundreds of charter flights. These are used mostly by German and British tourists, although holidaymakers come from all over Europe.

In most cases a charter flight ticket can only be bought as part of a package tour. However, it is sometimes possible to make a ticket-only purchase, usually following last-minute cancellations.

When buying an air ticket you should always enquire about current offers. Occasionally, some airlines offer very good bargains. Bargains are also to be had if you book your ticket on the Internet. However, it is difficult to find a bargain during the high seasons, such as the school summer holidays, Christmas or during the carnivals, which take place in February and March. Information can be found on the Internet or obtained from travel agents.

You can also travel to the islands by ship (the only option if taking a motorbike or car).

There are weekly departures from Cadiz to Tenerife and Gran Canaria. The voyage takes one-and-a-half to two days, depending on the destination.

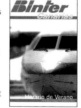
Brochure for Binter Canarias

FLIGHTS BETWEEN THE ISLANDS

ALL THE ISLANDS of the archipelago now have their own airports. Nevertheless, not all of them offer flights to all the other islands. For example, La Gomera only has flights to Tenerife and Gran Canaria. Most routes are served by Binter Canarias Airlines.

When hopping between the islands, it is a good idea to find out which airline provides the service. It is not a cheap option and some aircraft are very small, with a dozen or so seats. Often, the airline will not allow you to take large hand luggage. Travelling in a small, packed and stuffy aircraft can be a little unpleasant for people who suffer from claustrophobia or other health problems.

Flights between the islands are short. The shortest, between La Palma and El Hierro, takes 20 minutes; the longest – from La Palma to Lanzarote – 70 minutes.

Gran Canaria airport, next to the sea

Líneas Fred Olsen ferry

AIRPORTS

TENERIFE HAS TWO airports – **Los Rodeos** in northen Tenerife and **Reina Sofia** in southern Tenerife. Flights from Tenerife Norte go to all the other islands of the archipelago and the airport handles most of the scheduled flights to Tenerife. Reina Sofia is a more modern airport, and caters mainly for the heavier load of charter traffic.

El Hierro has a small airport – **El Llano del Cangrejo**. It is situated 12 km (7 miles) from the island's capital – Valverde, but it is difficult to get there by bus. It handles flights to Tenerife, La Palma and Gran Canaria.

La Gomera has recently acquired an airport – **Punta del Becerro**, situated not far from Playa de Santiago. The island has flights to Tenerife (Los Rodeos) and Gran Canaria only.

La Palma's airport is situated near Santa Cruz de La Palma. It handles flights to Gran Canaria, Lanzarote, Tenerife and El Hierro.

Gran Canaria has only one airport, situated between Las Palmas and Maspalomas. The airport has good bus links with both of the largest towns on the island. Gran Canaria has flights to all the other islands of the archipelago.

The **Guasimeta** airport on Lanzarote handles flights to Gran Canaria, Tenerife and La Palma. It is situated not far from Arrecife, which also has a bus station.

Fuerteventura has air links with Gran Canaria and Tenerife. A bus runs from the airport to Puerto del Rosario, 6 km (4 miles) away.

FERRIES

FERRIES PROVIDE an alternative form of inter-island transport, although crossings are not always direct and might require a change. Direct crossings to all the other islands, or crossings with a single change, run only from Tenerife, which is the hub of island-hopping by sea (*see inside back cover*). The most popular tourist resorts provide several daily crossings, by ferry or large, fast catamarans. These carry cars, buses and lorries as well as foot passengers. They also have bars, restaurants and cabins.

Logo for the Trasmediterranea line

When planning a tour around the archipelago you should remember that travelling by ferry is always much cheaper than flying. Although it takes longer it can be a very pleasant option.

Ticket prices for crossings offered by the two biggest companies serving inter-island routes – **Trasmediterranea** and **Líneas Fred Olsen** – are broadly similar. Slightly cheaper tickets are offered by **Armas** lines.

Ferry harbour in Las Palmas de Gran Canaria

Getting Around the Islands

DEPENDING ON YOUR plans for visiting the islands, you can choose one of many forms of transport. The bigger islands, such as Tenerife, Gran Canaria and Lanzarote, have efficient buses. Here you can travel by bus to almost any point on the island. Exploring some of the smaller islands means hiring a car, motorbike or bicycle. However, some places are best visited as part of an organized tour, with an experienced guide and driver.

Winding roads in the vicinity of Masca

ROADS

VISITORS TOURING the Canary Islands by car cannot but be impressed by the state of the roads. Many are newly built and smoothly surfaced. All major towns and villages can be reached by road, without any problem. Larger islands have their own motorways *(autopistas)*, running along the coast, which connect with the airports and major resorts.

Roads in the central, mountainous regions, on the other hand, are narrow and winding. They often lead through narrow tunnels. Problems can arise when two vehicles try to pass each other, particularly when one of them is a bus or a lorry. Sometimes a hidden oncoming vehicle signals its approach by blowing its horn.

Driving conditions may become dangerous in some areas when it is raining or foggy, as the roads can become slippery and the visibility limited.

Many scenic spots are accessible only by rough tracks or unmade roads, requiring a four-wheel-drive vehicle. The best way to visit them is to join an organized tour. A heavy rainfall can make these roads impassable.

The islands' roads are, in the main, well signposted, with clear signs for towns, major tourist attractions and viewpoints. El Hierro is the exception and you may have problems spotting the small, wooden signposts from a distance. In town, the well-signposted streets make historic sites and museums easy to find.

BUSES AND TAXIS

ON LARGER ISLANDS, such as Gran Canaria and Tenerife, there are no problems travelling by bus. You should, however, bear in mind that buses to some smaller towns or villages may run only once or twice a day and you might have problems finding a bus to get you back to your hotel or apartment.

Travelling from a small town or village to a major nightlife centre later in the evening may also be something of a problem.

Large towns have their own bus networks. These serve the town and its immediate environs.

Smaller islands have infrequent bus services, which, although sufficient for the locals, make it difficult to explore these places.

In towns and major tourist resorts it is easy to get a taxi. They are a much more convenient, although more expensive, form of transport than buses. Taxi drivers are obliged to turn on the meter at the start of the journey, and the sum displayed is the one you pay. Only when travelling to and from an airport is there an additional airport fee as well as a small luggage charge.

TOWN DRIVING

IF AT ALL possible, you should avoid driving in towns. Cities such as Las Palmas often experience traffic jams during the rush hours, and at other times. Cars parked by the pavements make driving conditions more difficult. It is also very difficult to find a parking space, particularly in city centres. Most car parks charge fees, and there are fines for non-payment.

Advertisement for one of the numerous car hire firms

CAR HIRE

ON ALL THE islands you can easily find a car hire firm. Major companies, including **Avis** and Hertz, as well as the local ones, including **Cicar**, have their desks at the airports. Car hire is generally very reasonable, but the price depends on many factors,

Tourist coach on La Gomera

An unorthodox form of transport on the islands

including the time of year, the size of the car and the length of hire. Advance booking also affects the price. It is worth comparing the prices quoted by various agencies and checking exactly what the quote includes.

When hiring a car you should carefully inspect its condition, as you will have to return it in the same state or pay a fine.

The terms and conditions of hire vary according to individual companies. There are no established rules regarding insurance, mileage or petrol. Check carefully before signing any contract. For an ordinary car the terms will probably include a provision ensuring that you do not drive on unmade roads, or take the car by ferry to another island. Hire cars must be returned to where they were collected, or to another agreed place.

Firms offering motorbikes for hire are few and far between. Crash helmets are obligatory, and for anything over 50cc you'll need to produce a driving licence.

BUYING PETROL

P ETROL ON THE islands is cheaper than on mainland Spain. Petrol stations offer all types of fuel, but most cars use unleaded petrol.

Petrol station pumps are generally operated by the staff. Only a few are automatic and open 24 hours. When touring the small islands, such as El Hierro, you

should remember that there are very few petrol stations, and that a car uses more fuel on mountainous terrain than on a flat road. It is therefore worth filling the tank before setting off.

RULES OF THE ROAD

T HE TRAFFIC regulations on the islands are generally the same as those of other European countries. Vehicles drive on the right-hand side of the road and there are few road signs specific to Spain or the islands. Speed limits, though not always obeyed by the Spaniards, are legally binding. On motorways the speed limit is 120 km/h (74 mph), on major roads, 90 km/h (55 mph) and in towns, 50 km/h (30 mph).

The fines for exceeding the speed limit are high, just as they are for drunken driving. The highest permitted blood alcohol level is 0.05 per cent (random breath testing is carried out). Safety belts are obligatory for passengers as well as drivers.

Road breakdown help point

DIRECTORY

CAR HIRE

CICAR
928 822 900.

Betacar
922 372 856.
w www.betacar.com

Avis
902 135 531.
w www.avis.com

BUS STATIONS

Gran Canaria
928 360 179.

Fuerteventura
928 850 951.

Lanzarote
928 811 522.

Tenerife
922 531 300.

La Gomera
922 141 101.

El Hierro
922 550 729.

La Palma
922 411 924.

MAPS

W HEN BUYING a map you should first check if it is up to date. This is important, in view of the continuing local road development programme. Should you fail to buy maps before leaving, you can always get the island's map from each car hire firm. Street maps can be obtained from tourist offices.

Cavalcade of jeeps at a mountain road stopping point

General Index

Acknowledgments

WIEDZA I ŻYCIE would like to thank the following people for their contribution to the preparation of this guide: Jürgen Bingel, Magdalena Borzęcka, Zbigniew Dybowski, Joanna Egert-Romanowska, Daniel Poch, Javier Lopez Silvosa, Damian Sosa.

FOR DORLING KINDERSLEY
PUBLLSHING MANAGER Helen Townsend
MANAGING ART EDITORS Kate Poole and Ian Midson
SENIOR EDITOR Jacky Jackson
EDITORIAL AND DESIGN ASSISTANCE Jill Benjamin, Marian Broderick, Jo Cowen, Helen Peters, Stewart Wild.

The Publisher would also like to thank all those who gave permission to reproduce photographs of their property and for allowing the use of photographs from archives.

AFP (Piotr Ufnal); Casa de Colón– Las Palmas de Gran Canaria; (Elena Acosta Guerrero, Ramon Gil); Casino Las Palmas –Las Palmas de Gran Canaria (Victoria Rivero); CORBIS (Małgorzata Gajdzińska); Fundacíon Césare Manrique (Bianca Visser); Hotel Rural Finca de Salinas – Yaiza; Hotel Santa Catalina– Las Palmas de Gran Canaria (Kati von Poroszlay); Loro Parque (Grettel Pérez Darias); Museo Arqueológico de Tenerife – Santa Cruz de Tenerife (Néstor Yanes); Museo de Cerámica– Casa Tafuriaste – La Orotavie (Antonio Cid Menchen); Museo de Historia de Tenerife – La Laguna (Ana Moreno, Jorge Gorrin Morales); Museo Etnografico Tanit– San Bartolomé (Remy de Quintana); Museo Municipal de Bellas Artes (María del Carmen Duque Hernández); Museo Néstor– Las Palmas de Gran Canaria (Pedro Luis Rosales Pedrero); Patronato de Turismo de Fuerteventura; Patronato de Turismo de Gran Canaria (Alfonso Falcón); Sociedad de Promocion de Las Palmas de Gran Canaria (Candelaria Delgado); ZEFA (Ewa Kozłowska); ZOOM s.c.

PICTURE CREDITS
t=top; tl=top left; tc=top centre, tr=top right; c=centre; cl=centre left; cr=centre right; cb=centre below; ca=centre above; clb=centre below left; crb=centre right below; cla=centre left above; cra=centre right above; b=bottom; bl=bottom left; bc=bottom centre; br=bottom right; bca=bottom centre above; bla=bottom left above; bra=bottom right above; blb=bottom left below; bcb=bottom centre below, brb=bottom right below, l=left; lc= left centre, r=right, ra=right above, rb=right below.

Every effort has been made to trace the copyright holders. Dorling Kindersley apologizes for any unintentional omissions and would be pleased, in such cases, to add an acknowledgment in future editions.

AFP: 22c.

CORBIS: 10t, 25b, 28, 71tr; Sean Aidan 22b; John Carter 23c; Jack Fields 111b; Robert Holmes 184–185; Robert Krist 25c; José F. Poblete 191b,; Roger Ressmeyer 150b; Nik Wheeler 24b, 122, 132, 137t.

DORLING KINDERSLEY: 16b, 17tl, 35bl, 40; Sven Larrson, 56t, 166cla, 166cra, 166cb, 166bcb, 167tr, 167cb, 167bl, 188c, 182c; Max Alexander 189t, 190c; David Cannon 22t; Philip Gatward 121cb; Neil Lukas 191c, 192tr; Brian Pitkin 182b; Kim Sayer 14bl, 24cr, 26b, 39tl, 41t, 44c, 62t, 81b; Linda Whitwam 17tr.

HOTEL SANTA CATALINA – LAS PALMAS DE GRAN CANARIA: 178c.

FUNDACÍON CÉSARE MANRIQUE: 85b.

ANDRZEJ LISOWSKI 120b, 123b. LORO PARQUE: 114t, 114c, 114b, 115t, 115ca, 115cb, 115b, 178b.

CARLOS MINGUEL:16t, 16tl, 16lc, 16lb, 17c, 17bl, 17br. PAWEŁ MURZYN: 36–37. MUSEO ARQUEOLÓGICO DE TENERIFE – SANTA CRUZ DE TENERIFE: 30cb, 31br. MUSEO NÉSTOR – LAS PALMAS DE GRAN CANARIA: 48b.

ORONOZ: 30–31, 35t.

ROBERT G. PASIECZNY: 15tc, 15tr, 15bl, 15bc 31tl, 32ca, 38ca, 44tl, 49t, 51c, 52t, 64b, 65b, 67t, 68t, 69t, 70c, 71tl, 72c, 74t, 75c, 76b, 77br, 78t, 78c, 81t, 82t, 94c, 95b, 97t, 100c, 106t, 108t, 117t, 119t, 119bl, 137b, 138c, 140, 141t, 143t, 154t, 154b, 164t, 164b, 165b, 180t, 181c, 182t, 186c, 196b. PIOTR PASZKIEWICZ: 26t, 54t, 54b, 123t. PATRONATO DE TURISMO DE GRAN CANARIA: 179b. ÁNGEL GÓMEZ PINCHETTI: 46t, 46c, 46b, 47t, 47cb, 47b. MAGDALENA POLAK: 130t, 149cl, 149cr, 149b.

MARIA ÁNGELES SANCHEZ: 23b, 20c, 21b, 27b, 128b, 149t, 150c. SOCIEDAD DE PROMOCION DE LAS PALMAS DE GRAN CANARIA: 4b, 20t, 20b, 21t, 21c, 179t.

ANDRZEJ ZYGMUNTOWICZ AND IRENEUSZ WINNICKI: 5c, 166ca, 166clb, 166crb, 167tr, 167ca, 167cl, 167cr, 167bla, 167blb.

JACKET
Front - DK PICTURE LIBRARY: lc; Kim Sayer rb; B. Zaranek bl; cl; Andrej Zygmuntowicz cr; GETTY IMAGES: Richard Passmore ra; PICTURES COLOUR LIBRARY: Sven Larrson main image. Back - DK PICTURE LIBRARY: P. Wojcik tl, br. Spine - DK PICTURE LIBRARY: Robert Pasioczny b; CORBIS: Michael T. Sedam t.

All other images © DORLING KINDERSLEY.
For further information see: www.DKimages.com

SPECIAL EDITIONS OF DK TRAVEL GUIDES

DK Travel Guides can be purchased in bulk quantities at discounted prices for use in promotions or as premiums. We are also able to offer special editions and personalized jackets, corporate imprints, and excerpts from all of our books, tailored specifically to meet your own needs.

To find out more, please contact:
(in the United States) **SpecialSales@dk.com**
(in the UK) **Sarah.Burgess@dk.com**
(in Canada) DK Special Sales at **general@tourmaline.ca**
(in Australia)
business.development@pearson.com.au

Phrase Book

IN AN EMERGENCY

Help!	¡Socorro!	soh-**koh**-roh
Stop!	¡Pare!	**pah**-reh
Call a doctor!	¡Llame a un médico!	yah-meh ah oon **meh**-dee-koh
Call an ambulance!	¡Llame a una ambulancia!	yah-meh ah **oonah** ahm-boo-**lahn**-thee-ah
Call the police!	¡Llame a la policía!	yah-meh ah lah poh-lee-**thee**-ah
Call the fire brigade!	¡Llame a los bomberos!	yah-meh ah lohs bohm-**beh**-rohs
Where is the nearest telephone?	¿Dónde está el teléfono más próximo?	dohn-deh ehs **tah** ehl teh-**leh**-foh-noh mahs **prohx**-ee-moh
Where is the nearest hospital?	¿Dónde está el hospital más próximo?	dohn-deh ehs-**tah** ehl ohs-pee-**tahl** mahs **prohx**-ee-moh

COMMUNICATION ESSENTIALS

Yes	Sí	see
No	No	noh
Please	Por favor	pohr fah-**vohr**
Thank you	Gracias	**grah**-thee-ahs
Excuse me	Perdone	pehr-doh-neh
Hello	Hola	**oh**-lah
Goodbye	Adiós	ah-dee-**ohs**
Good night	Buenas noches	bweh-nahs noh-chehs
Morning	La mañana	lah mah-**nyah**-nah
Afternoon	La tarde	lah **tahr**-deh
Evening	La tarde	lah **tahr**-deh
Yesterday	Ayer	ah-**yehr**
Today	Hoy	oy
Tomorrow	Mañana	mah-**nya**-nah
Here	Aquí	ah-**kee**
There	Allí	ah-**yee**
What?	¿Qué?	keh
When?	¿Cuándo?	**kwahn**-doh
Why?	¿Por qué?	pohr-**keh**
Where?	¿Dónde?	**dohn**-deh

USEFUL PHRASES

How are you?	¿Cómo está usted?	**koh**-moh ehs-**tah** oos-**tehd**
Very well, thank you.	Muy bien, gracias.	mwee bee-**ehn grah**-thee-ahs
Pleased to meet you.	Encantado de conocerle.	ehn-kahn-**tah**-doh deh koh-noh-**thehr**-leh
See you soon.	Hasta pronto.	ahs-tah **prohn**-toh
That's fine.	Está bien.	ehs-**tah** bee-**ehn**
Where is/are ...?	¿Dónde está/están ...?	**dohn**-deh ehs-**tah**/ehs-**tahn**
How far is it to ...?	¿Cuántos metros/ kilómetros hay de aquí a ...?	**kwahn**-tohs **meh**-trohs/kee-**loh**-meh-trohs **eye** deh ah-**kee** ah
Which way to ...?	¿Por dónde se va a ...?	pohr **dohn**-deh seh bah ah
Do you speak English?	¿Habla inglés?	**ah**-blah een-**glehs**
I don't understand	No comprendo	noh kohm-**prehn**-doh
Could you speak more slowly please?	¿Puede hablar más despacio por favor?	pweh-deh ah-**blahr** mahs dehs-pah-thee-oh pohr fah-**vohr**
I'm sorry.	Lo siento.	loh see-**ehn**-toh

USEFUL WORDS

big	grande	**grahn**-deh
small	pequeño	peh-**keh**-nyoh
hot	caliente	kah-lee-**ehn**-teh
cold	frío	**free**-oh
good	bueno	**bweh**-noh
bad	malo	**mah**-loh
enough	bastante	bahs-**tahn**-teh
well	bien	bee-**ehn**
open	abierto	ah-bee-**ehr**-toh
closed	cerrado	thehr-**rah**-doh
left	izquierda	eeth-key-**ehr**-dah
right	derecha	deh-**reh**-chah
straight on	todo recto	toh-doh **rehk**-toh
near	cerca	**thehr**-kah
far	lejos	**leh**-hohs
up	arriba	ah-**ree**-bah
down	abajo	ah-**bah**-hoh
early	temprano	tehm-**prah**-noh

late	tarde	**tahr**-deh
entrance	entrada	ehn-**trah**-dah
exit	salida	sah-**lee**-dah
toilet	lavabos, servicios	lah-**vah**-bohs sehr-**bee**-thee-ohs
more	más	mahs
less	menos	**meh**-nohs

SHOPPING

How much does this cost?	¿Cuánto cuesta esto?	**kwahn**-toh kwehs-tah ehs-toh
I would like ...	Me gustaría ...	meh goos-ta-**ree**-ah
Do you have?	¿Tienen?	tee-**yeh**-nehn
I'm just looking.	Sólo estoy mirando, gracias.	soh-loh ehs-**toy** mee-**rahn**-doh grah-thee-ahs
Do you take credit cards?	¿Aceptan tarjetas de crédito?	ah-**thehp**-tahn tahr-**heh**-tahs deh **kreh**-dee-toh
What time do you open?	¿A qué hora abren?	ah **keh** oh-rah **ah**-brehn
What time do you close?	¿A qué hora cierran?	ah keh oh-rah thee-**ehr**-rahn
This one.	Éste	**ehs**-teh
That one.	Ése	**eh**-seh
expensive	caro	**kahr**-oh
cheap	barato	bah-**rah**-toh
size, clothes	talla	**tah**-yah
size, shoes	número	**noo**-mehr-oh
white	blanco	**blahn**-koh
black	negro	**neh**-groh
red	rojo	**roh**-hoh
yellow	amarillo	ah-mah-**ree**-yoh
green	verde	**behr**-deh
blue	azul	ah-**thool**
antiques shop	la tienda de antigüedades	lah tee-**ehn**-dah deh ahn-tee gweh-**dah**-dehs
bakery	la panadería	lah pah-nah-deh-**ree**-ah
bank	el banco	ehl **bahn**-koh
book shop	la librería	lah lee-breh-**ree**-ah
butcher's	la carnicería	lah kahr-nee-theh-**ree**-ah
cake shop	la pastelería	lah pahs-teh-leh-**ree**-ah
chemist's	la farmacia	lah fahr-**mah**-thee-ah
fishmonger's	la pescadería	lah pehs-kah-deh-**ree**-ah
greengrocer's grocer's	la frutería la tienda de comestibles	lah froo-teh-**ree**-ah lah tee-**yehn**-dah deh koh-mehs-**tee**-blehs
hairdresser's	la peluquería	lah peh-loo-keh-**ree**-ah
market	el mercado	ehl mehr-**kah**-doh
newsagent's	el kiosko de prensa	ehl kee-**ohs**-koh deh **prehn**-sah
post office	la oficina de correos	lah oh-fee-**thee**-nah deh kohr-**reh**-ohs
shoe shop	la zapatería	lah thah-pah-teh-**ree**-ah
supermarket	el supermercado	ehl soo-pehr-mehr-**kah**-doh
tobacconist	el estanco	ehl ehs-**tahn**-koh
travel agency	la agencia de viajes	lah ah-**hehn**-thee-ah deh bee-**ah**-hehs

SIGHTSEEING

art gallery	el museo de arte	ehl moo-**seh**-oh deh **ahr**-teh
cathedral	la catedral	lah kah-teh-**drahl**
church	la iglesia la basílica	lah ee-**gleh**-see-ah lah bah-**see**-lee-kah
garden	el jardín	ehl hahr-**deen**
library	la biblioteca	lah bee-blee-oh-**teh**-kah
museum	el museo	ehl moo-**seh**-oh
tourist information office	la oficina de turismo	lah oh-fee-**thee** nah deh too-**rees**-moh
town hall	el ayuntamiento	ehl ah-yoon-tah-mee-**ehn**-toh
closed for holiday	cerrado por vacaciones	thehr-**rah**-doh pohr bah-kah-thee-**oh**-nehs
bus station	la estación de autobuses	lah ehs-tah-thee-**ohn** deh owtoh-**boo**-sehs
railway station	la estación de trenes	lah ehs-tah-thee-**ohn** deh **treh**-nehs

Staying in a Hotel

Do you have a vacant room?	¿Tiene una habitación libre?	tee-**eh**-neh oo-nah ah-bee-tah-thee-**ohn lee**-breh
double room	habitación doble	ah-bee-tah-thee-**ohn doh**-bleh
with double bed	con cama de matrimonio	kohn **kah**-mah deh mah-tree-**moh**-nee-oh
twin room	habitación con dos camas	ah-bee-tah-thee-**ohn** kohn dohs **kah**-mahs
single room	habitación individual	ah-bee-tah-thee-**ohn** een-dee-vee-doo-**ahl**
room with a bath	habitación con baño	ah-bee-tah-thee-**ohn** kohn bah-nyoh
shower	ducha	doo-chah
porter	el botones	ehl boh-**toh**-nehs
key	la llave	lah **yah**-veh
I have a reservation.	Tengo una habitación reservada.	tehn-goh oo-na ah-bee-tah-thee-**ohn** reh-sehr-**bah**-dah

Eating Out

Have you got a table for …?	¿Tiene mesa para …?	tee-**eh**-neh meh-sah pah-**rah**
I want to reserve a table.	Quiero reservar una mesa.	kee-eh-roh reh-sehr-**bahr** oo-nah **meh**-sah
The bill please.	La cuenta por favor.	lah **kwehn**-tah pohr fah-**vohr**
I am a vegetarian	Soy vegetariano/a	soy beh-heh-tah-ree-**ah**-no/na
waitress/ waiter	camarera/ camarero	kah-mah-**reh**-rah kah-mah-**reh**-roh
menu	la carta	lah **kahr**-tah
fixed-price menu	menú del día	meh-**noo** dehl **dee**-ah
wine list	la carta de vinos	lah **kahr**-tah deh **bee**-nohs
glass	un vaso	oon **bah**-soh
bottle	una botella	oo-nah boh-**teh**-yah
knife	un cuchillo	oon koo-**chee**-yoh
fork	un tenedor	oon teh-neh-**dohr**
spoon	una cuchara	oo-nah koo-**chah**-rah
breakfast	el desayuno	ehl deh-sah-**yoo**-noh
lunch	la comida/ el almuerzo	lah koh-**mee**-dah/ ehl ahl-**mwehr**-thoh
dinner	la cena	lah **theh**-nah
main course	el primer plato	ehl pree-**mehr plah**-toh
starters	los entremeses	lohs ehn-treh-**meh**-sehs
dish of the day	el plato del día	ehl **plah**-toh dehl **dee**-ah
coffee	el café	ehl kah-**feh**
rare (meat)	poco hecho	poh-koh **eh**-choh
medium	medio hecho	**meh**-dee-oh **eh**-choh
well done	muy hecho	mwee **eh**-choh

Menu Decoder

al horno	ahl **ohr**-noh	baked
asado	ah-**sah**-doh	roast
el aceite	ah-**thee-eh**-teh	oil
las aceitunas	ah-theh-**toon**-ahs	olives
el agua mineral	ah-gwa mee-neh-**rahl**	mineral water
sin gas/con gas	seen gas/kohn gas	still/sparkling
el ajo	**ah**-hoh	garlic
el arroz	ahr-**rohth**	rice
el azúcar	ah-**thoo**-kahr	sugar
la carne	**kahr**-neh	meat
la cebolla	theh-**boh**-yah	onion
el cerdo	**therh**-doh	pork
la cerveza	thehr-**beh**-thah	beer
el chocolate	choh-koh-**lah**-teh	chocolate
el chorizo	choh-**ree**-thoh	spicy sausage
el cordero	kohr-**deh**-roh	lamb
el fiambre	fee-**ahm**-breh	cold meat
frito	**free**-toh	fried
la fruta	**froo**-tah	fruit
los frutos secos	**froo**-tohs **seh**-kohs	nuts
las gambas	**gahm**-bahs	prawns
el helado	eh-**lah**-doh	ice cream
el huevo	oo-**eh**-voh	egg
el jamón serrano	hah-**mohn** sehr-**rah**-noh	cured ham

el jerez	heh-**rehz**	sherry
la langosta	lahn-**gohs**-tah	lobster
la leche	**leh**-cheh	milk
el limón	lee-**mohn**	lemon
la limonada	lee-moh-**nah**-dah	lemonade
la mantequilla	mahn-teh-**kee**-yah	butter
la manzana	mahn-**thah**-nah	apple
los mariscos	mah-**rees**-kohs	seafood
la menestra	meh-**nehs**-trah	vegetable stew
la naranja	nah-**rahn**-hah	orange
el pan	pahn	bread
el pastel	pahs-**tehl**	cake
las patatas	pah-**tah**-tahs	potatoes
el pescado	pehs-**kah**-doh	fish
la pimienta	pee-mee-**yehn**-tah	pepper
el plátano	**plah**-tah-noh	banana
el pollo	**poh**-yoh	chicken
el postre	**pohs**-treh	dessert
el queso	**keh**-soh	cheese
la sal	sahl	salt
las salchichas	sahl-**chee**-chahs	sausages
la salsa	**sahl**-sah	sauce
seco	**seh**-koh	dry
el solomillo	soh-loh-**mee**-yoh	sirloin
la sopa	**soh**-pah	soup
la tarta	**tahr**-tah	pie/cake
el té	teh	tea
la ternera	tehr-**neh**-rah	beef
las tostadas	tohs-**tah**-dahs	toast
el vinagre	bee-**nah**-greh	vinegar
el vino blanco	**bee**-noh **blahn**-koh	white wine
el vino rosado	**bee**-noh roh-**sah**-doh	rosé wine
el vino tinto	**bee**-noh **teen**-toh	red wine

Numbers

0	cero	**theh**-roh
1	uno	**oo**-noh
2	dos	dohs
3	tres	trehs
4	cuatro	**kwa**-troh
5	cinco	**theen**-koh
6	seis	says
7	siete	**see**-eh-teh
8	ocho	**oh**-choh
9	nueve	**nweh**-veh
10	diez	dee-**ehth**
11	once	**ohn**-theh
12	doce	**doh**-theh
13	trece	**treh**-theh
14	catorce	kah-**tohr**-theh
15	quince	**keen**-theh
16	dieciséis	dee-eh-thee-**seh-ees**
17	diecisiete	dee-eh-thee-see-**eh**-teh
18	dieciocho	dee-eh-thee-**oh**-choh
19	diecinueve	dee-eh-thee-**nweh**-veh
20	veinte	**beh**-een-teh
21	veintiuno	beh-een-tee-**oo**-noh
22	veintidós	beh-een-tee-**dohs**
30	treinta	**treh**-een-tah
31	treinta y uno	**treh**-een-tah ee **oo**-noh
40	cuarenta	kwah-**rehn**-tah
50	cincuenta	theen-**kwehn**-tah
60	sesenta	seh-**sehn**-tah
70	setenta	seh-**tehn**-tah
80	ochenta	oh-**chehn**-tah
90	noventa	noh-**vehn**-tah
100	cien	thee-**ehn**
101	ciento uno	thee-**ehn**-toh **oo**-noh
102	ciento dos	thee-**ehn**-toh dohs
200	doscientos	dohs-thee-**ehn**-tohs
500	quinientos	khee-nee-**ehn**-tohs
700	setecientos	seh-teh-thee-**ehn**-tohs
900	novecientos	noh-veh-thee-**ehn** tohs
1,000	mil	meel
1,001	mil uno	meel **oo**-noh

Time

one minute	un minuto	oon mee-**noo**-toh
one hour	una hora	oo-na oh-rah
half an hour	media hora	**meh**-dee-a **oh**-rah
Monday	lunes	**loo**-nehs
Tuesday	martes	**mahr**-tehs
Wednesday	miércoles	mee-**ehr**-koh-lehs
Thursday	jueves	hoo-**weh**-vehs
Friday	viernes	bee-**ehr**-nehs
Saturday	sábado	**sah**-bah-doh
Sunday	domingo	doh-**meen**-goh

Canary Island Ferry Routes

LA PALMA

Santa Cruz
de La Palma

LA GOMERA

San Sebastián
de La Gomera

LA GOMERA

Los Cristianos

TENERIFE

Santa Cruz
de Tenerife

Puerto de la Estaca

EL HIERRO

Atlantic Ocean

FERRY LINES

TRASMEDITERRANEA
W www.trasmediterranea.net

Gran Canaria
Las Palmas de Gran Canaria
928 474 482, FAX 928 474 121.

Fuerteventura
Puerto del Rosario
928 850 877, FAX 928 852 408.
Morro Jable
928 540 250.

Lanzarote
Arrecife
928 811 019.

Tenerife
Santa Cruz de Tenerife
922 842 200, FAX 922 842 244.
Los Cristianos
922 796 178, FAX 922 796 179.

La Gomera
San Sebastián de La Gomera
922 870 802, FAX 922 871 324.

El Hierro
Puerto de la Estaca
922 550 905, FAX 922 550 129.

La Palma
Santa Cruz de La Palma
922 118 265,
FAX 922 418 252.

LÍNEAS FRED OLSEN
W www.fredolsen.es

Tenerife
Santa Cruz de Tenerife
922 290 011.
Los Cristianos
922 790 556.

La Gomera
San Sebastián de La Gomera
922 871 007.

La Palma
Santa Cruz de La Palma
922 415 433.

NAVIERA ARMAS
W www.naviera-armas.com

Gran Canaria
Las Palmas de Gran Canaria
928 300 600.

Fuerteventura
Puerto del Rosario
928 851 542.
Morro Jable
928 542 113.
Corralejo
928 867 080.

Lanzarote
Arrecife
928 824 931.
Playa Blanca
928 517 912.

Tenerife
Santa Cruz de Tenerife
922 534 052.

La Palma
Santa Cruz de La Palma
922 417 482.

LÍNEAS MARÍTIMAS ROMERO

La Graciosa
928 842 070.